Freedom

Also Available from Bloomsbury

Sex and the Failed Absolute, Slavoj Žižek
Disparities, Slavoj Žižek
Antigone, Slavoj Žižek
Hegel in A Wired Brain, Slavoj Žižek
Christian Atheism, Slavoj Žižek
Surplus-Enjoyment, Slavoj Žižek
Against Progress, Slavoj Žižek
Zero Point, Slavoj Žižek

Freedom

A Disease Without Cure

Slavoj Žižek

BLOOMSBURY ACADEMIC
LONDON • NEW YORK • OXFORD • NEW DELHI • SYDNEY

BLOOMSBURY ACADEMIC
Bloomsbury Publishing Plc, 50 Bedford Square, London, WC1B 3DP, UK
Bloomsbury Publishing Inc, 1359 Broadway, 12th Floor, New York, NY 10018, USA
Bloomsbury Publishing Ireland, 29 Earlsfort Terrace, Dublin 2, D02 AY28, Ireland

BLOOMSBURY, BLOOMSBURY ACADEMIC and the Diana logo are trademarks of Bloomsbury Publishing Plc

First published in Great Britain 2023
Paperback edition first published 2025
Reprinted 2025 (three times)

Cover image: Fluid color abstract background
(© worawit chutrakunwanit / Alamy)
Cover design: Ben Anslow

A catalogue record for this book is available from the British Library.

A catalog record for this book is available from the Library of Congress.

ISBN: HB: 978-1-3503-5712-9
PB: 978-1-3505-5916-5
ePDF: 978-1-3503-5713-6
eBook: 978-1-3503-5714-3

Typeset by RefineCatch Limited, Bungay, Suffolk
Printed and bound in Great Britain

For product safety related questions contact productsafety@bloomsbury.com.

To find out more about our authors and books visit www.bloomsbury.com and sign up for our newsletters.

Contents

Introduction

Move Your Buridan's Ass!

A Miracle in China

In November 2021, the general public in China debated the story of Chen Zi, a migrant worker who dropped out of college as a sophomore and worked for 10 years for a pittance as a machine repairman in a camera factory, wearing a blue dust-free suit that exposed his eyes to work on an assembly line. Secretly, after 12 hours of daily repetitive and debilitating work, he learned English, began reading Heidegger, and translated into Chinese Richard Bolter's *Introduction to Heidegger*. After he finished some other translations, he asked online if he could publish the books to prove that he could go to college. His offer was rejected, but his post was discovered by the media and became a hot topic on the internet.[1]

Is there something liberating in this dedication to Heidegger or is it a false way out? It is easy to imagine the orthodox Marxist answer: assembly line workers do not need Heidegger as an antidote, what they need is to change their miserable conditions of work. Heidegger appears a really bad choice, and for obvious reasons. Lately, after the publication of Heidegger's *Black Notes*, attempts abound to exclude him from the list of philosophers to be taken seriously on account of his anti-Semitism and Nazi links. For this very reason, one should insist that Heidegger remains pertinent: even when he is at his worst, unexpected links open themselves up. In the mid-1930s, Heidegger said: "there are human beings and human groups (Negroes like, for example, Kaffirs) who have no history [. . .] however, animal and plant life has a thousand year long and eventful history [. . .] within the human region, history can be missing, as with Negroes".[2] ("Kaffir" was at the time of apartheid an ethnic slur used to refer to black Africans in South Africa.) The quoted lines are strange, even by Heidegger's standards: so animals and plants do have history, but "Negroes" do not? "Animal and plant life has a thousand year long and eventful history"—but for sure not in the strict Heideggerean sense of the epochal disclosures of Being . . . Plus where do then stand countries like China or India which are also not historical in Heidegger's specific sense?

Should then the case of Grant Farred, a noted contemporary Black philosopher who teaches at Cornell, be dismissed as a simple case of misunderstanding? Farred's short book *Martin Heidegger Saved My Life*[3] was written in reaction to a racist encounter: in the Fall of 2013, while he was raking leaves outside his home, a white woman stopped by and asked him "Would you like another job?", obviously mistaking him for a paid gardener of the rich family which lived in the house. Farred sarcastically responded: "Only if you can match my Cornell faculty salary." In order to understand what happened, Farred turned to Heidegger: "Heidegger saved me because he gave me the language to write about race in such a way as I'd never written it before. Heidegger enabled me to write in this way because he has made me think about how to think."[4] What he found so useful in Heidegger was the notion of language as a "house of being": not the abstract-universal language of science and state administration but language rooted in a particular way of life, language as the medium of an always-unique life-experience which discloses reality to us in a historically specific way. It is easy to imagine how such a stance enables a subject to resist being swallowed into a global universe of technological domination . . . however, is this the way to fight what is often called the "Americanization" of our lives? To answer this question, we have to think—and, as Farred repeatedly points out, this is what he learned from Heidegger, not just to think but to think about thinking.

To make it clear, I am not a Heideggerian. But what I do know is that we live in a unique moment which gives rise to the urgency to think. Ours is not a peaceful time which provides the opportunity to comfortably withdraw into reflection on the world but a time when our survival itself as humans is under threat from different directions: the prospect of total digital control, which plans to invade our mind itself ("wired brain"), uncontrollable viral infections, effects of global warming . . . We are all affected by these threats, so-called ordinary people even more than others. So we should celebrate miracles like the one with Chen Zi—they demonstrate that philosophy is much more than an academic discipline, it is something that can all of a sudden interrupt the course of our daily life and make us perplexed. Alain Badiou opens up his *True Life* with the provocative claim that, from Socrates onward, the function of philosophy is to "corrupt the youth," to alienate them from the predominant ideologico-political order.[5] Such "corruption" is needed today especially in the liberal-permissive West where most people are even not aware of the way the establishment controls them precisely when they appear to be free—the most dangerous unfreedom is the unfreedom that we experience as freedom. None other than Goethe already knew this: "None are more hopelessly enslaved than those who falsely believe they are free."[6] Is a "free" populist who works on destroying the thick social network of customs really free? Mao Zedong wrote in 1957: "Let a hundred flowers bloom; let a hundred schools of thought contend."[7] Today, we should say: let a hundred Chen Zi's study philosophy—only in this way we will find a way out of our sad predicament.

No Free Choice Without Being Chosen

We are all afraid that new dangers pose a threat to our hard-won freedoms, so what deserves special attention is precisely the notion of freedom. It is not enough to defend freedom, what is even more needed is to take a step back and reflect upon what we mean by freedom. Authoritarian and totalitarian regimes often characterized political opponents as mentally ill (and treated them accordingly). In the good old Soviet times, the Serbsky Institute in Moscow (which after 1990 went on doing the same thing under a new name, the Serbsky Centre) was the psychiatric flagship for punitive political control; its psychiatrists developed painful drug methods to make detainees talk and extract testimony for use in national security investigations. Underpinning the power of psychiatrists to incarcerate people was an invented political mental disorder known as "*vyalotekushchaya*" ("sluggish schizophrenia"). Psychiatrists described the person suffering this condition as somebody appearing quite normal most of the time but who would break out with a severe case of "inflexibility of convictions," or "nervous exhaustion brought on by his or her search for justice," or "a tendency to litigation" or "reformist delusions." The underlying premise was that a person had to be *insane* to be against the existing Soviet Communist order, and the treatment involved intravenous injections of psychotropic drugs that were so painfully administered that patients became unconscious.

Although, of course, this notion (and practice) are to be unconditionally rejected, we should nonetheless endorse the idea that there is something "crazy," something of a madness, in radical freedom—Kant and Hegel knew this, they were both aware that freedom is at its most radical a disease, something that parasitizes on our organic wellbeing, something destructive and self-destructive, or, to put it in Freud's terms, something that operates "beyond the pleasure-principle." However, in contrast to the ideology of the Serbsky Institute, they were also aware that this "disease" of freedom is the very foundation of our "normal" social existence, which is why our "normal" life is irreducibly exposed to the threat of freedom. In Kant, there is an exact homology with the moral Law, which is the *ratio cognoscendi* of our freedom, the only proof that I can act autonomously (independently of pathological reasons); however, it is at the same time experienced as a foreign traumatic intruder into our immanent inner life, i.e. as something that functions "beyond the pleasure principle."[8] Let us be more precise here: freedom is not just something which can be distorted, which can undergo a disease; freedom *is* at its most basic a disease, which is why—as Kant put it—the human being is an animal which needs a master to discipline/educate it. Which is the dimension upon which discipline and education work? Kant seems to claim that it is our animal nature:

> Discipline or training changes animal nature into human nature. An animal is already all that it can be because of its instinct; a foreign intelligence has already taken care of everything for it.

> But the human being needs his own intelligence. He has no instinct and must work out the plan of his conduct for himself. However, since the human being is not immediately in a position to do this, because he is in a raw state when he comes into the world, others must do it for him."[9]

However, the need for discipline is not just grounded negatively, in the lack of an instinctual firm base; discipline is also needed because humans display an "unnatural" savagery (*Wildheit*) or passion for freedom specific to human nature:

> Savagery or unruliness, *Wildheit* is independence from laws. Through discipline the human being is submitted to the laws of humanity and is first made to feel their constraint. Thus, for example, children are sent to school initially not already with the intention that they should learn something there, but rather that they may grow accustomed to sitting still and observing punctually what they are told, so that in the future they may not put into practice actually and instantly each notion that strikes them . . . Now by nature the human being has such a powerful propensity towards freedom that when he has grown accustomed to it for a while, he will sacrifice everything for it.[10]

The predominant form of appearance of this weird "savagery" is passion, an attachment to a particular choice so strong that it suspends rational comparison with other possible choices—when we are in the thrall of a passion, we stick to a certain choice whatever it may cost. And, as the subdivision "On the inclination to freedom as a passion" tells us, "For the natural human being this is the most violent [*heftigste*] inclination of all."[11] Passion is as such purely human: animals have no passions, just instincts. The Kantian savagery is "unnatural" in the precise sense that it seems to break or suspend the causal chain which determines all natural phenomena—it is as if in its terrifying manifestations, noumenal freedom transpires for a moment in our phenomenal universe. Freud's *Unbehagen in der Kultur* (uneasiness in, discontent with, culture) could and should thus be paraphrased as "discontent with freedom": we never feel at ease in freedom, the more we are free, the more we dwell in anxiety. Freedom is one of those deceiving notions that appear self-evident, but the moment we try to dissect them we get caught in ambiguities and contradictions. I think the best illustration of these ambiguities is the situation imagined in the expression "Buridan's ass."

The three basic meanings of the term "ass" in English (donkey; a stupid person; the part of the body a person sits on) nicely come together in this expression: a stupid donkey who is equally hungry and thirsty is sitting on its ass midway between a stack of hay and a pail of water (or, in another version, midway between the two exact same stacks of hay)—it dies of both hunger and thirst since it cannot make a decision which of the two to choose. (In digital electronics, something similar appears as "metastability": when a circuit must decide between two states based on an input that is in itself undefined (neither zero nor one), it gets stuck, i.e., it spends more time than it should in this "undecided" state.) Far from being a pathological exception, the stance of the Buridan's ass is in some sense the Degree Zero of freedom: if a clear calculation tells us what to do, we just follow the calculation of reasons, there is no doubt or oscillation and, consequently, no freedom. But if, in a choice between equivalents, we just follow reason, we die. All radical decisions are undecidable, only the decision itself makes the reasons for it palpable and apparent?

If there is a free choice it is that of a love object, we cannot be ordered to love somebody; however, once fully in love, we experience it as our fate—it holds us in its clutches, no matter how hard we try we cannot escape it. This is why we can (usually) enumerate reasons why we fell in love, but these reasons appear as reasons only after we are already in love—we are never in a comfortable external position in which we can compare reasons to fall in love with different people and decide whom to choose. Kierkegaard says exactly the same about faith: I do not acquire faith in, say, Christ after comparing different religions and deciding the best reasons to speak for Christianity—there are reasons to choose Christianity, but these reasons appear only after I have already chosen, i.e., taken the leap of faith. To see the reasons for belief, one already has to believe. And, let's go to the end here, the same holds for Marxism: it is not that, after objectively analysing history, I became a Marxist—my decision to be a Marxist (the experience of a proletarian position) makes me see the reasons for it, i.e., Marxism is the paradox of an objective "true" knowledge accessible only through a subjective partial position.

We thereby touch the ultimate politico-theological dimension of the present book. In our conscious experience, we directly jump from the non-decision of Buridan's ass to the certainty that we have discovered our fate. The purely virtual moment of decision (free choice) which never occurs in the present of our reality is the moment of radical freedom, of "freedom as such"—I am paraphrasing here the title of Walter Benjamin's famous essay "On Language As Such and on the Language of Man." His point is not that human language is a species of some universal language "as such" which comprises also other species (the language of gods and angels?, animal language?, the language of some other intelligent beings out there in space?, computer language?, the language of the DNA?): there is no actually existing language other than human language—but, in order to comprehend this "particular" language, one HAS to introduce a gap that separates the actually existing language from language "as such" (the pure structure of language deprived of the insignia of the human finitude, of erotic passions and mortality, of the struggles for domination and the obscenity of power).

Language is the basic medium of freedom—not just language as the medium which allows us to think and say what we want, but also what Lacan called *lalangue*, language in all its non-intended ambiguities and wordplays—*lalangue* opens up the space in which we can resist the hegemonic discourse of power. In today's China, the Grass Mud Horse or Cǎonímǎ is an internet meme based on a pun: it is a play on the Mandarin words *cào nǐ mā*, literally "fuck your mother". Cǎonímǎ is an exemplary case of the resistance discourse of Chinese internet users, a mascot of netizens in China fighting for free expression, inspiring poetry, photos and videos, artwork, lines of clothing, and more. As such, it is part of a broader Chinese internet culture of spoofing, mockery, punning, and parody known as *e'gao*, which includes video mash-ups and other types of *bricolage*.[12]

What this means is that "freedom as such" and "language as such" are radically opposed: "language as such" is a pure asubjective structure, with no desire inscribed into it and, consequently, no freedom at work in it—this structure gets subjectivized only through the idiosyncrasies of *lalangue*. The same split between "as such" and experienced reality is at work also in freedom: beyond (or, rather, beneath) free acts of an actual subject there is the abyss of "pure" freedom. The status of "language as such" is symbolic, a stable structure, while the status of "freedom as such" is that of an impossible/Real, a singularity popping out and disappearing. The whole mystery of subjectivity resides in the co-dependence of these two opposed moments.

From a properly Hegelian perspective, we should not limit freedom to a predicate of some entity: at the highest point of freedom, freedom itself is the subject and we—fighting for freedom—are its predicates, instruments even, as in the refrain of an old German Communist song from the 1930s "*Die Freiheit hat Soldaten!*" (Freedom has its soldiers!) has it. It may appear that such an identification of a particular unit as the military instrument of Freedom itself is the very formula of the "totalitarian" temptation: we do not just fight for (our understanding of) freedom, we serve freedom, it is freedom itself which immediately avails itself of us . . . The way seems open to terror: who would be allowed to oppose freedom itself? However, the identification of a revolutionary military unit as a direct organ of freedom cannot simply be dismissed as a fetishist short circuit: this is true of the authentic revolutionary explosion. What happens in such an "ecstatic" experience is that the subject who acts is no longer a person, but, precisely, an *object*. And it is this dimension of identifying with an object which justifies the use of the term "theology": "theology" is here a name for what is, in a revolutionary subject, beyond a mere collection of individual humans. In our ordinary daily lives, we are free, freedom is a human property, but in an authentic revolutionary situation, freedom itself becomes a subject and acts through us—we reduce ourselves to its objects. To make this religious component even clearer: at the level of subjective freedom, I (an agent-subject) *make a free choice*; but at the level of freedom itself acting, I am not the agent of choice, *I am myself chosen*. As Deleuze put it somewhere apropos Leibniz?, "I really choose only if I am chosen."[13] So yes, we should shamelessly admit the point often made against the Marxist notion of revolutionary agent: it is *chosen* in the religious sense of the term.

At this highest point when we are reduced to objects, freedom and necessity coincide, but we are as far as possible from becoming just a cog in the structure that determines us. Free decisions are only possible within a structure which is in itself subjectivized through an immanent inconsistency. Agnes Sligh Turnbull wrote: "If a diplomat says 'yes,' he means 'perhaps.' If he says 'perhaps,' he means 'no.' And if he says 'no,' he's the hell of a diplomat."[14] What makes this triad (a diplomat can say yes, perhaps, or no) a *structure* (in the strict structuralist sense) is the cut between the second and the third statements: while the first two explain the real meaning of a claim (yes means perhaps, perhaps means no), the third one changes the terrain from real meaning to the direct disqualification—a diplomat who says no is a bad diplomat. A true diplomat is thus defined by an imbalance between what he says and what he means: he never says no, but he also never means yes. In other words, what makes this triad a structure is that the third logical variation (when a diplomat says no, he means yes) is excluded, and what fills its lack is the direct reference to the subject of enunciation—structure is never flatly "objective," it always includes a moment of subjectivization.

The Odds of Freedom

However, this notion of radical freedom is clearly an exception: our daily experience of freedom has many shades, from simple choices (which movie to see?, which commodity to buy?) to difficult and painful decisions of engaging oneself in a political struggle, from our subjective experience of being free ("I can think and do what I want") to social freedom in all its complexity and ambiguity ("I am free if I can publicly express my opinions and organize, together with others, my life in the way I find appropriate for my well-being and dignity—in short, I am free if my voice matters in how the society I live in is organized"). But a totally different approach to freedom opens up with modern science: are we (humans) really free in the sense that what we are doing is not fully determined by neuronal and other processes of which we are not aware? In short, is there a free will, and is the notion of free will compatible with scientific determinism?

Until now, at least, this different approach was limited to the scientific domain: the fact that I experience myself as free and that I strive to live in a society which offers a space for my freedom was perceived as fully compatible with the fact that my intimate experiences as well as social activity are neuronally and biologically determined. But today, with the latest advances in digital control and brain sciences, our intimate self-experience and our social activity can be controlled and regulated to such a degree that the liberal notion of a free individual becomes obsolete and even meaningless: the scientific determinism which grounds the technological control of our lives is more and more not just a theory but a social and political fact that directly affects our intimate self-experience.

All these levels have to be analysed in their interconnection. The self-experience of a free inner life should be, of course, supplemented by an account of the Freudian unconscious (which is simultaneously a social fact): is the Unconscious an agency of determinism, or is it (as Schelling and Lacan thought) the site of the most radical free decision? Brain sciences raise the question of freedom to a new level: are we free at all, is our free will compatible with scientific determinism, and if it is, in what precise sense can we claim this? Within a social space, we are always caught in the tension between abstract and concrete freedom, and thereby with the "alienated" institutions which mediate our freedom: market, state, and representative democracy. Are they an irreducible condition of our freedom or do they also function as an obstacle to it? Our immersion in the digital universe clearly indicates how free circulation in virtual space gives birth to new non-transparent forms of domination. And, last but not least, what is the lesson of our ecological crises with regard to freedom? How will we be obliged to reinvent (or limit) the contours of our freedom?

The present booklet is accordingly divided into two parts: "Freedom as Such" deals with freedom as its own subject, while "Human Freedom" deals with the mess of our social lives in which we are free (or not) in different ways. "Freedom as Such" does not only stand for the abstract-formal structure of freedom, it also stands for concrete social situations in which this abstraction is directly realized in what cannot but appear as a ridiculous excess that violates all particular rules—such situations are freedom at its most dangerous, and simultaneously at its most promising as a way towards emancipation. But how will this emancipation look? Since capitalism implies permanent self-revolutionizing—are we aware of how thoroughly our lives changed in the last fifty years?—my wager is that, perhaps, the time has come to re-conceive Communism as a *counter-revolution*, as an effort to establish a new stable order.

*

I dedicate this book to Wolfgang Kieling, a West German actor who died in 1988 in the German Democratic Republic—why? The official name of the foreign intelligence service of the Ministry of State Security (*Stasi*), the main security agency of the German Democratic Republic headed by Markus Wolf, was Hauptverwaltung Aufklärung (HVA, The Main Directorate for Reconnaissance); in German, the main meaning of Aufklärung is "enlightenment," which, of course, gave birth to many ironic comments. Although HVA was, without doubt, a very dark organization, it didn't wholly escape what one cannot resist calling, following Adorno and Horkheimer, *die Dialektik der* Aufklärung ("the dialectic of enlightenment"): there were (rare, true) people who, if not collaborated with it, went over to the GDR for proper ethico-political reasons. For me, the most fascinating case is that of Wolfgang Kieling, the well-known West German movie and TV actor who played also in some Hollywood productions. His biggest role in Hollywood is that of Hermann Gromek in Hitchcock's *Torn Curtain*. Gromek is a Stasi officer who suspects that Armstrong (Paul Newman), the movie's hero, did not sincerely defect to the East, so he follows Armstrong to a lone farm where Armstrong went to make preparations to return to the West via an escape network. Gromek realizes that Armstrong is a double agent, and as he is calling the police, a tortuous struggle commences that ends with Gromek being brutally slain by Armstrong—by far the best scene in the movie which demonstrated, as Hitchcock put it, how difficult it is to really kill a man: Gromek's head is pushed into a gas oven where he slowly suffocated, desperately waving his hands … Here comes the big surprise: during the post-production of the movie in Hollywood in late 1965, the Watts race riots occurred which were brutally suppressed by the police, leaving Kieling disgusted with American society. As a result, after the film was released, he defected to East Germany in real life, calling the United States "the most dangerous enemy of humanity in the world today" and guilty of "crimes against the Negro and the people of Vietnam."[15] The irony of his case is supreme: the production of a movie about a fake defection to the East led to an actual defection to the East … A truly dialectical approach to the Cold War has to give space also to such peculiarities which disturb the simple opposition between democracy and totalitarianism.

Freedom as Such

1
Freedom and Its Discontents

Freedom versus Liberty

I remember how, more than a decade ago, my younger son teased me. We were eating lunch at a large table, and I asked him if he could pass me the small bottle of salt that was on his side of the table; he answered, "Of course I can" . . . and did nothing. When I repeated my request, he snapped back with childish impudence: "You asked me if I *can* do it, and I answered you—you didn't tell me that I should really do it!" Who was in this situation more free, me or my son? In a sense—if we understand freedom as the freedom of choice—my son was more free: he had at his disposal an additional choice of how to understand my question, either literally (am I able to do it?) or in the usual everyday sense (as a request for reasons of politeness formulated as a question). I renounced this choice and automatically relied on the usual sense. However, let us try to imagine a world in which most people would act like my son: we would never know for sure what our partner in conversation wants to say and would lose an immense amount of time with pointless interpretations.

Are we not facing in our political life in the last decades a similar situation? Even when Donald Trump and his alt-Right populists do not violate explicit laws, they ignore the unwritten rules and customs. In Slovenia, my own country, there was two years ago a conflict concerning the nomination of Slovene members of the European court: the Rightist government took literally its purely formal function of taking cognizance of the proposed names and acted as if it effectively had to decide and make a choice—exactly like my son who took my request "Can you pass me the salt?" literally and didn't do it. Trump's Republicans are doing something similar in the US: the American legal system stipulates as an exceptional measure that, when in one of the federal states the outcome of elections is not clear, this state's congress can directly nominate electors; in the Republican interpretation, this means that if the Republican-dominated congress doesn't like an electoral result it can directly nominate electors . . . One of the conditions of political democracy is that all political agents speak the same language—say, that they understand in a similar way the electoral rules, so that even when the electoral outcome doesn't fit them, they accept it. If this doesn't happen, we find ourselves close to a civil war. And the same holds for international politics: all sides are expected to speak the same language when they talk about freedom and occupation.

However, things are never as simple as that: we may speak the same language while each of us gives it a specific spin. The finale of Act I of Mozart's *Don Giovanni* begins with Don Giovanni's powerful appeal to all present "Viva la liberta!", repeated forcefully by all, interrupting the melodic flow, as if the music got stuck at this point of excessive engagement—but the catch is, of course, that, although the entire group is enthusiastically unified around the call to freedom, each subgroup projects into "liberta" its own dreams and hopes, or, to quote Etienne Balibar: "Sociability is therefore the unity of a real agreement and an imaginary ambivalence, both of which have real effects."[1] Imagine a situation of political unity where all sides unite under the same Master-signifier ("freedom"), but every particular group projects a different meaning into this universality (freedom of property for some, anarchic freedom outside the state law for others, social conditions which allow individuals to actualize their potentials for yet another group . . .). It is crucial here that affect is invested already in the universal notion: we passionately participate in the struggle for "freedom" although our idea of freedom is not the same as that of others—passion is abstract-universal, not particular. What we have to avoid here is the pseudo-Marxist reduction of "freedom" to an illusion which conceals the conflict of multiple "real" meanings—the unity of agreement is real, it has performative efficiency.

We should even go a step further here: every figuration of freedom is in itself plural and full of inconsistencies, but what if the gap that separates the universal notion of freedom from the multiple meanings freedom has for different groups is the gap that constitutes (actual) freedom? Concretely, the fact that for me as a political agent the freedom for which I fight is at a distance from its particular content makes it possible for me to freely change the content of freedom that is attached to my idea of freedom. In English, this tension that cuts across the notion of freedom is indicated by two words, "freedom" and "liberty," which seem to refer to the same content (in Slovene, my own language, we also have two terms: "svoboda" and "prostost"). Numerous attempts to draw a distinction between the two brought no clear result—here is a quote from Wikipedia:

> Broadly speaking, liberty is the ability to do as one pleases, or a right or immunity enjoyed by prescription or by grant (i.e. privilege). It is a synonym for the word freedom. In modern politics, liberty is the state of being free within society from control or oppressive restrictions imposed by authority on one's way of life, behaviour, or political views. In philosophy, liberty involves free will as contrasted with determinism. In theology, liberty is freedom from the effects of "sin, spiritual servitude, [or] worldly ties". Sometimes liberty is differentiated from freedom by using the word "freedom" primarily, if not exclusively, to mean the ability to do as one wills and what one has the power to do; and using the word "liberty" to mean the absence of arbitrary restraints, taking into account the rights of all involved. In this sense, the exercise of liberty is subject to capability and limited by the rights of others. Thus liberty entails the responsible use of freedom under the rule of law without depriving anyone else of their freedom. Freedom is more broad in that it represents a total lack of restraint or the unrestrained ability to fulfil one's desires. For example, a person can have the freedom to murder, but not have the liberty to murder, as the latter example deprives others of their right not to be harmed. Liberty can be taken away as a form of punishment. In many countries, people can be deprived of their liberty if they are convicted of criminal acts.[2]

Let us then take a risk and fix this opposition as the one between what Hegel called "abstract freedom" and what he called "concrete freedom." Abstract freedom is the ability to do what one wants independently of social rules and customs, to violate these rules and customs, even to act against one's own substantial nature in an explosion of "radical negativity," exemplarily in a revolt or revolutionary situation. Such an explosion takes place when I do something crazy "out of nowhere," which surprises me also—recall Ang Lee's *Lust, Caution* from 2007. In 1942 Shanghai occupied by Japan, the Kuomintang undercover agent Chia Chi is given the task to seduce Yee, the head of the secret police department under the puppet government responsible for capturing and executing Chinese resistance agents who are working for the KMT. Her advances to become Yee's mistress are apparently reciprocated, and the two engage in a passionate love affair, with Chia caught in an inhuman emotional conflict, sexually and emotionally bound to a man whom she is plotting to assassinate. Yee invites Chia to an exclusive jewellery shop to give her an expensive ring, and this provides the resistance a chance to get at Yee without his bodyguards. When she puts on the ring, she suddenly and impulsively changes her mind and quietly urges him to leave. Understanding her meaning, Yee immediately flees the shop and escapes the assassination attempt. By the end of the day, most of the resistance group are captured. Emotionally in turmoil, Yee signs their death warrants and the resistance group members, including Chia Chi, are led out to a quarry and executed . . .[3] The important thing is not to interpret Chia Chi's sudden decision as an expression of some "deeper" unconscious determinism, even less as the final twist in her oscillation between the patriotic duty and sexual love where love prevails: her impulsive decision is the outburst of an "imp of perversity" at its purest, like Mersault's decision to kill an anonymous Arab in Camus's *L'Étranger*.

In contrast to such explosions, "concrete freedom" is the freedom located within and sustained by a set of social rules and customs. With regard to anti-vaxxers in the Covid pandemic, the freedom to choose being vaccinated or not is of course a formal kind of freedom; however, to reject vaccination effectively implies limiting my actual freedom as well as the freedom of others. Within a community, being vaccinated means I am a much lesser threat to others (and others to me), so I can to a much greater degree exercise my social freedoms to mix with others in the usual way. My freedom is only actual as freedom within a certain social space regulated by rules and prohibitions. I can walk freely along a busy street because I can be reasonably sure that others on the street will behave in a civilized way towards me, will be punished if they attack me, if they insult me, etc.—and it is exactly the same with vaccination. Of course, we can strive to change the rules of common life—there are situations when these rules can be relaxed, but also strengthened (as in the conditions of a pandemic), but a domain of rules is needed as the very terrain of our freedoms.

Therein resides the Hegelian difference between abstract and concrete freedom: in a concrete life-world, abstract freedom changes into its opposite since it narrows our actual exercise of freedom. Let us take the case of freedom to speak and communicate with others: I can only exert this freedom if I obey the commonly established rules of language (with all their ambiguities and inclusive of the unwritten rules of messages between the lines). What a society in its public discourse doesn't find satisfying is its specific repressed—unwritten rules, obscene supplements which are socially not recognized but necessary. The space of ideology, of customs that regulate our daily interactions, is thus ambiguous and inconsistent. There are prohibitions we are expected to violate, but discreetly, not in public. And there are freedoms that are given to us *on condition that we don't use them*—we are given a free choice if we make the right choice. (For example, in my country, if I have a dinner with my friend who is poor, when the bill arrives, he is expected to insist that he will pay his share, but I am expected to insist that I will pay, so he quickly accepts that I will pay.) But we also have prohibitions which are themselves prohibited, i.e., which cannot be publicly announced. For example, in a hard Stalinist regime, it was of course prohibited to openly criticize the Leader, but it was also prohibited to publicly announce this prohibition. Nobody publicly said that it is prohibited to criticize Stalin, and the one saying this publicly would instantly disappear.

The appearance of freedom of choice which conceals a redoubled domination is structurally similar to this paradox of prohibited prohibition. A free choice where you are ordered what to choose is not just an abstract presupposition—in our late-capitalist permissiveness it is more and more becoming part of our daily reality:

> Today's version of "I command you to freely sign this document!" – Company tells employees: work "voluntary" overtime or go to jail! After workers organized to refuse overtime voluntary shifts, the employer filed a labor complaint that resulted in the action being labeled an illegal strike. /. . ./ Not only must you do it, you must also *choose* to do it, actively *desire* to do it. You must not only obey, you must *love* obeying and publicly demonstrate this, prove it. /. . ./ Like the example of the postmodern permissive parent who manipulates the child not only to visit grandma, but to also want to visit grandma. The message is: "you have to do this, and you have to enjoy doing it too!"[4]

Every order of culture implies its obscene underground, what one is not allowed to talk about publicly. This space of the obscene operates at multiple levels, from rumours about the dark side of the private life of political leaders and the use of dirty language and indecent insinuations to cases which are much more "innocent" and as such even more crucial—here is an extreme case of the prohibition of publicly stating the obvious. In the last years of his life, Deng Hsiao-Ping officially retired, but everybody knew that he continued to pull the strings of power. When one of the high Chinese party apparatchiks referred to Deng as de facto leader of China in an interview with a foreign journalist, he was nonetheless accused of publicly disclosing a state secret and severely punished. So a state secret is not necessarily what only a few are allowed to know—it can also be something that everybody knows—everybody except what Lacan calls the big Other, the order of public appearance . . . In this way, we violate what Kant called the "transcendental formula of public law": "All actions relating to the right of other men are unjust if their maxim is not consistent with publicity." A secret law, a law unknown to its subjects, would legitimize the arbitrary despotism of those who exercise it—compare with this formula the title of a recent report on China: "Even what's secret is a secret in China."[5] Troublesome intellectuals who report on political oppression, ecological catastrophes, rural poverty, etc., got years of prison for betraying a state secret. The catch is that many of the laws and regulations that make up the state-secret regime are themselves classified, making it difficult for individuals to know how and when they are in violation.

This secrecy of the prohibition itself serves two different purposes which should not be confused. Its commonly admitted role is that of universalizing guilt and fear: if you do not know what is prohibited, you cannot even know when you are violating a prohibition, which makes you potentially guilty all the time. Of course, except at the climax of the Stalinist purges when, effectively, everyone could be found guilty, people *do* know when they are doing something that will annoy those in power. The function of prohibiting prohibitions is thus not to give rise to "irrational" fear, but to let the potential dissidents (who think they can get away with their critical activity, since they are not breaking any laws, but only doing what laws guarantee them—freedom of the press, etc.) know that, if they annoy those in power too much, they can be punished at the power's will.

But there is another function of prohibiting prohibitions which is no less crucial: that of *maintaining the appearances*—and we all know how absolutely crucial appearances were in Stalinism: the Stalinist regime reacted with total panic whenever there was a threat that appearances will be disturbed: there were, in the Soviet media, no black chronicles, no reports on crimes and prostitution, not to mention workers or public protests. This prohibiting of prohibitions is far from being limited to Communist regimes: it is operative also in today's "permissive" capitalism. A "postmodern" boss insists that he is not a master but just a coordinator of our joint creative efforts, the first among equals; there should be no formalities among us, we should address him by his nickname, he shares a dirty joke with us ... but, in all this, he *remains our master*. In such a social link, relations of domination function through their denial: we are not only obliged to obey our masters, but we are also obliged to act as if we are free and equal, as if there is no domination—which, of course, makes the situation even more humiliating. Paradoxically, in such a situation, the first act of liberation is to demand from the master that he acts as one: one should reject false collegiality from the master and insist that he treats us with cold distance, as a master ... No wonder all this sounds vaguely Kafkaesque—Kafka effectively wrote that "it is an extremely painful thing to be ruled by laws that one does not know,"[6] thereby bringing out the implicit superego obscenity of the famous legal principle that "ignorance (of the law) is not an excuse." Derrida is thus fully justified in emphasizing the self-reflexivity of the prohibition with regard to the Law—the Law not only prohibits, it is ITSELF prohibited:

> The law is prohibition: this does not mean that it prohibits, but that it is itself prohibited, a prohibited place /. . ./ one cannot reach the law, and in order to have a rapport of respect with it, one must not have a rapport with the law, one must interrupt the relation. One must enter into relation only with the law's representatives, its examples, its guardians. These are interrupters as much as messengers. One must not know who or what or where the law is.[7]

In one of his short fragments, Kafka himself pointed out how the ultimate secret of the Law is that *it does not exist*—another case of what Lacan called the inexistence of the big Other. This inexistence, of course, does not simply reduce the Law to an empty imaginary chimera; it rather makes it into an impossible Real, a void which nonetheless functions, exerts influence, causes effects, curves the symbolic space ... In every social situation, freedom thus works in an ambiguous way. On the one hand, we have what Marxists like to dismiss as a mere formal freedom: equality in the terms of law can cover and legitimize brutal submission and exploitation. (Marx was nonetheless fully aware that form matters: only the declaration of formal freedom opens up the way to demand actual rights and freedoms.) On the other hand, a subject who is effectively free (in the sense of power to decide) can claim that he is just doing his duty and in this way avoid full responsibility for his acts. (One can also evoke one's own culture in this way: I act as a racist, but it's not my guilt, it is part of the culture into which I was born ...)

This is what I call the structure of inherent transgression: a social space is not just the space of what is permitted but also the space of what is repressed, excluded from public space, and simultaneously necessary for this public space to reproduce itself. This is what "acheronta movebo" (move the underground) as a practice of the critique of ideology means: not directly changing the explicit text of the Law, but, rather, intervening into its obscene virtual supplement. For example, one should ask here a naive, but nonetheless crucial question: why does the Army universe so strongly resist publicly accepting gays into its ranks? There is only one consistent answer possible: not because homosexuality poses a threat to the alleged "phallic and patriarchal" libidinal economy of the Army community, but, on the contrary, because the libidinal economy of the Army community itself relies on a thwarted/disavowed homosexuality as the key component of the soldiers' male-bonding.

From my own experience, I remember how the old infamous Yugoslav People's Army was homophobic to the extreme (when someone was discovered to have homosexual inclinations, he was instantly turned into a pariah, treated as a non-person, before being formally dismissed from the Army), yet, at the same time, everyday army life was excessively permeated with the atmosphere of homosexual innuendos. Say, while soldiers were standing in line for their meal, a common vulgar joke was to stick a finger into the ass of the person ahead of you and then to withdraw it quickly, so that when the surprised person turned around, he did not know who among the soldiers behind his back sharing a stupid obscene smile did it. A predominant form of greeting a fellow soldier in my unit, instead of simply saying "Hello!", was to say, "Smoke my prick!" ("Puši kurac!" in Serbo-Croat); this formula was so standardized that it completely lost any obscene connotation and was pronounced in a totally neutral way, as a pure act of politeness.

The key point not to be missed here is how this fragile co-existence of extreme and violent homophobia with thwarted, i.e. publicly non-acknowledged, "underground" homosexual libidinal economy, bears witness to the fact that the discourse of the military community can only be operative by way of censoring its own libidinal foundation. Do we not encounter a strictly homologous self-censoring mechanism, outside the confines of military life, in the contemporary conservative populism with its sexist and racist bias? Against the image, all-present in cultural criticism, of a radical subversive discourse or practice "censored" by the Power, one is even tempted to claim that today, more than ever, the mechanism of censorship intervenes predominantly to enhance the efficiency of the power discourse itself. The language we speak is, of course, not ideologically neutral, it embodies many prejudices and makes it impossible for us to formulate clearly certain uncommon thoughts—as, again, Hegel knew it, thinking always occurs in language and it brings with itself a common-sense metaphysics (view of reality), but to truly think, we have to think in a language against this language. Among the best jokes about philosophy is the one reported on Twitter by Mira Assaf Kafantaris: "When I told my 4 years old son that I am not a medical doctor but a doctor of philosophy, he retorted with: 'Is philosophy an illness?'" This is what philosophy effectively is: an illness, a dysfunctional behaviour of the human mind. In some sense, the late Wittgenstein was right: philosophical problems arise out of the improper use of language, so the solution is to make them disappear by returning to proper use of everyday language . . . The problem is, of course, that this is impossible to do since misuse is inscribed into the very heart of language—into its very notion, as Hegel would have put it. The rules of language can be changed in order to open up new freedoms, but the trouble with Politically Correct newspeak clearly shows that direct imposition of new rules can lead to ambiguous results and give birth to new, more subtle forms of racism and sexism.

The contours of "concrete freedom" are, of course, historically variable: they depend on the predominant mode of social customs. Milena Zupančič, a Slovene journalist and anthropologist, caused a scandal by the frank description of Slovene sexual customs a century ago:

> A male specialty was also little pocket knives, often slightly twisted and with a not too sharp blade, sold by the traveling merchants from Dalmatia. A gentleman told me that, when he was a kid, he was always intrigued why his father didn't allow him to peel apples with this knife. Later he of course learned that men, who didn't wash themselves, used them to scratch from their penises the dirt which bothered them before they laid down to their wife to do their conjugal duty.[8]

When an injustice happens, its historicist relativization by way of evoking specific circumstances ("he lived in another epoch when it was normal to be a racist or anti-feminist, so we shouldn't judge him by today's standards") is wrong—we should do precisely that, *measure the past wrongs by today's standards.* We should be shocked by how women were treated in past centuries, by how benevolent "civilized" people owned slaves, etc. The lie of the historicist relativism resides in the fact that it is not truly historical: its position of enunciation is that of pure metalanguage, i.e., it is as if I exempt myself from all specific epochs and assume that I can occupy a neutral position from which I can compare different epochs.

This brings us to the profound historicity of the predominant notion of freedom: to simplify it to the utmost, in traditional societies freedom does not refer to equality—freedom means that each person should be free to play their specific role in the hierarchic order. In modern societies, freedom is linked to abstract legal equality and personal liberty (a poor worker and his rich employer are equally free); from the mid-19th century, freedom is more and more linked to social circumstances which enable me to actualize it (minimal welfare, free education, healthcare, etc.). Today the accent is on "freedom of choice", which implies that we ignore how the very frame of choices is imposed on individuals, which choices are de facto privileged, etc. However, Hegel knew very well that there are moments of crisis when abstract freedom has to intervene. In the December 1944 issue of *The Atlantic*, Sartre wrote:

> Never were we freer than under the German occupation. We had lost all our rights, and first of all our right to speak. They insulted us to our faces.... And that is why the Resistance was a true democracy; for the soldier, as for his superior, the same danger, the same loneliness, the same responsibility, the same absolute freedom within the discipline.[9]

This situation full of anxiety and danger was freedom, not liberty—liberty was established when postwar normality returned. And in Ukraine today, those who fight the Russian invasion are free and they fight for liberty—but can we still maintain clearly this distinction? Are we not more and more approaching a situation in which millions of people think that they have to act freely (violate the rules) in order to protect their liberty? I don't have in mind here only the Leftist anti-establishment uprisings, but also—today more than ever—the Rightist populist revolts! Did the Trumpian crowd not invade The Capitol on January 6, 2021, to protect their liberty? No wonder that there was a mix of fascination and horror present in the Left-liberal reaction to the protesters breaking into The Capitol—"ordinary" people breaking into the sacred seat of power, a carnival that momentarily suspended our rules of public life ... there was a little bit of envy in their condemnation of the event. So does this mean that the populist Right stole from the Left the last resort of their resistance to the existing system, the popular attack on the seat of power? Is our only choice the one between parliamentary elections controlled by corrupted elites and uprisings controlled by populist Right?

Regulating Violations

The embarrassing paradox we are compelled to accept here is that, from the moral standpoint, the most comfortable way to maintain one's high ground is to live in a moderately-authoritarian regime. One can softly (following the unwritten rules) oppose the regime (without really posing a threat to it), so that one can be assured of one's upright moral stance without risking a lot. Even if one does suffer some disadvantages (some jobs are out of reach, one can be prosecuted), such minor punishments only provide the aura of a hero. And even if the punishment gets harsher, one's moral compass is never thrown into chaos: one knows clearly one's duty, one knows that those in power are morally wrong and responsible for all troubles. But once democracy arrives, we all enter the domain of disorientation: choices are no longer so clear. For example, in Hungary in the mid-1990s, the liberal ex-dissidents had to make a difficult choice: should they enter into a coalition with ex-Communists to prevent the conservative Right taking power? This was a strategic decision where simple moral reasoning is not enough. That's why many political agents in post-Socialist countries long for the old times when choices were clear—in despair, they try to return to the old clarity by equating their actual opponent with old Communists. In Slovenia, the ruling conservative nationalists still blame ex-Communists for all the present troubles—for example, they claim that the high number of anti-vaxxers is the result of continuing Communist legacy; at the same time, the Left-liberal opposition claims that the ruling conservative nationalists govern in exactly the same authoritarian way as the Communists did before 1990. So the first gesture of a new politics is to fully admit this disorientation and to assume the responsibility for difficult strategic choices.

Here we stumble upon another paradox of political freedom: we should be very precise with regard to what the majority really wants—what if they don't really want to be free (in the sense of really choosing in elections), what if they care more for the appearance of freedom? In a "normal" democracy, the majority wants to maintain the appearance of freedom and dignity, it wants the electoral procedure to go on as if they are really making a free choice, but they simultaneously want to be discreetly told (by the media, experts, "public opinion") what choice to make. The rare moments when people really have to make a hard choice are usually perceived as the moments of the "crisis of democracy," the moments of anxiety when the very continuous order is threatened.

Between the two extremes of liberty and freedom there is a tension between the universality of Law and its species in the sense that particular species function as attempts to formulate the exception to the universal law—this exception can also be conceived as a space of freedom. Let's take the case of Islam: Mansur Tayfuri[10] brought out the deep ambiguity of Al-Anfal (or "haram") which characterizes the entire history of Islam, from Muhammad's time to our present. Al-Anfal stands for a set of things and acts that are "sacred" and should as such remain out of our reach; it mainly refers to what warriors should not do in a captured territory: rape or take others' women, loot their property and land, etc. But, as it is always the case with religious prohibitions, they see precisely what the victorious warriors desire most, so that it is de facto impossible to abstain from violating Al-Anfal. Tayfuri demonstrates that the establishment of a caliphate (the institution governing a territory under Islamic rule) served precisely the function of resolving this tension. The leader of a caliphate (caliph) has the right to allow his (selected) subjects the right to violate some rules of haram (to take women as personal slaves—a right which was recently practiced in

ISIS—etc.). Through this right to make the illicit lawful as a "favour" reserved for the Muslims, the caliphate constructed itself by projecting on God its own desire for the booty.

Tayfuri thus deploys nothing less than what we could call the "political economy of Islam"—something that is crucial for every religious edifice which, as soon as it becomes an actual power edifice, has somehow to legitimize the violation of its own sacred prohibitions. Immediately after Buddha's death, even Buddhism found ways to legitimize killing in a war (for example, as a way to prevent a greater evil . . .). The task of a religion is no longer just to enforce its prohibitions but primarily to legitimize the vast domain of exceptions to the Law, which only makes the reign of Law liveable. In Christianity, this systemization of exceptions was done by St Augustine and Thomas Aquinas; in Hinduism, it was done by *The Laws of Manu*, one of the most exemplary texts of ideology in the entire history of humanity. While its ideology encompasses the entire universe, inclusive of its mythic origins, it focuses on *everyday practices as the immediate materiality of ideology*: how (what, where, with whom, when . . .) we eat, defecate, have sex, walk, enter a building, work, make war, etc. Here, the text uses a complex panoply of tricks, displacements and compromises whose basic formula is that of universality with exceptions: in principle, yes, but . . . *The Laws of Manu* demonstrates a breath-taking ingenuity in accomplishing this task, with examples often coming dangerously close to the ridiculous. For example, priests should study the Veda, not trade; in extremity, however, a priest can engage in trade, but he is not allowed to trade in certain things like sesame seed; if he does it, he can only do it in certain circumstances; finally, if he does it in the wrong circumstances, he will be reborn as a worm in dog shit . . . The general formula of this procedure is to state one general rule, to which the whole of the subsequent treatise constitutes nothing but a series of increasingly specific exceptions. A specific injunction is stronger than a general one. In other words, the great lesson of *The Laws of Manu* is that the true regulating power of the law does not reside in its direct prohibitions, in the division of our acts into permitted and prohibited, but in *regulating the very violations of prohibitions*: the law silently accepts that the basic prohibitions are violated (or even discreetly solicits us to violate them); and then, once we find ourselves in this position of guilt, it tells us how to reconcile the violation with the law by way of violating the prohibition in a regulated way . . . The whole point of law is to regulate its violations: without violations, there would have been no need for the law.

Tayfuri's analysis is thus fully relevant today not just for our approach to Islam—our social reality here and now is full of the cases of granting exceptions as a special favour: wars are legitimate if they are proclaimed "humanitarian actions to protect peace," violations of women's and gay rights are tolerated if they are proclaimed to be a component of a specific "way of life," etc. So when you read Tayfuri's book, don't think just about Isis or Taliban, think about all those moments when our own "developed" societies do exactly the same.

How—if at all—can we break out of this predominant logic of moral imperatives (a universal rule with an exception: don't kill—BUT you can do it when you are in a just war, when you are defending your family from a murderer . . .)? In the terms of Lacan's formulas of sexuation, universality with exception is masculine, so what if we turn it around into the feminine version? When Antigone justifies why she unconditionally wants to perform the burial rites for her brother, the "law" she refers to is not a universality allowing no exceptions ("all humans have the right to burial, including my brother"): she begins with a chaotic absence of rules ("I would let all the bodies rot if the burial goes against the decision of public power"), and then adds an unconditional BUT ("but when my brother's funeral is at stake, I insist on it").

Freedom, Knowledge, Necessity

The obvious counter-argument here is: are these cases of freedom in all their diversity not constrained to our socio-symbolic universe? Isn't there the domain of facts which we are not free to choose, which simply are out there in their stupid being? Science is discovering (not inventing or creating) natural laws—we, humans, can get to know (some of) these laws, we cannot change them . . . We enter here the question of the relationship between freedom, necessity and knowledge. The Spinozean-Marxist tradition was unfortunately under the sign of Friedrich Engels's definition (he attributes it to Hegel) of freedom as insight into necessity: "I am free when I know the necessity and act upon it, like when I know natural laws and can exploit them in changing objects for my purposes . . ."[11] What immediately arises here is the follow-up questions: but are my purposes not also determined by necessity? If I know necessity, does this affect in any way necessity, or is my knowledge just an epiphenomenon and necessity realizes itself independently of it? Or is my knowledge itself determined by natural necessity? Does it matter that I know it? Engels relies on the model of what Hegel called "external teleology": the industrial exploitation of nature for our purposes which has nothing to do with the exploited objects (if, knowing physical laws, I stream water to produce electricity, this use is not immanent to the flow of water). Hegel says something different: for him, freedom is the "truth" of necessity, sublated (*aufgehobene*) necessity. What this means is at least that knowing a necessity, becoming aware of it, has a performative dimension: the very act of recognizing necessity actualizes it—the purest constative (just recognizing what there is) is the strongest performative. Is this not the case especially when the agency that takes note of something "really happening" is some figure of the "big Other" like the bureaucratic state agency? A friend from Slovenia told me of the tragic end of a young woman who wanted to change her sex to male; she went through all the procedures and, on the day she got by post the official confirmation that she was now a man, she took her life . . . It is too easy to speculate about the reasons that pushed her to do it (was realizing her deepest desire too much for her? etc.)—what we should note is just the weight of the symbolic act, of the inscription of my chosen identity into the official big Other. What drew her to suicide was not any change in her bodily or interpersonal reality (her parents and friends were supportive of her decision) but the mere final step of the state agency registering what she did.

The minimal gap between "what really happens" and its symbolic registration opens up the space for the opposite no less paradoxical case: what about necessity as Fate which realizes itself ONLY through being known? This paradox opens up an unexpected space of freedom: not of a freedom within the space of fate (in the sense that fate determines us, but not wholly, that we keep a margin of freedom), but a more radical freedom of changing fate itself. Recall the Arab story about the "appointment in Samara" retold by W. Somerset Maugham:[12] a servant on an errand in the busy market of Baghdad meets Death there; terrified by its gaze, he runs home to his master and asks him to give him a horse, so that he can ride all the day and reach Samara, where Death will not find him, in the evening. The good master not only provides the servant with a horse, but goes himself to the market, looks for Death and reproaches it for scaring his faithful servant. Death replies: "But I didn't want to scare your servant. I was just surprised about what was he doing here when I have an appointment in Samara tonight ..." What if the message of this story is not that a man's demise is impossible to avoid, that trying to twist free of it will only tighten its grip, but rather its exact opposite, namely that if one accepts fate as inevitable one can break its grasp? It was foretold to Oedipus's parents that their son would kill his father and marry his mother, and the very steps they took to avoid this fate (exposing him to death in a deep forest) made sure that the prophecy would be fulfilled—without this attempt to avoid fate, fate could not have realized itself. Daniel Gilbert wrote: "The fact that we can make disastrous decisions even as we foresee their consequences is the great, unsolved mystery of human behavior."[13] Instead of trying to resolve this mystery with the psychoanalytic notions of death drive and pleasure-in-pain, we can consider the possibility that the very fact of foreseeing the disastrous consequences and trying to avoid them makes the disaster happen. There is an important lesson in this about how ideology functions today. Economic or social determinists like to emphasize how social processes are objective trends which actualize themselves independently of our awareness or ignorance of them—our knowledge is just a secondary epiphenomenon. My Hegelian counterpoint is that some of these processes can go on *only if the individuals caught in them have a wrong notion of them*: "consciousness" is necessary, but it has to be a "wrong consciousness."

We should add yet another twist to this complex interconnection of factual necessity, knowledge and freedom: knowledge alone doesn't guarantee that I will act accordingly. Not only can I act in disavowal of what I know, knowledge itself can serve as the fetish that allows me to disavow the reality known to me. Today, ideology functions less and less like a symptom and more and more like a fetish. The symptomal functioning makes ideology vulnerable to ideologico-critical procedure: in the classic Enlightenment way, when an individual caught in ideology understands the hidden mechanism of ideological deception, the symptom disappears, the spell of ideology is broken. In the fetishist functioning, ideology works in a cynical mode, it includes a distance towards itself—or, to repeat Sloterdijk's old formula of cynical reason: "I know what I am doing, but I am nonetheless doing it."[14] As Alenka Zupančič wrote, in a cynical mode, the fetishist disavowal "I know very well, but . . . (I don't really believe it)" is raised to a higher reflexive level: fetish is not the element to which I hold so that I can act ignoring what I know—fetish is *this knowledge itself*. The cynical reasoning is: "I know very well what I am doing, so you cannot reproach me that I don't know what I am doing."[15]

Martin Luther's SIMUL JUSTUS ET PECCATOR is deeply ambiguous. It can mean that, once you really assume that you are a sinner, you are already beyond sin. (In the same way, for some Marxists, when you experience yourself as a reified object of exchange in a capitalist society, you are already a subject, i.e., only a subject can experience him/herself as such.) But it can also mean that, say, I am a dishonest pig, and I openly confess this, counting on the fact that my addressee will take my confession as a proof that I am not a dishonest pig. I had years ago a corrupted professor who told us students: "I know I am a dishonest pig!", and I was tempted to answer him with a version of the old Marx Brothers joke: "This guy is saying he is a dishonest pig, and he acts like one, but this shouldn't deceive you, he really is a dishonest pig!" So admitting that I am a dishonest pig can be itself a fetish obfuscating the fact that I really am a dishonest pig—my addressee should reply to me: "Why are you telling me that you are a dishonest pig when you really are a dishonest pig?" Or, with regard to global warming: "Why are you saying that we have to act now and change our way of life when we really have to act now and change our way of life?"

This is how in today's capitalism the hegemonic ideology includes (and thereby neutralizes the efficiency of) critical knowledge: critical distance towards the social order is the very medium through which this order reproduces itself. Just think about today's explosion of art biennales (Venice, Kassel ...): although they usually present themselves as a form of resistance towards global capitalism and its commodification of everything, they are in their mode of organization the ultimate form of art as a moment of capitalist self-reproduction. But this inclusion of critical self-distance is just one of the cases of how freedom of choice can act as a factor preventing the choice of actual change. In a wonderful comment on Italo Svevo's *Zeno's Consciousness*, Alenka Zupančič[16] shows how the very reference on a permanent freedom of choice (my awareness that I can stop smoking any time I want) guarantees that I will never actually do it—the possibility of stopping smoking is what blocks actual change, it allows me to accept my continuous smoking without a bad conscience, so that the end of smoking is constantly present as the very resource of its continuation. As Zupančič perspicuously notes, we should just imagine a situation in which the subject would be under the sway of the following order: you can smoke or not, but once you start to smoke you have no choice, you are not allowed to end—many fewer people would choose to smoke under this condition ... When I can no longer tolerate the hypocrisy of this endless excuse, the next step consists in an immanent reversal of this stance: I decide to smoke and I proclaim this to be the last cigarette in my life, so I enjoy smoking it with a special surplus provided by the awareness that this is my last cigarette ... and I do this again and again, endlessly repeating the end, the last cigarette. The problem with this solution is that it only works (i.e., the surplus-enjoyment is only generated) if, each time that I proclaim this to be my last cigarette, I sincerely believe it is my last cigarette, so that this strategy also breaks down. In Svevo's novel, the next step is that the subject's analyst (who, until now, tried to convince Zeno that smoking is dangerous for physical and mental health) changes his strategy and claims that Zeno should smoke as much as he wants since health is not really a problem—the only pathological feature was Zeno's obsession with smoking and his passion to stop doing it. So what should end is not smoking but the very attempt to stop smoking. Predictably (for anyone with analytic experience), the effect of this change is catastrophic: instead of finally feeling relieved and able to smoke (or not) without guilt, Zeno is totally perturbed and desperate. He smokes like crazy and nonetheless feels totally guilty without getting any narcissistic satisfaction from this guilt. In despair, he breaks down—whatever he does turns out to be wrong, neither prohibitions nor permissiveness work, there is no way out, no pleasurable compromise, and since smoking was the focus of his life, even smoking loses its sense, there is no point in it, so in total despair—not as a great decision—he *stops smoking* . . . The way out emerges unexpectedly when Zeno accepts the total hopelessness of his predicament. And this same matrix should also be applied to the prospect of radical political change.[17] True freedom occurs when we are forced to choose something that will determine the rest of our life, our Fate. This also happens in politics: true freedom is when we choose the contours of our "liberty" that will determine our entire life. Apropos the Ukrainian war, they are choosing the contours of their liberty—there will be no undoing it, no "let's go back and redo the choice" . . .

Freedom to say NO

We should make here a step further and accept that the cynical saying "Talk what you want, just do what I order you!" is false: even the most permissive cynical tolerance of talking is intercepted by numerous particular prohibitions. This is why freedom is not just the ability to do what I will, it is the autonomy of the universal with regard to its species: I experience my freedom when I, say, desire a dessert but cannot decide which one, so I oscillate and float—if I know what I want and directly grab it, there is no freedom in it, I just do what my (socially mediated, of course) nature is telling me. It is this autonomy that opens up the space for metaphoric substitutions in which a universal can stand for a particular, as in a video that went viral on social media in mid-March 2022 showing a woman being arrested by the Russian police for holding up a small piece of paper that read "two words" ("два слова" in Russian), which, of course, referred to the forbidden slogan "no to war" ("нет войне" in Russian). At its extreme, absence (void) itself can be "determinate," i.e., it can refer to a specific content—Russian police also arrested demonstrators who protested with blank signs: a video that received millions of views shows a woman holding a blank sign among a group of people before police officers approach her and escort her away from the crowd.[18] This substitution worked because everybody knew at that point what is prohibited in Russia: to publicly reject the war against Ukraine.

This is why another aspect of the subjectivization of a structure is that, in it, not only can something be missing (since it is not there where we expect it to be) but this missing itself can be missing—subjective desire is, at its most basic, always such a redoubled missing. Let me mention yet again the coffee-without joke from *Ninotchka* in which the waiter replies to the customer who wants coffee without cream: "Sorry, we ran out of cream, so, instead of coffee-without-cream, I can only bring you coffee-without-milk."[19] But we should go on with the joke: how does the customer react to the waiter's explanation? He should reject the waiter's offer because what he wants is coffee-without-cream—he is, say, tempted by cream and, as a compulsive gesture of sacrifice, wants to be deprived precisely of cream, not of milk, so what only counts as his object of desire is coffee without cream; in short, he wants the sacrifice of cream to be inscribed into what he gets: more than coffee itself he wants *no cream*. This is why, if the customer gets coffee-without-milk instead of coffee-without-cream, he will miss not the cream but *not having cream*. This is how differentiality works in the symbolic universe: only in this universe can we miss not only saying something but also not saying something—or, as one of the heroes says in the BBC series on gay life in the 1980s *It's a Sin* says: "We miss you not sayin' it." That's why, as Benjamin Libet argued decades ago, the most basic mode of freedom is that of a NO, of blocking what I spontaneously want to do, not a positive decision to do something.[20]

The lesson of this mess is that, as Libet put it, freedom is grounded in a NO, which ultimately means that the ultimate act of freedom is to renounce what one desires most. Recall Edith Wharton's *Age of Innocence*: Newland sticks to the customs (of marriage to May) and sacrifices what he desires more than anything else, but if he were to abandon May and escape to Paris to Olenska, or if he were to secretly pursue his affair with Olenska, he would not be truly free but simply follow his social dispositions. At the novel's end, the old Newland is told by his son that May told him she trusts her husband because he gave up what he praised her most for, and this information makes him avoid meeting Olenska now that he is free to join her (since May died). Newland also knows that May manipulated him: aware of his passion, she visited Olenska and told her that she is pregnant with her husband, making sure that Olenska will not pose a threat to her marriage. In contrast to this manipulation, Newland (not May) embodies the "age of innocence": if he were to act like May, he would simply cheat on his wife and discreetly pursue the affair with Olenska. While Wharton clearly sees the repression and broken lives caused by the reigning customs, she avoids any easy call for liberation: her broken heroines and heroes resist the easy way out because *they are free* . . .[21] But, again, are they free? What if their freedom is just an illusory self-experience? Until now, we have only talked about freedom as a social category, freedom in our socio-symbolic space—what if this freedom is a "user's illusion" of human beings who are effectively determined by anonymous (non-subjective) neuronal mechanisms? The moment has come to tackle this question directly.

2
Is There Such a Thing as "Free Will"?

From its very origins, philosophy dealt with freedom: how does human freedom fit into the general order of things? If there is no place for it in the order of nature, is it a gift to us, humans, from a higher being? Is "free will" just an illusory self-experience or can it be explained by evolutionary theory?

Determinism and its Vagaries

Since we live in the era of science, let's begin with the predominant stance of the natural sciences, deterministic naturalism. In nature (conceived in a scientific way) there is no space for free will, free will is a nonsense, and it is also naive to look for a space of freedom in the indeterminacy of nature discovered by quantum mechanics—freedom is not contingency but a free decision, i.e., the determinism of a free decision. With regard to quantum mechanics, freedom does not reside in the openness of the wave function but in the experimenting scientist's decision on what to measure which leads to the collapse of the wave function—this free choice (which takes place in our ordinary reality) is unaccounted for in quantum mechanics, and here enter the partisans of superdeterminism, who claim the only adequate way to resolve the problematic status of measurement that plagues quantum mechanics in its entire history is to assert the general interrelatedness of nature (reality)—the measuring process is part of the same reality as the measured phenomena. From this standpoint of deterministic naturalism, freedom is a "user's illusion": "freedom" refers to a subjective experience of doing what one wants, acting in a not-oppressed state, but this can be easily combined with determinism—I do what I will, but what I will is determined.

Benjamin Libet's (deservedly) famous experiment[1] is usually taken to demonstrate that there is no free will: even before we consciously decide (say, to move a finger), the appropriate neuronal processes are already underway—which means that our conscious decision just takes note of what is already going on (adding its superfluous authorization to a *fait accompli*). However, although Libet's results are clear, it is not clear what they are arguments FOR: Libet himself doesn't interpret them as a proof that there is no free will, he just moves free will to another level—he attributes to consciousness the veto power to stop the process already underway, so there seems to be at least the freedom to BLOCK our spontaneous decisions. And yet, as determinist critics of Libet have pointed out, what if our very ability to veto the automatic decision is again conditioned by some "blind" neuronal processes? There is, however, a third, more radical option: what if, prior to our conscious decision, there already was an *unconscious* decision that triggered the "automatic" neuronal process itself?

If freedom doesn't contradict natural laws, i.e., if the same event can be described as naturally determined and (at a higher level experienced as) free, what remains of freedom? It may appear that the only way to save freedom is to presume that there is a genuine contingency at a lower level of natural processes, and our free decision makes a choice in the space of this contingency. However, this solution doesn't work because it is clearly dualist: it explains (more or less, with all reservations) how a free decision does not necessarily contradict the realm of natural laws, but it does not explain how this freedom (which is a free determination, not a contingency) arises in nature.

Due to its reduction of the human psyche itself to an object of technological manipulation, biogenetics is therefore effectively a kind of empirical instantiation of what Heidegger perceived as the "danger" inherent to modern technology. Crucial here is the interdependence of man and nature: by reducing man to just another natural object whose properties can be manipulated, what we lose is not (only) humanity but *nature itself*. In this sense, Francis Fukuyama was right: humanity itself relies on some notion of "human nature" as what we inherited, as simply given to us, the impenetrable dimension in/of ourselves into which we are born/

thrown. The paradox is thus that there is man only insofar as there is impenetrable inhuman nature (Heidegger's "earth"): with the prospect of biogenetic interventions opened up by the access to the genome, the species freely changes/redefines *itself*, its own coordinates; this prospect effectively emancipates humankind from the constraints of a finite species, from its enslavement to "selfish genes." This emancipation, however, comes at a price:

> With interventions into man's genetic inheritance, the domination over nature reverts into an act of taking-control-over-oneself, which changes our generic-ethical self-understanding and can disturb the necessary conditions for an autonomous way of life and universalistic understanding of morals.[2]

How, then, do we react to this threat? Habermas's logic is here: since the results of science pose a threat to our (predominant notion of) autonomy and freedom, one should curtail science. The price we pay for this solution is the fetishist split between science and ethics ("I know very well what science claims, but, nonetheless, in order to retain (the appearance of) my autonomy, I choose to ignore it and act as if I don't know it"). This prevents us from confronting the true question: *how do these new conditions compel us to transform (reinvent or abandon) the very notions of freedom, autonomy, and ethical responsibility?* From a Kierkegaardian standpoint, we should also consider the opposite split:

> *I know very well that I am free and as such responsible for my acts, but in order to avoid the burden of this responsibility, I pretend that I believe in scientific determinism which enables me to say "sorry that I did that evil act, but it isn't my responsibility, it is the combination of my genetic structure and environment."*

The same point is made in more common terms by cultural critics from Fukuyama to Bill McKibben, worried about how the latest techno-scientific developments (which potentially make the human species able to redesign and redefine itself) will affect our being-human—the call we hear is best encapsulated by the title of McKibben's book: "enough." Humanity as a collective subject has to put a limit and freely renounce further "progress" in this direction.

McKibben endeavours to empirically specify this limit: somatic genetic therapy is still this side of the "enough" point, one can practice it without leaving behind the world as we have known it, since we just intervene into a body formed in the old "natural" way; germ line manipulations lie on the other side, in the world beyond meaning.[3] When we manipulate the psychic and bodily properties of individuals before they are even conceived, we pass the threshold into full-fledged planning, turning individuals into products, preventing them from experiencing themselves as responsible agents who have to educate/form themselves through the effort of focusing their will, thus obtaining the satisfaction of achievement—such individuals no longer relate to themselves as responsible agents ... But ignorance is not freedom. If I can influence my stances through bio-chemical and genetic interventions, this means that if I don't do it I am already determined by other bio-chemical and genetic factors. If we don't manipulate pre-born babies' genes, it is chance and not freedom that decides.

We can add another twist here: freedom is not just user's illusion, a false appearance, it is the "freedom" (minimal autonomy) of appearance itself with regard to its natural base/ground. This brings us to the next notion of freedom grounded in the vision of multiple layers of reality: out of a basic level which can be described by elementary physics, higher levels spontaneously emerge, each with its own immanent structure and causality: plants, animal life, human social and spiritual reality. Within Marxism, this vision was elaborated by Georg Lukács in his late "ontology of social being."[4] Lukács's starting point is his attempt to grasp human labour as the elementary form of teleology: in human labour, nature overcomes itself, its determinism, since natural processes become moments of the process of the material realization of human goals. Against Aristotelian or Hegelian idealism, which subordinates the totality of nature to a spiritual Telos, Lukács as a materialist sees social labour as the primary domain of teleology, a domain which remains a small part of nature and arises spontaneously out of biological processes. Although this "ontology of social labour" cannot be reduced to a version of the Stalinist dialectical materialism, it remains one in the series of big evolutionary visions of the cosmos as the ontological hierarchy of levels (matter, plants, animal life and human spirit as the highest level known to us), all too close to Nicolai Hartmann's ontology (and Lukács does refer positively to Hartmann). And it is interesting to note that even Quentin Meillassoux falls into this trap and pays a fateful price for his suspension of the transcendental dimension: the price of the regression to a naive-realist ontology of spheres or levels in the style of Nicolai Hartmann: material reality, life, thought.

The dilemma here is: is the relative autonomy of the higher spheres an actual fact of nature or is it just a simplification that pertains to the limitation of our description of reality, so that in a full description of nature no mention of higher levels would be needed? Daniel Dennett tries to resolve this deadlock with his version of a dualist ontology of physics and design: the two basic levels of reality are the deterministic physical level and the "higher" level of design.[5] Here is his own simple and clear example: imagine a two-dimensional grid of pixels, each of which can be ON or OFF (full or empty, black or white). Each pixel has eight neighbours, the four adjacent pixels and the four diagonals. This "universe" changes between each tick of the clock according to the following rule: for each of the cells in the grid, count how many of its eight neighbours are ON; if the answer is three, the cell is ON in the next instant whatever its current state; under all other conditions, the cell is OFF in the next instant. With the succession of instants, nothing "moves" here, individual cells are just going ON and OFF in a totally deterministic way. However, the moment we step back and consider larger patterns, surprising things happen. We discover that some forms (three pixels vertically or horizontally ON) behave like "flashers," flip-flopping back and forth from horizontal to vertical; some other forms like a square of four pixels just remain the way they are; other forms, like some five-pixel configurations, behave like "gliders," swimming, amoeba-like, across the plane. What, however, happens, when another configuration encroaches upon the first one? We get "eaters" (forms which swallow another form), "puffer trains," some forms vanish, etc., etc. Another ontological level thus emerges which, although grounded in physical reality, obeys its own rules:

> At the physical level there is no motion, only ON and OFF, and the only individual things that exist, pixels, are defined by their

> fixed spatial location /. . ./. At the design level we suddenly have the motion of persisting objects; it is one and the same glider (though composed each generation of different pixels) that has moved southeast /. . ./, changing its shape as it moves; and there is one less glider in the world after the eater has eaten it. /. . ./ Whereas the individual atoms—the pixels—flash in and out of existence, ON and OFF, without any possibility of accumulating any changes, any history that could affect their later history, larger constructions can suffer damage, a revision of structure, a loss or gain of material that can make a difference in the future.[6]

This dualism evokes many other, similar ones, in modern philosophy: Wittgenstein's opposition between things (objects) and what happens to them (what is the case, "*was der Fall ist*") in *Tractatus*, Deleuze's opposition between being and the flux of becoming, Alexis Meinong's opposition between objective reality and objects which correspond to different intentional attitudes (desiderata, etc.). It is easy to imagine other similar examples, like the running message on an electronic publicity board, where the message seems to "run across," the same letter or word moving from left to right, although, in physical reality, only fixed light-points are going ON and OFF; or the proverbial "movement" of the "same" shape of a sand-mountain during a storm in a desert (the shape seems to move, although individual pieces of sand merely change their positions within a very short scope of space). What we can do is thus to study the rules which predict the behaviour of these larger configurations at the design level, without bothering to compute the physical level: how should a glider be structured to avoid being "eaten" by another, etc. When we let the game develop in more complex ways, forms of behaviour appear which, from our human perspective, we cannot but describe as "intentional": some gliders seem to "avoid" being eaten or annihilated, etc.:

> Speaking of these smallest avoiders as if they 'knew' anything at all involves a large dose of poetic license /. . ./ but it is still a useful way of keeping track of the design work that has gone into them. /. . ./ Enriching the design stance by speaking of configurations as if they 'know' or 'believe' something, and 'want' to accomplish some end or other is moving up from the simple

> *design stance* to what I call the intentional stance. /…/ this permits us to think about them at a still higher level of abstraction, ignoring the details of just how they manage to store the information they 'believe' and how they manage to 'figure out' what to do, based on what they 'believe' and 'want.' We just assume that however they do it, they do it rationally—they draw the right conclusions about what to do next from the information they have, given what they want. It makes life blessedly easier for the high-level designer, just the way it makes life easier for us all to conceptualize our friends and neighbors (and enemies) as intentional systems.[7]

The model of this "as if" approach is, of course, the Darwinian evolution, where organisms act "as if" they strive for survival, "as if" they intentionally try to choose and develop the best organs and survival strategies, although, "in itself," the process is purely mechanic and senseless. (Does the notion of "memes" also not imply an intentional stance in the precise Dennettian sense of the term? When we talk about how memes use us, humans, in order to reproduce themselves, this is not a true ground-level naturalistic explanation of culture, but an explanation that offers itself when we observe the development of culture in the "as if" attitude of intentionality.) Does, then, "intentional stance" not function as a kind of Kantian "regulative idea"? Does it not imply that we do not describe reality directly as it is, but in an "as if" mode, imputing to it a teleology which cannot ever be fully proven? No wonder Damasio directly resorts to the formula of fetishist disavowal—we know, but nonetheless:

> Long before living beings had anything like a creative intelligence, even before they had brains, it is as if nature decided that life was both very precious and very precarious. *We know* that nature does not operate by design and does not decide in the way artists and engineers do, *but* this image gets the point across.[8]

Darwinism is THE anti-teleological thought, so the enigma remains: why do Darwinists, to get their point across, need the image of the very ideology they oppose? We are effectively dealing here with *supposed* knowledge, with a version of what Lacan called the "subject supposed to know." However, the greatness of Darwinism is that it provides a precise account of HOW the appearance of purposeful behaviour can emerge from a senseless mechanistic process, while this dimension is lacking in Dennett, and this failure is not without ironic consequences: when Dennett points out how we can perceive the "intentional stance" that inheres to a natural process—say, the avoidance of a threat—only if we speed up the slow natural movement ("Along the way there was much avoidance and prevention, but at a pace much too slow to appreciate unless we artificially speed it up in imagination."[9]), he thereby celebrates the same manipulation that the notorious Catholic anti-abortion movie *The Silent Scream* resorted to, that of a foetus being cut and dragged out in an abortion procedure: by reproducing the event in a fast-forward mode, the film creates the impression that the foetus is acting with a purpose, desperately trying to avoid the knife . . .

The problem with Dennett's dual ontology is: does it really reach "all the way down"? Is then the "teleological" causality of motivation (I did something because I aimed to achieve some goal) just an epiphenomenon, a mental translation of a process which can (also) be fully described at a purely physical level of natural determinism, or does such a "teleological" causation effectively possess a power of its own and fill in the gap in direct physical causality? In mechanistic materialism, the zero-level to which all "higher" forms of natural interaction, up to life and the human mind, can be reduced was conceived as the multiplicity of atomic parts moving in the infinite empty space—if we were able to know in detail their movements, everything else could be explained. However, 20th-century physics identifies as this zero-level not reality as we know it but a much more flurry proto-reality of quantum waves which includes irreducible chance and unpredictability. (With regard to the fact that there are some unexpected homologies between quantum proto-reality and the symbolic universe, I tried to argue that, in the guise of human spirit, i.e., in the symbolic domain, this "repressed" proto-reality returns within the order of reality.)

Is there negativity in nature? Of course not in the sense of self-conscious reflexivity, but in the sense that the massive presence of an In-itself is not the ultimate fact of nature. What Sartre describes so well in his *Nausea*[10] as the disgusting impenetrability of natural objects that resist subjective appropriation is not nature in itself but a mirror-image of subjectivity, something that subjectivity projects onto nature as its counter-image. The lesson of quantum physics is that there is something that precedes the mechanic reality of particles: wave oscillations which are in some sense pre-ontological; they "collapse" into the reality we dwell in—in quantum physics itself, these waves are conceived as a form of void. The conclusion that imposes itself is that the gradual stratification of nature into mechanic, organic, and the spiritual has to be supplemented by a preceding level.

Rewriting the Past

One can also sustain the space of freedom by way of directly limiting the domain of universal natural laws: either there is an exception in the order of nature itself when its laws are suspended (singularity, Big Bang), or there is a sphere radically different from the domain of nature (spirit, human soul). This is one of the ways Catholics make a compromise with the theory of evolution: it can explain the development of life on earth, but it cannot account for the emergence of human soul when god directly conferred spirit on humans. At the opposite end of this account of freedom in terms of an exception to the universal laws of nature there is the idea that, although there is no exception, nothing outside nature, nature is in itself "non-all," inconsistent, composed of multiple causal networks, and this multiplicity of imperfect causal chains opens up to the subject the space not to operate in pure freedom but to determine/choose the causal link that determines it. BUT how far should we go here? Does such retroactive causality not operate only in the domain of the symbolic order where, effectively, our free acts are not simply outside the chain of reasons, they happen because of gaps in the chains of reasons, and in this sense, we can change the past—to quote T.S. Eliot:

> what happens when a new work of art is created is something that happens simultaneously to all the works of art which

> preceded it. The existing monuments form an ideal order among themselves, which is modified by the introduction of the new (the really new) work of art among them. The existing order is complete before the new work arrives; for order to persist after the supervention of novelty, the *whole* existing order must be, if ever so slightly, altered; and so the relations, proportions, values of each work of art toward the whole are readjusted; and this is conformity between the old and the new. /. . ./ the past should be altered by the present as much as the present is directed by the past.[11]

Let us take the example of Shakespeare: a great staging of *Hamlet* today is not just a new interpretation of the play, it, in a way, fills the gaps in Shakespeare's original itself—when writing it, Shakespeare didn't know fully what he was saying, the play is full of inconsistencies, open towards the future. Recall also the ridiculously ingenious Christian reply to the Darwinist challenge. One of Darwin's contemporaries proposed an absurdly perspicuous reconciliation between the Bible and evolutionary theory: the Bible is literally true, the world was created *c.* 4000 BC—so how can we explain the fossils? They were directly created by God as fossils, to give humanity a false sense of opening, of living in an older universe—in short, when God created the universe, he created traces of its imagined past. Post-Kantian transcendentalism answers the challenge of objective science in a similar way: if, for the theological literalists, God directly created fossils in order to expose men to the temptation of denying the divine creation, i.e., to test their faith, the post-Kantian transcendentalists conceive the spontaneous everyday "naive" notion of objective reality existing independently of us as a similar trap, exposing humans to the test, challenging them to see through this "evidence" and grasp how reality is transcendentally constituted. We should nonetheless insist that the Christian solution—meaningless as a scientific theory, of course—contains a grain of truth: it provides an implicit adequate theory of ideology. Does every ideology not also directly create fossils, i.e., does it not create an imagined past which fits the present?

And the same holds for politics. When, in 1953, Chou En Lai, the Chinese prime minister, was in Geneva for the peace negotiations to end the Korean War, a French journalist asked him what does he think about the French Revolution; Chou replied: "It is still too early to tell." In a way, he was right: with the disintegration of the East European "people's democracies" in the late 1990s, the struggle for the historical place of the French Revolution flared up again. The liberal revisionists tried to impose the notion that the demise of Communism in 1989 occurred at exactly the right moment: it marked the end of the era which began in 1789, the final failure of the revolutionary model which first entered the scene with the Jacobins. The battle for the past goes on today: if a new space of radical emancipatory politics will emerge, then the French Revolution was not just a deadlock of history.

At every historical conjuncture, the present is not only present, it also encompasses a perspective on the past immanent to it—say, after the disintegration of the Soviet Union in 1991, the October Revolution is no longer the same historical event, i.e., it is (for the triumphant liberal-capitalist view) no longer the beginning of a new progressive epoch in the history of humanity, but the beginning of a catastrophic misdirection of history which reached its end in 1991. Or let's take the passage from Lenin to Stalin: once Stalinism emerged, Lenin's epoch changes its meaning, it becomes retroactively determined by what comes after—either Stalinism appears as a necessary consequence of Lenin's rule, or we emphasize how Stalinism involved a radical break with Lenin. However, if we really want to "liberate" Lenin from Stalin's shadow, we should avoid both these extremes (Stalin as the truth of Lenin; Stalin as a break, no continuity with Lenin) and try to abstract from Stalin's towering presence altogether, focusing on Lenin's period as it was in itself, with all the ambiguities that it involved, inclusive of its dark potentials (intuited exemplarily by Platonov's two great novels, *Chevengur* and *Foundation Pit*).

The counter-argument is here again that such a retroactive determination of causes which (I choose to) determine me is limited to symbolic networks: only within the symbolic space can I "change the past"—the past is factually what it was, but I can re-inscribe it into a different context, or simply act as if a part of the past didn't happen. In the first season of (the otherwise revolting) *Sex and the City*, there is a nice detail. Samantha spends the night with a young lover in the apartment of Charlotte where she is temporarily staying, without telling this to Charlotte. In the middle of the night, Charlotte stumbles upon the half-dressed boy in the corridor and tells him: "I am going to a bathroom, and when I come out, you will not be here, and we will never talk about this!" This is how *Ungeschehenmachen* (undoing something) can work in everyday life: you just make a deal with another or others to act as if something didn't happen. Unexpectedly, Louis Althusser himself (in his late manuscripts from 1980) engaged in this path, linking overdetermination with underdetermination:

> Of course there are . . . "possibilities" within social determination, if only because there are several different orders of social determination and because this creates a play—of gaps, blank spaces, or margins (des lacunes, des blancs, des marges) in which the subject may find his path determined or not determined by social constraints; but this non-determination is an effect, a sub-effect (sous-effet), of determination, of determinations; what I called not only overdetermination (surdétermination), but underdetermination (sous-détermination) . . . .[12]

However, a couple of pages later, Althusser wisely limits this "freedom of choice" to interpellation, i.e., to the assuming of (recognizing oneself in) symbolic identity:

> The interpellation of the individual as subject, which makes him an ideological subject, is realized not on the basis of a single ideology, but of several ideologies at once, under which the individual lives and acts his practice. These ideologies may be very "local", such as a subject in his family and at work, in his immediate relations with his family and friends or his peers; or they may be broader, "local" in the broad sense, either "regional" or "national". Such ideologies are, for the most part, always initially inherited from the past, the tradition. What results is a play and a space of multiple interpellations in which the subject is caught up, but which (as contradictory play and as space) constitutes the "freedom" of the individual subject, who is simultaneously interpellated by several ideologies that are neither of the same kind nor at the same level; this multiplicity

> explains the "free" development of the positions adopted by the subject-individual. Thus the individual has at his disposal a "play of manoeuvre" between several positions, between which he can "develop", or even, if you insist, "choose", determine his course, although this determination is itself determined, but in the play of the plurality of interpellations … The theory of the ISAs is therefore quite the contrary of a determinist theory in the superficial sense of the term.[13]

However, this grounding of subject's freedom in multiple (and conflicting, even) interpellations is not enough—there has to be a zero-level subject beneath the subject guaranteed its symbolic identity through interpellation. Althusser's own example of interpellation contains more than his theorization gets out of it. Althusser evokes an individual who, while carelessly walking down the street, is suddenly addressed by a policeman: "Hey, you there!" By answering the call—that is, by stopping and turning round towards the policeman—the individual recognizes-constitutes himself as the subject of Power, of the big Other-Subject: ideology

> "transforms" the individuals into subjects (it transforms them all) by that very precise operation which I have called interpellation or hailing, and which can be imagined along the lines of the most commonplace everyday police (or other) hailing: "Hey, you there!"
>
> Assuming that the theoretical scene I have imagined takes place in the street, the hailed individual will turn round. By this mere one-hundred-and-eighty-degree physical conversion, he becomes a subject. Why? Because he has recognized that the hail was "really" addressed to him, and that "it was really him who was hailed" (and not someone else). Experience shows that the practical transmission of hailings is such that they hardly ever miss their man: verbal call or whistle, the one hailed always recognizes that it is really him who is being hailed. And yet it is a strange phenomenon, and one which cannot be explained solely by "guilt feelings," despite the large numbers who "have something on their consciences."
>
> Naturally for the convenience and clarity of my little theoretical theatre I have had to present things in the form of a

> sequence, with a before and an after, and thus in the form of a temporal succession. There are individuals walking along. Somewhere (usually behind them) the hail rings out: "Hey, you there!" One individual (nine times out of ten it is the right one) turns round, believing/suspecting/knowing that it is for him, i.e. recognizing that "it really is he" who is meant by the hailing. But in reality these things happen without any succession. The existence of ideology and the hailing or interpellation of individuals as subjects are one and the same thing.[14]

The first thing that strikes the eye in this passage is Althusser's implicit reference to Lacan's thesis on a letter that "always arrives at its destination": the interpellative letter cannot miss its addressee since, on account of its "timeless" character, it is only the addressee's recognition/acceptance that constitutes it as a letter. The crucial feature of the quoted passage, however, is the double denial at work in it: the denial of the explanation of interpellative recognition by means of a "guilt feeling," as well as the denial of the temporality of the process of interpellation (strictly speaking, individuals do not "become" subjects, they "always-already" are subjects).[15] This double denial is to be read as a Freudian denial: what the "timeless" character of interpellation renders invisible is a kind of atemporal sequentiality that is far more complex than the "theoretical theatre" staged by Althusser on behalf of the suspicious alibi of "convenience and clarity." This "repressed" sequence concerns a "guilt feeling" of a purely formal, "non-pathological" (in the Kantian sense) nature, a guilt which, for that very reason, weighs most heavily upon those individuals who "have nothing on their consciences." That is to say, in what, precisely, consists the individual's first reaction to the policeman's "Hey, you there!"? In an inconsistent mixture of two elements: (1) why me, what does the policeman want from me? I'm innocent, I was just minding my own business and strolling around ...; however, this perplexed protestation of innocence is always accompanied by (2) an indeterminate Kafkaesque feeling of "abstract" guilt, a feeling that, in the eyes of Power, I am a priori terribly guilty of something, although it is not possible for me to know what precisely I am guilty of, and for that reason—since I don't know what I am guilty of—I am even more guilty; or, more pointedly, it is in this very ignorance of mine that my true guilt consists.[16]

What we have here is thus the entire Lacanian structure of the subject split between innocence and abstract, indeterminate guilt, confronted with a non-transparent call emanating from the Other ("Hey, you there!"), a call where it is not clear to the subject what the Other actually wants from him ("Che vuoi?"). In short, what we encounter here is interpellation prior to identification. Prior to the recognition in the call of the Other by means of which the individual constitutes himself as "always-already"-subject, we are obliged to acknowledge this "timeless" instant of the impasse in which innocence coincides with indeterminate guilt: the ideological identification by means of which I assume a symbolic mandate and recognize myself as the subject of Power takes place only as an answer to this impasse. So what remains "unthought" in Althusser's theory of interpellation is the fact that prior to ideological recognition we have an intermediate moment of obscene, impenetrable interpellation without identification, a kind of vanishing mediator that has to become invisible if the subject is to achieve symbolic identity, i.e., to accomplish the gesture of subjectivization. In short, the "unthought" of Althusser is that there is already an uncanny subject that precedes the gesture of subjectivization. This gap is addressed by the hysterical question which undermines the identity conferred by interpellation: "Why am I what you are saying that I am?"

Since desire is hysteric and metonymic, since it targets the gap beyond or between demands, what "not giving up on one's desire" amounts to is precisely the readiness to give up ("betray") any specific object, to pass from one to another object because no determinate object is "that"—or, as Lacan put it in his seminar *Encore*: "*Je te demande de refuser ce que je t'offre parce que c'est pas ça*" ["I demand from you (ask you) to reject what I offer you because it is not that"] (session of February 9, 1972). A case from everyday life: when I get mad at somebody my fury is triggered by some insignificant detail, and when the target of my fury gives me a perfectly reasonable and convincing explanation that my grudge is totally unfounded, I am disappointed and explode even more, as if I was somehow cheated ... It is the same in politics: when widespread protests focus on a specific demand which effectively functions as the condensation of a much deeper dissatisfaction with the existing order, and those in power wisely concede on this point, the protesters are quite justified in going on with their activity, aware that "this is not that" . . .

Beyond the Transcendental

But can we simply oppose symbolic retroactivity and external reality which stupidly is at it—or, as Lacan condenses "c'est comme ca," *sekomsa*. We should bear in mind that reality is never given to us directly but always within a certain symbolic frame, and this holds also for any scientific approach to reality. What this means is that our self-perception as free and responsible agents is not just a necessary illusion, but the a priori of every scientific knowledge, however determinist the content of this knowledge is. So when Sabine Hossenfelder dismisses free will (and the claim that the denial of free will destroys science itself) as non-scientific nonsense, she misses the point of her critics, the point nicely formulated in Michael Egner's (theologically inclined) critique:

> Hossenfelder is wrong to deny the reality of free will. I think her critique of physicists who deny superdeterminism because it denies free will has salience, but the denial of free will is self-refuting regardless of the issues in theoretical physics. Free will is a precondition for all science, all reasoning, and all claims to know the truth. As noted above, if free will is not real [then] all of our actions, including our investigations of reality, are determined by the laws of nature which in themselves are not propositions and have no truth value. Thus, if free will is not real, human thought has no access to truth. To deny free will is to assert it, and any denial of free will on any basis whatsoever is nonsensical. If we lack free will, we have no justification whatsoever to believe that we lack free will.[17]

We are dealing here with a case of what is usually referred to as pragmatic contradiction: the very practice of a scientific community (which relies on rational argumentation) addresses us as free-thinking beings who could be convinced by arguments. Even the most positivist and reductionist science is in itself a normative activity, it tries to make us accept facts as truths, and when we convince someone that he has no free will, what he is saying is: "Ok, you convinced me, I freely admit I have no free will ..." Our approach to reality always has to rely on some transcendental horizon; "transcendental" is the philosopher's technical term for a frame which defines the coordinates of reality. For example, the transcendental approach makes us aware that, for a scientific naturalist, only spatio-temporal material phenomena regulated by natural laws really exist, while for a premodern traditionalist, spirits and meanings are also part of reality, not only our human projections. The symbolic universe in which we dwell is "transcendental": it is not an object in the world since it provides the very frame of how we approach objects. This is what the object-oriented-ontology gets wrong when it points out that subject is not the centre of the world but just one among the objects in the world, which is why it cannot transcendentally constitute the entirety of reality: as it is clear already in Kant, "transcendental" names a fundamental limitation of our approach to reality—it is precisely because we are one of the objects within the world that we cannot observe reality (inclusive of ourselves) "objectively," i.e., that our approach to reality is constrained by our particular standpoint.

In this sense, there is nothing outside the symbolic Matrix since we (subjects) *cannot step out of ourselves*, we cannot as it were stand on our shoulders and draw a clear line of distinction between what only appears to us and what belongs to "things in themselves." "Transcendental" does not signal a superiority of subject but precisely its limitation: everything we experience, interact with, appears within a horizon of meaning or symbolic space into which we are "thrown," as Heidegger would have put it. When Heidegger characterizes a human being as "being-in-the-world," this does not mean that we are an object in the world. It means that, because of our limitation, we cannot ever fully self-objectivize ourselves: we cannot perceive and analyse ourselves as just another object in the world precisely because we are always-already IN the world.

Does this mean that the symbolic universe as the transcendental horizon that regulates our approach to reality is our ultimate point of reference, something behind or beneath which we cannot reach? What eludes reality (constructed/mediated by the big Other) is the Real in the Lacanian sense, something that resists symbolization.[18] David Chalmers[19] argues that virtual reality is genuine reality: virtual worlds are not second-class worlds, we can live a meaningful life in virtual reality—we may even be in a virtual world already. The difference between ordinary "real" reality and virtual reality is secondary and will gradually, with the further development of digital media, become irrelevant since humans will be able to pass from one to another reality, each offering a space into which we will be able to totally immerse ... While I accept that our access to "real" reality is always-already virtually-mediated by some symbolic network, I don't think this simple multiplication of realities works: what makes "real" reality different from virtual realities is not that it is in itself more "real" but that it is traversed by an immanent impossibility, that it stumbles upon something that eludes it, while digital/virtual realities are constrained only by the immanent rules of their construction. I propose here to read Chalmers's title "reality+" in the same way one should read "LGBT+": is + just a stand-in for the missing positions (like "and others"), or can one be directly a +? The properly dialectical answer is: yes, the subject is inscribed into a series of its possible identities precisely as a +, as an excess that eludes every identification. What this means is that subject is a + and simultaneously a –, a lack in the signifying chain: it is the excess itself which functions as a lack. And the same goes for reality: there are not simply "many realities" but many "realities+", and this excess is inscribed into "real reality" as a minus, as its constitutive lack.

However, the fact that a hermeneutic horizon through which we approach reality cannot be reduced to or explained by this reality does not imply that we are free to choose this horizon: on the most basic level, we are thrown into this horizon, this horizon always-already here determining how we perceive reality. So, again, our highest freedom (independence with regard to factual reality) coincides with destiny: the passage from the traditional view of reality and the modern scientific view of reality just happened as what Heidegger calls an "event," it did not arise as the "free choice" of an agent but is here as our fate. Insofar as "event" remains the ultimate dimension of freedom, we should note here that Heidegger disconnects freedom and will: freedom at its highest is not an affair of our free will. Is then this horizon the unsurpassable fact of our lives? Psychoanalysis shows the way beyond. Here Heidegger misses the point when, in his *Zollikoner Seminare*, he dismisses Freud as a causal determinist:

> He postulates for the conscious human phenomena that they can be explained without gaps, i.e. the continuity of causal connections. Since there are no such connections "in the consciousness," he has to invent "the unconscious," in which there have to be the causal links without gaps.[20]

This interpretation may appear correct: is it not that Freud tries to discover a causal order in what appears to our consciousness as a confused and contingent array of mental facts (slips of tongue, dreams, clinical symptoms) and, in this way, to close the chain of causal links that run our psyche? Is the whole point of "free associations" in the analytic treatment not to prove that they are *not* free but determined by unconscious causal chains? However, Heidegger completely misses the point here: as Freud repeatedly emphasizes, the unconscious is not an objective causal texture, *the subject is fully responsible for it*. In this sense, Freud notes with some irony that psychoanalysis is worse than Catholic confessions: in a confession, I have to admit all that I know, while in the analytic treatment I also have to admit what I don't know . . . The Freudian "unconscious" is grounded in the traumatic encounter of an Otherness whose intrusion precisely *breaks*, interrupts, the continuity of the causal link: what we get in the "unconscious" is not a complete, uninterrupted, causal link, but the repercussions, the after-shocks, of a traumatic interruption. What Freud calls "symptoms" are ways to deal with a traumatic cut, while "fantasy" is a formation destined to cover up this cut. Human freedom is ultimately not a user's illusion only if it is grounded in this catastrophe.

Pascalean Wager

In this sense (and in this sense only) freedom cannot be reduced to human freedom: it refers to the abyssal break whose dimension can be circumscribed only in terms of theology. The notion of "Christian materialism" thus has to be taken quite literally: only the specifically Christian notion of the Fall as the self-division of God can save materialism from the clutches of what Derrida called the "metaphysics of presence," of the notion of the universe as an all-encompassing global order, inclusive of all its inconsistencies and antagonisms. Crazy as it may sound, sometimes it is only a materialist theology that can help us break out of philosophical idealism—as can be proven by a close reading of Pascal's wager, a practical argument for the belief in God formulated by Blaise Pascal in his *Pensées* (1657–1658).

Pascal applied elements of game theory to show that belief in the Christian religion is rational. He argued that people can choose to believe in God or can choose to not believe in God and that God either exists or he does not. Under these conditions, if a person believes in the Christian God and this God actually exists, they gain infinite happiness; if a person does not believe in the Christian God and God exists, they receive infinite suffering. On the other hand, if a person believes in the Christian God and God does not exist, then they receive some finite disadvantages from a life of Christian living; and if a person does not believe in this God and God does not exist, then they receive some finite pleasure from a life lived unhindered by Christian morality. As Pascal states, "Let us weigh the gain and the loss in wagering that God is. Let us estimate these two chances. If you gain, you gain all; if you lose, you lose nothing. Wager, then, without hesitation that He is."[21]

Although Pascal addresses a person who is uncertain about God's existence, the semantic space of his wager is composed of two axes (I know there is god / I know there is no god; I choose to follow god / I choose against god), the combination of which allows four stances. The first two are ordinary: the common religious stance (I know there is god, and I follow and obey him), and the secular philosophical stance (I know there is no god, and I act accordingly, not caring for the afterlife). These two stances are, as Lacan put it, indifferent, with no deep engagement. The other two are much more interesting: due to their obviously paradoxical nature, they imply a strong subjective engagement. The third one—I know there is no god but I act as if there is one—is the stance of benevolent cynical goodness; it can assume many different forms, from moralist benevolence (even if there is no god let's act as if he exists, our life will be better . . .) to capitalist speculation. A capitalist knows there is no Market protecting him with its invisible hand, but he puts his wager on it, hoping that he will be touched by a contingent grace of profit—capitalism is definitely more Jansenist than Protestant.[22]

In contrast to these three stances, the only authentic one, the one enacted by a psychoanalytic subject, is the fourth one: knowing that god/the Other exists (that I am caught in its chain), I put my wager against him/it, and in exchange I get hell. What is this hell? Lacan put it clearly: "human desire is hell and this is the only way to understand something. Which is why there is no religion with no place for hell. Not desiring hell is a form of *Widerstand*, of resistance."[23] Desire is hell—heaven simply means a universe without desire. "Hell" is not another reality full of horrors, "hell" is the reality we live in, the reality of our lives structured by the inconsistency of our desires, the reality in which we desire what we do not want and do not even know what we desire. Lacan's formula "do not compromise your desire" means precisely this: remain faithful to your hellish desire to the end, accept that god himself is hellish, that he also does not dwell in perfect happiness.

What one should advocate is thus the materialist procedure of the immanent self-undermining of a religious edifice—the claim that god is evil or stupid can be much more unsettling than the claim that there is no god since the first claim destroys the very notion of divinity. Let's take *The Rapture* (1991, written and directed by Michael Tolkin, in which Mimi Rogers superbly plays Sharon, a young LA woman who works during the day as a phone operator endlessly repeating the same questions in a small cubicle among dozens of others, while in the evenings she engages in swinging orgies. Bored and dissatisfied at leading such an empty life, Sharon becomes a member of a sect which preaches that the end of times and the Rapture are imminent; turning into a passionate believer, she begins to practice a new, pious lifestyle, gets married to Randy, one of her previous swinging partners, and has a daughter Mary with him. Six years later, when Randy, now also a devoted Christian, is shot to death by a madman, this senseless catastrophe makes her and her daughter even more convinced that the Rapture is soon approaching. Sharon believes God told her to go with Mary to a nearby desert camping place and wait there until the two are taken into heaven where they will be united with Randy. Foster, a well-meaning, nonbelieving patrol officer, takes care of them there during their long wait when they run out of food. Mary gets impatient and proposes to her mother that they simply kill themselves in order to go to heaven and join Randy immediately. After a couple of weeks, Sharon also loses patience, decides to do the unspeakable and follows Mary's advice to stop her suffering; however, after shooting Mary, she is unable to take her own life afterwards, knowing that suicides are not allowed into heaven. She confesses her act to Foster who arrests her and takes her to a local jail . . .

Until this point, the story moves along "realist" lines, and one can easily imagine a possible "atheist" ending: bitter and alone, deprived of her faith, Sharon realizes the horror of what she had committed, and is maybe saved by the good policeman. Here, however, events take a totally unexpected turn: in the jail cell, Rapture happens, literally, in all naivety, including bad special effects. First, deep in the night, Mary appears with two angels, and then, early in the morning, while Sharon sits in her cell, a loud trumpet blast is heard all around and announces a series of supranatural events—prison bars fall down, etc. Escaping from the jail, Sharon and Foster drive out into the desert, where signs of Rapture multiply, from dust storms up to the horsemen of the apocalypse running after and around the car. Next, Sharon and Foster are both "raptured," transported to a purgatory-like landscape where Mary approaches them from heaven and pleads with Sharon to accept God, to declare that she loves God—by just doing this she will be able to join Mary and Randy in heaven. Foster, although until now an atheist, quickly seizes the opportunity, says that he loves God and is allowed entrance to heaven, but Sharon refuses, saying that she cannot declare her love for a god who acted so cruelly towards her family for no reason at all. When Mary asks her if she knows for how long she will be confined to the purgatory, condemned to be there alone, Sharon replies: "Forever." Sharon's resistance to God, her refusal to declare her love for him, is thus an authentic ethical act. It would be totally wrong to say that she rejects the *false* god and that, in an authentically Christian version of the film, the true Christ should appear at the end, proclaim her a true believer precisely because she refused to declare that she loves the false god. The true temptation to be resisted is thus to declare our love for a god who doesn't deserve it *even if he is real*. For a vulgar materialist, all this cannot but appear as an empty mental experiment; however, for a true materialist, it is only in this way that we really renounce God—by way of renouncing him not only insofar as he doesn't really exist, but even if he is real. In short, the true formula of atheism is not "god doesn't exist" but "god not only doesn't exist, he is also stupid, indifferent, and maybe outright evil"—if we do not destroy the very fiction of god from within, it is easy for this fiction to prolong its hold over us in the form of disavowal ("I know there is no god, but he is nonetheless a noble and uplifting illusion").

We are thus reading the truth of the Pascalean wager as the exact opposite of a call to put our bets on God—it is a crazy wager against God whose existence is accepted. Is this choice a simple nonsense? No, because the wager of my choice is that the Other ("God") is in itself inconsistent, antagonistic, that there is a lack in the Other—and with her simple "Forever," Sharon is addressing this very lack. As a subject, I am a subject of the signifier, caught in the signifying chain, but my very existence (or, rather, insistence) bears witness to a lack in the Other, to an obstacle which prevents the Other's closure into a consistent One. I as a subject am a living proof that the Other is not complete but cracked, that the Other doesn't know what it wants, that the impenetrable Other is impenetrable also to itself. Here fantasy enters: fantasy, a fantasy formation, is the way we try to obfuscate this crack in the Other. This paradoxical constellation is another way to formulate the "pragmatic contradiction" of predetermination and freedom: I know I am predetermined, but I put my wager against this and act as free.

It is easy to see why, even if I accept that my acts are fully predetermined, so that my free will is an illusion, it is still rational to struggle with myself to do what I consider to be the right thing: my acts may be totally predetermined but I don't know in what way, so what if I am also predetermined to passionately engage in ethical struggles with myself? This, of course, opens up a paradoxical possibility: that, perhaps, the only way to break out of predetermined fate is to do nothing actively, to abstain from all struggle, and totally surrender to fate. According to the standard view, the past is fixed, what happened has happened, it cannot be undone, and the future is open, it depends on unpredictable contingencies. What we should propose here is a reversal of this standard view: the past is open to retroactive reinterpretations, while the future is closed since we live in a determinist universe. This doesn't mean that we cannot change the future; it just means that, in order to change our future we should first (not "understand" but) change our past, reinterpret it in such a way that opens up towards a different future from the one implied by the predominant vision of the past. This is why radical acts of freedom are possible only under the condition of predestination: in predestination, we know we are predestined, but we don't know how we are predestined, i.e., which of our choices is predetermined, and this terrifying situation where we have to decide what to do, knowing that our decision is decided in advance, is perhaps the only case of real freedom, of the unbearable burden of a really free choice—we know that what we will do is predestined, but we still have to take a risk and subjectively choose what is predestined.

Since today's predominant notion of the big Other is that of the scientific knowledge which promises to provide a full causal explanation of my thinking and acting, leaving no space for freedom, the psychoanalytic subject's answer to today's big Other, scientific/determinist knowledge, is to conceive my freedom not just as a "user's illusion" but as something in which that gap in the Other resonates. This is why freedom is ultimately a crazy wager, a risky jump ahead of oneself: we do not wait to be free, but in a short-circuit we act as if we already are free. This brings us back to the topic of Buridan's ass: the wager on freedom is not grounded in reasons, in a free act we do something ignoring reasons or even acting against reasons.

Does this mean that we are free only in crazy practical acts not grounded in theory? Let us take the relationship between psychoanalytic theory and practice as a properly dialectical one: theory is not only the theory of clinical practice but simultaneously the theory of the ultimate failure of the practice (as Freud put it, clinical practice would be fully possible only in a situation in which it would no longer be needed). In this sense, Lacan said that clinical practice is the Real-impossible of psychoanalysis (in contrast to theory). This does not mean that theory is just talk, words, while practice takes place in the actual world where we really encounter psychic pain and suffering—it means almost the opposite. The aspect of impossibility of the clinical practice can only be demarcated through theory—without the theoretical gaze, clinical practice functions like any other practical endeavour, a profession following its rules. And the same goes for revolutionary activity. In his long poem "Lenin," Mayakovsky, THE poet of the Soviet Revolution, wrote: "Our dialectics / weren't derived / from Hegel's cunning. / Through battle's din / it burst into our verse / when bullets from our guns / sent bosses running / the same as we / had run from theirs at first." As a card-carrying Hegelian, I am tempted to add: this—not reading Hegel—is one of the reasons why the Soviet revolution ended up in Stalinism. Lenin's well-known aphorism from his *Philosophical Notebooks*—"It is impossible completely to understand Marx's *Capital*, and especially its first chapter, without having thoroughly studied and understood the whole of Hegel's *Logic*. Consequently, half a century later none of the Marxists understood Marx!!"[24]—should thus be taken quite literally (and applied to Lenin himself until 1915).

This brings us to the ambiguity of the formula $-*a*, the empty subject confronted to the *objet a*. Subject is voided, emptied of all substantial content by the signifying order; however, this void is correlative to the *objet a* which stands for the void in the Other itself, and, simultaneously, for the excess for which there is no place in the Other—this is why $-*a* is simultaneously the formula of a fantasy which fills in this void. Let us elaborate this point through one of my guilty pleasures, *Bulletproof Monk* (Paul Hunter, 2003, with Chow Yun-Fat in the main role)[25] which opens up in 1943 Tibet where a young monk is told he has fulfilled a series of prophecies that mark him as his master's successor; he is entrusted with guarding a scroll with the power to keep whoever possesses it young, immune to injury and so powerful that he can rule the world. The monk, who also learns he must one day find his own successor to pass the scroll onto, is forced to flee when Nazi German soldiers, led by Colonel Strucker, attack his temple and murder his master in search of the scroll.

Sixty years later, in New York, the nameless monk witnesses a young pickpocket named Kar fleeing from police as well as from members of a local gang who do not like him pickpocketing on their turf. When, on a subway station, a young girl falls into the path of an oncoming train, Kar and the monk rescue her. After they introduce themselves to each other, Kar steals the scroll from the monk and runs away; the monk pursues Kar, believing he may have fulfilled the first prophecy. When Kar finds himself fighting the local gang's leader, he meets a roguish young woman among them named Jade, whom he falls in love with. The following day, Jade attends a museum exhibition presided over by a beautiful yet disconcerting young blonde woman, later revealed to be Strucker's granddaughter Nina, who secretly spearheads his ongoing hunt for the scroll.

After a series of twists and turns, Strucker, dressed in his old uniform, regains his youth (he has read the scroll); however, he finds that the scroll's last verse, which the monk reveals he memorized, is missing. Before Strucker can scan the monk's brain for it, Kar arrives and distracts him, allowing the monk to break free and fight Strucker alongside Kar, knocking him off the roof and onto live electrical wires. Believing that Strucker has been dealt with, the pair reunite with Jade. The contents of the scroll transfer to Kar, as he has fulfilled the third prophecy. Strucker, still alive, attempts to kill Kar but is killed himself by a falling statue. Kar is surprised to find Jade alive after seemingly being shot by Strucker: like Kar, she also fulfilled the three prophecies, and the scroll's power is transferred to her as well. The monk, now aged, meets with Kar and Jade the next day, giving each one half of the final verse, deeming them inseparable . . . The ridicule of this ending cannot but strike the eye: in the best Hollywood tradition, the Oriental "unity of the opposites" appears in today's New York as the unity of a love couple.

Is there some emancipatory potential in the fact that the next master-protector is an ordinary young delinquent, the lowest figure in our society irradiating no simple deep wisdom? Yes, because the only condition s/he has to meet is that his acts fit the prophecy, which is here another name for contingency; the master-protector is not qualified by his/her properties, it can be anybody who happens to meet the conditions of the prophecy, so that his/her eventual wisdom comes from the symbolic place s/he happens to find him/herself in. No, because the obvious big question opened up by the movie remains unanswered: the content of the scroll has to be hidden since if it is known it gives to the one who knows it unlimited power—*why is then the scroll not simply destroyed*? Why must it be *kept* as a secret? There is only one consistent answer: this "secret" has no definite content, it is what Hitchcock would have called a pure MacGuffin, what matters is solely the *form* of a secret. The "power" exhibited by the evil person supposed to "know the secret" (like Strucker in the film) is not grounded in any real knowledge but only in the aura of possessing a secret. This is where *Bulletproof Monk* fails: it continues to imply that the secret contained in the scroll refers to some actual knowledge—in clear contrast to authentic Buddhism which is based on the insight into how the ultimate secret is that there is no secret. For a dialectical-materialist theory, the question is why is such a structure of "secret" constitutive of our ideological space, why can we not simply abolish it? And the answer is provided by the peculiar status of *objet a*, the object-cause of desire.

To put it in well-known Lacanian terms, the shift to be accomplished here is the shift from alienation to separation: from the subject being erased/voided by the Other ($)—and in this narrow sense separated from the Other—to the emergence of *objet a* as an excess, of a point at which *the Other is separated from itself*. What is absolutely to be avoided here is the Feuerbachian-early Marxian formula according to which the separation of God from man is an effect of the separation of man from himself, so that God vanishes when humans appropriate their essence, their authentic potentials. In theological terms, the space of freedom is opened when I (a believer alienated in God as the absolute master) discover that God himself is already separated from himself—which happens at its purest in Christianity only, when in Christ God separates himself from himself. The paradox of the proposed wager is that I do not wager on God's perfection but on God's imperfection, on his failure and inconsistency—or, as Chesterton put it: "Christianity is the only religion on earth that has felt that omnipotence made God incomplete. Christianity alone has felt that God, to be wholly God, must have been a rebel as well as a king."[26] Freud was well aware of this paradox when, in his *The Ego and the Id*, he wrote: "If anyone were to put forward the paradoxical proposition that normal man is not only far more immoral than he believes but also far more moral than he knows, psycho-analysis, on whose findings the first half of the assertion rests, would have no objection to raise against the second half."[27]

Alenka Zupančič applied this same paradox to Kant's notion of freedom: we are not only much less free than we believe, we are also much more free than we know. Where I believe that I am free (in the sense of experiencing myself as a spontaneous agent), Kant has no problem in admitting that, in principle, all my spontaneous acts are conditioned by "pathological" causes—in psychoanalysis, free associations prove this abundantly. But where the subject goes to the end in his reduction denouncing the spontaneity of his "inner life," he stumbles upon a freedom that reaches well beyond "doing what I feel or want." This also affects Kant's notion of autonomy: where I act freely, do what I want, I am enslaved to my pathological motivations. I am really and autonomous when I do something I simply cannot not do it.[28] How, exactly, are we to understand this? NOT in the Spinozean way of freedom as known necessity: in Spinoza (and his followers like Althusser) there is no place for pure *cogito*, science is a knowledge which does not imply any subjective position, or, as Lacan put it, sciences forecloses subject. But Lacan's "there is no meta-language" means precisely that there is no external-asubjective position of knowledge available to us—which subject is then implied by a scientific discourse? Here we have to introduce the difference between the subject of enunciation and the subject of the enunciated: freedom as subjective experience, spontaneous feeling of acting, is imaginary, determined by the unconscious Other, it concerns the subject of the enunciated—in Kant's terms, this freedom is always ruled by pathological motivations and thus reducible to causality. But when we accept that this spontaneous freedom is imaginary, determined by pathological causal mechanisms, what remains is the empty subject deprived of its pathological content—and this is the Cartesian cogito. This subject cannot be grounded in natural determinism because it arises as an "answer of the real," as a reaction to a traumatic cut. The claim that the subject we are dealing with here "doesn't really exist" is of course in some basic sense true: we will never discover the subject as an element in our reality, in the same way that the frame doesn't exist in the within picture it enframes. More precisely, the subject doesn't exist "objectively," but it also doesn't exist in itself, as an isolated solipsist monad: it exists only for another subject, it comes to be through stumbling upon the abyss of another's desire, through not knowing what the Other wants from it. We encounter in reality elements which appear to signal another subject's presence (artificial buildings, writings . . .) and subject is what we presuppose to be implied by these artefacts. That's why Artificial Intelligence is so disturbing: it can generate objects which we are accustomed to perceive as the expression of another subject. The title of a recent CNN report—"AI won an art contest, and artists are furious"[29]—tells it all. But this doesn't not mean that, even in the case of "real" other subjects, we can ever be sure: subject is as such a presupposition, the moment we can fully objectivize it it is no longer a subject.

3
Indivisible Remainder and the Death of Death

The Standpoint of the Absolute

Did we not regress to a crazy mixture of Gnosticism and Hegelian speculation, ending up in a topic of the Absolute which is clearly out of place in our post-Hegelian universe? Was Hegel not the last one who dared to talk about the Absolute in this way? But in what precise sense *did* he talk about the Absolute? In his short text, "The Return of Metaphysics: Hegel vs Kant," Robert Pippin provides a succinct description of his (Kantian, in my view) reading of Hegel:

> Hegel's basic claim had three components. The first is the claim that a priori knowledge of the world, the ordinary spatio-temporal world, is possible; knowledge about that world, but achieved independently of empirical experience. The second component is where all the interpretive controversies begin. It is the claim that this a priori knowledge, while in some sense ultimately about the world, consists in thinking's or reason's knowledge of itself; thinking's understanding of thinking or, as Hegel designates, a "science of pure thinking." . . . Hegel's enterprise takes as its topic the categories or thought determinations" (*Denkbestimmungen*) necessary for thought to have determinate objective content, an enterprise that at the same time specifies the determinations inherent in the possible determinacy of being itself. That means it is a metaphysics, one based on the "identity" in this sense, of "thinking and being." This is not a knowledge of any nonsensible reality, it is a knowledge of any intelligible reality, the only kind there is. It is a revival of the great principle of classical philosophy: to be is to be intelligible. Thinking's knowledge of itself is knowing

> what could be intelligible and therewith a knowledge of what could be.[1]

Sum ergo cogito is thus the formula of transcendental idealism: whatever there is has to appear within the structure of *Denkbestimmungen* deployed in logic, so that "I am" is already a statement within the space of thinking, i.e., only a thinking being can say "I am." But is this the ultimate limit of our thought? How to unite this with Hegel's claim that philosophy is its time conceived in concepts? Can, say, quantum mechanics still be fully covered by Hegel's matrix of all possible thought-determinations?

But does Hegel really follow Kant's insight that, even if our thinking cannot reach reality in itself, it has one object fully accessible to it—thinking itself? Pippin's idea is that, based on this insight, Hegel simply extends it to all possible objects and thus elevates it into metaphysics: whatever we think is circumscribed by the form-determinations of our thinking. However, Hegel's "reversal" of Kant is much more refined and radical. Kant's position is that the intractable thing that resists our cognitive grasp is reality "in itself," while thinking can clearly analyse itself and bring out its own immanent structure—antinomies and inconsistencies only arise when thinking is applied to reality beyond the scope of our experience. Hegel's position is that inconsistencies and "contradictions" are immanent to thinking, so that they emerge already when thinking tries to think itself, its own immanent structure—our thinking "reaches" reality precisely because its immanent "contradictions" mirror contradictions in/of reality itself. The failure of thinking to grasp reality is immanent to reality itself.

The predominant liberal reading of Hegel with its focus on reconciliation seems to remain within the horizon of the old Hegelian English joke: "I tried to read Hegel but found out that I Kant."[2] (We ignore here the potential obscenity of "Kant" which can be associated to "can't" as well as to "cunt.") They read Hegel, but their reading remains within the Kantian boundaries. Terry Pinkard correctly located the limit of the Kantian appropriations of Hegel into their uneasiness with the notion of the Absolute:

> to the extent that Hegel's legacy depends on his embrace of the necessity of "the absolute," Hegel's legacy in political theory at

> least remains troubled. Jürgen Habermas, for example, has consistently argued that although there are many independent items in Hegel's system worthy of further independent development on their own, his deeper commitment to some kind of "absolute" nonetheless has various authoritarian and antidemocratic implications that are not mere prejudices of his own time but which follow from the reliance on the "absolute." . . . the Hegelian emphasis on the absolute and on history as the self-articulation of the absolute has been argued to be Hegel's Achilles Heel, the real point at which the Hegelian system plunges into irretrievability for those after him.[3]

This point seems obvious: does the talk about the "Absolute" in such a direct way as Hegel practises it, positing the Absolute not in some Beyond out of our reach but as the topic of fully rational analysis, not belong to another era, the era which was dealt a mortal blow with the rise of modern empirical sciences and secular societies? In the "Preface" to his *Hegel: A Biography* (2000), Pinkard concisely deploys how all philosophical and political misunderstandings about Hegel originate in the wrong reading of his notion of the Absolute:

> Hegel is one of those thinkers just about all educated people think they know something about. His philosophy was the forerunner to Karl Marx's theory of history, but unlike Marx, who was a materialist, Hegel was an idealist in the sense that he thought that reality was ultimately spiritual, and that it developed according to the process of thesis/ antithesis/ synthesis. Hegel also glorified the Prussian state, claiming that it was God's work, was perfect, and was the culmination of all human history. All citizens of Prussia owed unconditional allegiance to that state, and it could do with them as it pleased. Hegel played a large role in the growth of German nationalism, authoritarianism, and militarism with his quasi-mystical celebrations of what he pretentiously called the Absolute.
>
> Just about everything in the first paragraph is false except for the first sentence.
>
> What is even more striking is that it is all clearly and demonstrably wrong, has been known to be wrong in scholarly

circles for a long time now, and it still appears in almost all short histories of thought or brief encyclopedia entries about Hegel.[4]

From the Hegelian standpoint, it is easy to see how this "clearly and demonstrably wrong" opinion imputes to Hegel a decidedly pre-Hegelian notion of the Absolute as something that is even more substantial than what we are facing as objective reality, a true In-itself that encompasses all and is beyond the scope of our representation. For Hegel, however, the minimal determination of "absolute" is self-relating: an entity which never simply and directly interacts with its environment (or is "influenced" by it)—it reflexively determines itself the mode of this interaction, the mode of how it is determined by its others. This, incidentally, is also the minimal determination of freedom: I am free if I minimally determine the conditions of my interaction with my environment. That's why life is the basic form of freedom: a living organism "constructs" its own environment, it selects parts of the environment (dangers, food, sexual partners) with which it interacts. That's why, in a living organism, the way I relate to an other is always also a way I relate to myself: I search for food because I need to survive, I search for a mate because I need to procreate . . . What this means is that, as a living organism, I am not just myself in my flat presence, I simultaneously APPEAR TO MYSELF in a certain mode (of hunger, of a drive to mate . . .) This is why the Absolute is not the true In-itself beyond objective reality—to arrive at the Absolute, what one has to add to the objective order is its appearance itself: one has to grasp how the subjective appearances and illusions of a thing that blur and misrepresent its "objective reality" are a moment of this thing itself, its necessary moment. We arrive at the absolute standpoint when we grasp how, if we subtract from a thing its illusory appearance, if we try to grasp a thing as it "really is in itself," this thing itself disintegrates. That's why Marx can be said to conceive capital as an absolute: he realized that the illusory way we experience capital (like commodity fetishism) is constitutive of its reality, that capital can only reproduce itself through this illusion. In this sense, as Hegel repeats again and again, the Absolute is the unity of the objective and the subjective: it is not a subjective notion that fits the objective (how things really are), it is the objective order which includes its subjective misrepresentations. In this sense, freedom is a subjective experience, but it is the very freedom (autonomy) of subjective experience with regard to "objective" reality that is the stuff of science. The very fact that we cannot ground it in "objective" reality is a negative proof of freedom.

Is, however, such a notion of the unity of the objective and the subjective enough to overcome being caught in a transcendental horizon? Things are here more difficult and impregnated by ambiguities than they may appear. The contrast between scientific realism and transcendental culturalism can be formulated in Spinoza's terms: if, for scientists, the name of the All is *Deus sive natura*, for culturalists it is *Deus sive cultura*, i.e., the cultural horizon ("episteme") is the ultimate reference of our knowledge. In the move from Kant to Hegel, we admit that our knowledge, when it tries to understand reality, gets involved in insoluble antinomies and paradoxes, but we then transpose these epistemological obstacles into reality itself, as it happens exemplarily from quantum mechanics (X is simultaneously particle and wave) and Marxism.

But, again, is this ontologization of epistemological antinomies and obstacles enough? Is there not also a zero-level of gnostic insight called by mystics "night of the world," confrontation with the abyss/crack that we "are" as the point at which only we touch the Real in itself?[5] This "night of the world" was called by Freud the unconscious "death drive," and, prior to Freud, Schelling developed the notion that the basic free decisions made by us are unconscious. So, with regard to Libet's experiment, from the Freudian standpoint, the basic underlying problem is that of the status of the Unconscious: are there only conscious thoughts (my belated conscious decision to move a finger) and "blind" neuronal processes (the neuronal activity to move the finger), or is there also an unconscious "mental" process? And, what is the ontological status of this unconscious, if there indeed is one? Is it not that of a purely virtual symbolic order, of a pure logical *presupposition* (the decision HAD TO BE MADE, although it was never effectively made in real time)? At the apogee of German Idealism, F.W.J. Schelling deployed the notion of the primordial decision-differentiation (*Ent-Scheidung*), the unconscious atemporal deed by means of which the subject chooses his/her eternal character which, afterwards, within his/her conscious-temporal life, s/he experiences as the inexorable necessity, "the way s/he always was":

> The deed, once accomplished, sinks immediately into the unfathomable depth, thereby acquiring its lasting character. It is the same with the will which, once posited at the beginning and led into the outside, immediately has to sink into the unconscious. This is the only way the beginning, the beginning that does not cease to be one, the truly eternal beginning, is possible. For here also it holds that the beginning should not know itself. Once done, the deed is eternally done. The decision that is in any way the true beginning should not appear before consciousness, it should not be recalled to mind, since this, precisely, would amount to its recall. He who, apropos of a decision, reserves for himself the right to drag it again to light, will never accomplish the beginning.[6]

This absolute beginning is never made in the present: its status is that of a pure presupposition, of something which always-already took place. In other words, it is the paradox of a *passive decision*, of passively assuming the Decision that grounds our being as the supreme act of freedom—the paradox of the highest free choice which consists in assuming that one is chosen. In his *Adieu à Emmanuel Levinas*, Derrida tries to dissociate the decision from its usual metaphysical predicates (autonomy, consciousness, activity, sovereignty . . .) and think it as the "other's decision in me": "The passive decision, condition of the event, is always, structurally, an other decision in me, a rending decision as the decision of the other. Of the absolutely other in me, of the other as the absolute who decides of me in me."[7] In psychoanalytic terms, this choice is that of the "fundamental fantasy," of the basic frame/matrix which provides the coordinates of the subject's entire universe of meaning: although I am never outside it, although this fantasy is always-already here, and I am always-already thrown into it, I have to presuppose myself as the one who posited it.

Schelling here just radicalizes Kant's notion of a primordial, atemporal, transcendental act by means of which we choose our "eternal character," the elementary contours of our ethical identity. And the link with Freud's notion of an *unconscious* decision is clear here: this absolute beginning is never made in the present, i.e., its status is that of a pure presupposition, of something which always-already took place. The topic of radical Evil, from Kant to Schelling, is an attempt to solve the enigma of how it is that we hold an evil person responsible for his deeds (although it is clear to us that the propensity to Evil is part of this person's "nature," i.e., that he cannot but "follow his nature" and accomplish his deeds with an absolute necessity), Kant and Schelling postulate a non-phenomenal transcendental, atemporal act of primordial choice, by means of which, each of us, prior to his temporal bodily existence, chooses his eternal character. Within our temporal phenomenal existence, this act of choice is experienced as an imposed necessity, which means that the subject, in his phenomenal self-awareness, is not conscious of the free choice which grounds his character (his ethical "nature")—that is to say, this act is radically unconscious.

Kant gets involved here in a difficult predicament: for him, we are not free when we just do what we want but only when we follow the moral law AGAINST our spontaneous tendencies (which enslave us to our pathological nature). However, in his detailed analysis of evil, Kant is compelled to distinguish between "ordinary" evil (the violation of morality on behalf of some "pathological" motivation, like greed, lust, ambition, etc.), "radical" evil and "diabolical" evil. It may seem that we are dealing with a simple linear graduation: "normal" evil, more "radical" evil and, finally, the unthinkable "diabolical" evil. However, upon a closer look, it becomes clear that the three species are not at the same level, i.e., that Kant confuses different principles of classification. "Radical" evil does not designate a specific type of evil acts, but an a priori propensity of the human nature (to act egotistically, to give preference to pathological motivations over universal ethical duty) which opens up the very space for "normal" evil acts, i.e., which roots them in human nature. In contrast to it, "diabolical" evil does designate a specific type of evil act: acts which are not motivated by any pathological motivation but are done "just for the sake of it," elevating evil itself into an a priori *non-pathological* motivation—something akin to Poe's "imp of perversity."

While Kant claims that "diabolical evil" cannot actually occur (it is not possible for a human being to elevate evil itself into a universal ethical norm), he nonetheless asserts that one should posit it as an abstract possibility. Interestingly enough, the concrete case he mentions (in Part I of his *Metaphysics of Mores*) is that of judicial regicide, the murder of a king executed as a punishment pronounced by a court: Kant's claim is that, in contrast to a simple rebellion in which the mob kills only the person of a king, the judicial process which condemns to death the king (this embodiment of the rule of law) destroys from within the very form of the (rule of) law, turning it into a terrifying travesty—which is why, as Kant put it, such an act is an "indelible crime" which cannot ever be pardoned. However, in a second step, Kant desperately argues that in the two historical cases of such an act (the killing of Charles I under Cromwell and the execution of the king in 1793 France), we were dealing just with a mob taking revenge . . . Why this oscillation and classificatory confusion in Kant? Because, if he were to assert the actual possibility of "diabolical evil," he would find it impossible to distinguish it from the Good—since both acts would be non-pathologically motivated, the *travesty* of justice would become indistinguishable from *justice itself*.

The Death of God

And Hegel? Far from dispelling the classificatory confusion present in Kant, Hegel elevates it into a principle—in his philosophy of right, he demonstrates how a travesty of justice is sublated into justice itself. And the same holds for Hegel's "absolute knowing," which is his name for accepting the full autonomy of all forms of Otherness, inclusive of nature. Decades ago, in the early years of modern ecology, some perspicuous readers of Hegel noted that Hegelian idealist speculation does not imply an absolute appropriation of nature—in contrast to its productive appropriation, speculation lets its Other be, it doesn't intervene into its Other. As Frank Ruda pointed out,[8] Hegel's Absolute Knowing is not a total *Aufhebung*—a seamless integration of all reality into the Notion's self-mediation; it is much more an act of radical *Aufgebung*—of giving up, of renouncing the violent effort to grab reality. Absolute Knowing is a gesture of *Entlassen*, of releasing reality, of letting-it-be and stand on its own, and, in this sense, it breaks with the endless effort of labour to appropriate its Otherness, the stuff that forever resists its grasp. Labour (and technological domination in general) is an exemplary case of what Hegel calls "spurious infinity," it is a pursuit which is never accomplished because it presupposes an Other to be mastered, while philosophical speculation is at ease, no longer troubled by its Other.

Schelling is thus wrong when he claims that Hegel's dialectical process is the process of full integration/sublation of all reality into the self-movement of the Idea, and that Hegel ignores the "indivisible remainder [*nie aufhebbare Rest*]" that resists this integration: for Hegel, such a remainder is the concluding moment/product of the dialectical process. To avoid repeating well-known examples (the monarch as a biologically determined head of state which is the ultimate rational totality), suffice it to mention nature itself. When Hegel's system of logic reaches its end and becomes a complete network of logical determinations, it "releases" itself into nature. Nature is for Hegel not the other of logic but logic/the idea itself in its otherness: the immediacy of nature is a proof that logical mediation is completed. Maybe a vague parallel with the credit scene in some movies may be of some help here: first we see just abstract lines, circles, which are gradually getting more concrete, with colours added, etc., and thus forming the image of a scene; when the drawing is completed, it changes into the actual shot of a real scene ... For Schelling, the indivisible remainder is the remainder of substantial reality that cannot be integrated into Idea, while for Hegel this remainder is the final product of Idea itself, the ultimate result of its self-relating negativity.

Etienne Balibar emphasizes the ambiguity of Hegel's formulas of self-relating negativity: negation of negation, death of death, the disappearance of disappearance itself ... They can be read as a return to positivity, a reconciliation (death of death as a return to life in Resurrection), or as an absolute annihilation, the erasure of erasure, the absence of absence itself where what was lost is no longer even experienced as something missing—in this second case, we can say, in Heidegger's style, that the ultimate meaning of death is the death of meaning itself. Hegel himself relies on this ambiguity when he says that

> the meaning attached to death is that through death the human element is stripped away and the divine glory comes into view once more—death is a stripping away of the human, the negative. But at the same time death itself is this negative, the furthest extreme to which humanity as natural existence is exposed; God himself is [involved in] this.[9]

How to read these last words? Through death, humanity in its natural existence (its decaying bodily reality, its finitude) is negated, so that the "divine glory" of the infinite and immortal Spirit can become visible without any finitude obfuscating the view. "But at the same time death itself is this negative": God is not a perfect full supreme Being that appears when finitude is stripped away, it is itself the absolute force of negativity, of "stripping away" all positive existence—in "God," the highest perfection coincides with the absolute power of destruction, so that, in the strongest sense possible, "God" is nothing but this negativity brought to the absolute, which means: to self-relation. And this means that God himself has to die; but since only mortal humans die, God has to appear as a human mortal—this is how "God himself is [involved in] this": what dies on the Cross is not a messiah of God, his earthly representative, but the God of beyond himself. So what can Resurrection mean then? The Spirit that survives in Resurrection is the Holy Spirit, the community [*Gemeinde*] of believers. Hegel goes to the end here: this is why he says that Resurrection is not an "objective fact" that can be verified by everyone, believer or non-believer. *Resurrection takes place only for believers, it is restricted to them*. Balibar noticed this key aspect of the "death of death":

> This restriction, almost a warning, is clearly expressed through the repeated use of "only" (nur) to inscribe the meaning of Tod des Todes in the realm of Faith only: God "maintains" himself in this process, and the latter [the death of God] is only the death of death. God rises again to life, and thus things are reversed. The resurrection is something that belongs just as essentially to faith. After his resurrection, Christ appeared only to his friends. This is not an external history for unbelievers; on the contrary, this appearance occurs only for faith.[10]

> The Resurrection is a subjective certitude about the presence of the "spiritual kingdom." However this subjective certainty does not lie in the individual: it exists only as a common or collective self-consciousness.[11]

The domain of community (*Gemeinde*) is therefore the proper region of Spirit: "the community itself is the existing Spirit, the Spirit in its existence, God existing as community."[12] What "God is love" means is: "No one has ever seen God; but, if we love one another, God lives in us and his love is made complete in us."[13] The beauty of this reversal is that Hegel fully endorses what is for common sense the standard argument against a resurrected God: that it is not a "real miracle" but something that happens only in the mind of believers, their imagination. His answer is: those who make this argument are looking for the resurrected God at the wrong place, as an entity in positive external reality. The resurrected God is *nothing but* the Holy Spirit, a presupposition posited by the believers: in it, *faith and the object of faith are one and the same*, so faith is not something that should be proven by facts. So the "death of death" does not mean that, after Resurrection, we all live in God eternally—it is also the other way round, God only lives in us, in our faith. And if this holds for God, it holds also for its opposite, Evil: evil is not nature as external to God, Evil is thoroughly spiritual, it is the necessary first appearance of Spirit, Spirit in its abstraction of substantial content, opposed to nature. Here, again, I disagree with Balibar, who claims that the distance between nature and Evil is a symptom of something that runs against Hegel's basic thesis: "Hegel always keeps a writing distance between the words *Natur* and *Böse*. 'Nature' is God's alienation, and 'evil' is God's alienation, but . . . caution!"[14] Balibar's implication is that, although for Hegel nature and Evil should be the same (alienation from God as the supreme Good), he symptomatically resists directly identifying them. I think that it is Balibar who is here symptomatically wrong. For Hegel, nature is NOT evil, evil is a spirit which excludes the wealth of nature and its substantial content, evil is thinking as such:

> It is cognition that first posits the antithesis in which evil is to be found. Animals, stones and plants are not evil, evil first occurs

> within the sphere of rupture or cleavage; it is the consciousness of being-myself in opposition to an external nature. [. . .] It is through this separation that I exist for myself for the first time, and that is where the evil lies. [. . .] So it is not the case that [rational] consideration has an external relationship to evil: it is itself what is evil.[15]

Brought to the end, this means that the supreme Evil is God himself insofar as he is considered as a substantial entity opposed to finite reality, separated from it. We should shamelessly repeat here Hegel's lines about the Beautiful Soul from his *Phenomenology*: evil God is his gaze itself which perceives reality around itself as evil, as irredeemably fallen. In other words, the "death of God" is not primarily the reconciliation between humanity and God, it is above all the reconciliation of God with himself—again, this is how "God himself is [involved in] this" . . . Does, then, this mean that Balibar is simply wrong, i.e., that there are no symptomatic ambiguities and twists in the Hegelian topic of the negation of negation? I think Balibar is right, it is just that the ambiguity has to be located at a somewhat different place. Is the "death of death" what Hegel calls *Ungeschehenmachen*, the "undoing" of something that happens?

> The undoing of what has been done cannot take place in a sensible manner; but in a spiritual manner or inwardly, what has been done can be undone.[16]

But what about death of God as death of death? Even if we see the speculative truth of the Holy Spirit as a *Gemeinde* in which faith coincides with its object, why does for ordinary believers (not speculative theologians) the appearance of externality persist, why do they remain transfixed on the Way of the Cross, on the sensual spectacle of Christ's long suffering and death? We can "undo" this fascination in philosophical speculation, but "the undoing of what has been done cannot take place in a sensible manner," which means that it persists as a non-conceptual moment keeping together the community of believers. (Hegel emphasizes that philosophy is only for the educated—for ordinary people, religion is the highest form of Spirit.) Is the image of suffering Christ, this "image to end all images," also an "indivisible remainder," and if yes, in what precise sense? Can it be united with a radical materialist perspective? Adrian Johnston noted:

> What if the ability to be radically skeptical, relativistic, or agnostic is afforded only to one who is omniscient and/or infinite (i.e., God)? Asked differently, what if, by attributing self-deception or self-doubt to God, Lacan means to place them beyond the reach of finite, mortal humans? What if the capacity to elevate oneself to one or more meta-levels over and above any initial first-order choice between theism and atheism, belief and unbelief, [. . .] is reserved exclusively for a being that would be omnipotent and eternal?[17]

While I basically agree with Johnston, I would add two provisos. Yes, sceptical doubt implies supreme arrogance: in it, the subject assumes the safe distance of an external observer to whom everything appears relative, historically conditioned, etc. But, following Hegel, we should distinguish here between *Zweifel* (doubt in the sense of doubting something) and *Verzweiflung* (a much more radical existential doubt/despair which affects the very core of my being). By attributing self-doubt to God, God is humanized/finitized, caught in a radical despair which undermines his very divinity. The second proviso: for reasons explained elsewhere in my writings, I also claim that direct atheism is not possible—to arrive at it, one has to pass through God's self-destruction.

Suicide as a Political Act

To orient ourselves in this mess, we should make a step beyond the ambiguity of "negation of negation" as it was formulated by Balibar (healing the wounds without any scars remaining; the reconciliation with wounds in their positive role) and add self-negation at its most radical: suicide. Can we imagine suicide as an emancipatory political act? The first association here of course is with public suicides as a protest against foreign occupation, from Vietnam to Poland in the 1980s—there is no place here to deal with this, or with the fact that, by way of largely ignoring global warming, humanity is unwillingly committing a collective suicide. Let us turn to more specific cases. In the last years, a suicidal proposal aroused a wide debate in South Africa. Derek Hook[18] reports how, in March 2016 Terblanche Delport, a young white academic, sparked outrage at a Johannesburg conference at the University of the Witwatersrand when he called on white people in South Africa "to commit suicide as an ethical act"—here are Delport's own words:

> The reality [in South Africa] is that most white people spend their whole lives only engaging black people in subservient positions—cleaners, gardeners, etc. My question is then how can a person not be racist if that's the way they live their lives? The only way then for white people to become part of Africa is to not exist as white people anymore. If the goal is to dismantle white supremacy, and white supremacy is white culture and vice versa, then the goal has to be to dismantle white culture and ultimately white people themselves. The total integration into Africa by white people will also automatically then mean the death of white people as white as a concept would not exist anymore.[19]

How, more concretely, are we to imagine the symbolic suicide of the South African whites? Donald Moss proposed a simple but problematic (for me, at least) solution: the racist whiteness is a parasitic formation which parasitizes on whites themselves:

> Whiteness is a condition one first acquires and then one *has*—a malignant, parasitic-like condition to which "white" people have a particular susceptibility. The condition is foundational, generating characteristic ways of being in one's body, in one's mind, and in one's world. Parasitic Whiteness renders its hosts' appetites voracious, insatiable, and perverse. These deformed appetites particularly target nonwhite peoples. Once established, these appetites are nearly impossible to eliminate.[20]

To get rid of their racist stance, whites have to get rid of the parasitic whiteness which is not part of their substantial nature but just parasitizes on them, which means that, in getting rid of their racism, they do not lose the substance of their being—they even regain it, obliterating its distortion . . . I prefer this to easy way out Hook's comment (inspired by Lacanian theory):

> Delport's rhetorical and deliberately provocative suggestion is perhaps not as counter-intuitive or crazy as it at first sounds. Arguably, it is the gesture of giving up what one is—the shedding of narcissistic investments, and symbolic and fantasmatic identities—that proves a necessary first step to becoming what one is not, but might become. This is the transformative potential of anxiety that clinicians work so hard to facilitate, and that I think can also be discerned—however fleetingly—in the instances of white anxiety discussed above: the potentiality that a new—and hitherto unthinkable—form of identification is being unconsciously processed and negotiated.[21]

What I nonetheless find problematic in these lines is the optimist turn: suicide does not mean the actual collective self-killing of the South African whites; it means a symbolic erasure of their identity which already points towards new forms of identity . . . I find it much more productive to establish a link between this idea of the whites' collective suicide and the idea of so-called afro-pessimism. Recall Fanon's claim that "the Negro is a zone of non-being, an extraordinarily sterile and arid region, an utterly declining declivity": is the experience that grounds today's "afro-pessimism" not a similar one? Is the insistence of afro-pessimists that Black subordination is much more radical than that of other underprivileged groups (Asians, LGBT+, women . . .), i.e., that Blacks should not be put into the series with other forms of "colonization," not grounded in the act of assuming that one belongs to such a "zone of non-being"? This is why Fredric Jameson is right when he insists that one cannot understand class struggle in the US without taking into account anti-Black racism: any talk which equalizes white and Black proletarians is a fake. (A point to be noted here is that, when the young Gandhi protested against the white rule in South Africa, he ignored the plight of the Black majority and just demanded the inclusion of Indians into the privileged White block.)

So what if we turn Delport's suggestion, radical as it may appear, around and propose that it is the Blacks in South Africa who should commit a collective symbolic suicide, to shed their socio-symbolic identity which is profoundly marked by white domination and resistance to it, and which contains its own fantasies and even narcissistic investments of victimization. (In the US, the Blacks are right in using the term "Victim!" to insult their Black opponents.) One can thus repeat exactly the same words: Blacks need to perform "the gesture of giving up what one is—the shedding of narcissistic investments, and symbolic and fantasmatic identities—that proves a necessary first step to becoming what one is not, but might become." Consequently, I see afro-pessimism not just as a recognition of dismal social reality but also and above all as something that announces, "the potentiality that a new—and hitherto unthinkable—form of identification is being unconsciously processed and negotiated." To put it brutally, let us imagine that, in one way or another, all the whites would disappear from South Africa—the ANC inefficiency and corruption would remain, and the poor Black majority would find itself even more strongly dislocated, lacking the designated cause of its poverty ... To revolutionize a system is never equal to just eliminating one of its parts, in the same way that the disappearance of Jews as the disturbing element never restores social harmony.

The key move has to be done by Blacks themselves—was Malcolm X not following this insight when he adopted X as his family name? The point of choosing X as his family name and thereby signalling that the slave traders who brought the enslaved Africans from their homeland brutally deprived them of their family and ethnic roots, of their entire cultural life-world, was not to mobilize the Blacks to fight for the return to some primordial African roots, but precisely to seize the opening provided by X, an unknown new (lack of) identity engendered by the very process of slavery which made the African roots forever lost. The idea is that this X which deprives Blacks of their particular tradition offers a unique chance to redefine (reinvent) themselves, to freely form a new identity much more universal than white people's professed universality. To put it in Hook's terms, Malcolm X proposes for Blacks themselves to bring to an end their deracination with a gesture of symbolic suicide, the passage through zero-point, in order to free the space for a new identity. Such a gesture would render white domination simply pointless, a solipsistic dream, a game missing a partner with whom it can be played. Was this not the reason why Malcolm X was treated as an enemy by all (opposed) sides in the conflict?

> At the time Malcolm spoke at the Audubon Ballroom on Feb. 21, 1965, he was a marked man—spied on by the F.B.I. and the police, denounced as a traitor by the Nation leadership, viscerally hated and beloved. Mr. Farrakhan declared him "worthy of death." A week before his assassination, his home in Queens was firebombed while he and his wife and four daughters slept inside.[22]

One cannot but note the cruel irony of the fact that—although, as is well known, Malcolm X found this new identity in the universalism of Islam—he was (in all probability) killed on the order of the organization called The Nation of Islam, an organization which used Islam to serve its limited ethnic identity:

> Was Malcolm your traitor or ours? And if we dealt with him like a nation deals with a traitor, what the hell business is it of yours? You just shut your mouth, and stay out of it. Because in the future, we gonna become a nation. And a nation gotta be able to deal with traitors and cutthroats and turncoats. The white man deals with his. The Jews deal with theirs.[23]

In short, Malcolm was killed because he blurred the clear line that separated "ours" from "yours"—he was killed to prevent the Blacks from committing the symbolic suicide that would open up the path to (not only) their emancipation. And even today we continue to live in the shadow of this failed suicide which keeps the Blacks in their subordinate position. The topic of failed suicide deserves special attention: as was pointed out by Alenka Zupančič, it presents an exemplary case of the "negation of negation" as a failure of negation itself. One of its most desperate versions is *Still Alice* (2014, written and directed by Richard Glatzer and Wash Westmoreland, based on the novel by Lisa Genova). It stars Julianne Moore as Alice Howland, a linguistics professor diagnosed with familial Alzheimer's disease shortly after her fiftieth birthday. As Alice's memory begins to fade, she memorizes words and sets a series of personal questions on her phone, which she answers every morning, plus she records a video message instructing her future self to commit suicide by overdosing on the pills when she can no longer answer the personal questions. Some time later, with her disease advancing, Alice opens the video with the suicide instructions; with some difficulty, she finds the pills and is about to swallow them, but when she is interrupted by the arrival of her caregiver, she drops the pills on the floor and forgets what she was doing—so even her suicide fails . . .[24] The paradox is here that Alice's suicide fails because of the very illness she wanted to escape from through it.

Is a hint in this direction (of "negation of negation" as the failed negation) not clearly discernible already in Freud's theory of dreams, symptoms, slips of the tongue, and other forms of the "return of the repressed": something repressed (negated, excluded from consciousness) returns as a broken/distorted cyphered message in which negation is negated, but not in a triumphant "synthesis"—it returns as a fragmentary compromise which is neither here nor there . . . But this "triad" is not the whole story: what complicates it is that we should add another moment at the beginning: what Freud calls the "primordial repression [*Ur-Verdraengung*]."

One of the best indicators of the dimension which resists the pseudo-Hegelian understanding of psychoanalytic treatment as the process of the patient's appropriation of repressed content is the paradox of perversion in the Freudian theoretical edifice: perversion demonstrates the insufficiency of the simple logic of transgression. The standard wisdom tells us that perverts practice (do) what hysterics only dream about (doing), i.e., "everything is allowed" in perversion, a pervert openly actualizes all repressed content—and nonetheless, as Freud emphasizes, *nowhere is repression as strong as in perversion*, a fact more than confirmed by our late-capitalist reality in which total sexual permissiveness causes anxiety and impotence or frigidity instead of liberation. (This repression of repression which occurs in perverse subjectivity is correlative to the prohibition of prohibition: it may appear that in perversion "everything is permitted," all repressed dirty fantasies can be brought out without impediments; however, what is rendered invisible in this space of the free flow of "perversities" is the very trauma, the Real of a basic impossibility, the gap which this flow tries to obfuscate.) This compels us to draw a distinction between the repressed content and the form of repression: the form remains operative even after the content is no longer repressed—in short, the subject can fully appropriate the repressed content, but repression remains. Why? Commenting on a short dream of one of his patients (a woman who first refused altogether to tell Freud the dream "because it was so indistinct and muddled") which revealed itself to refer to the fact that the patient was pregnant but was in doubts as to who the baby's father was (i.e., the parenthood was "indistinct and muddled"), Freud draws a key dialectical conclusion:

> the lack of clarity shown by the dream was a part of the material which instigated the dream: part of this material, that is, was represented in the form of the dream. The form of a dream or the form in which it is dreamt is used with quite surprising frequency for representing its concealed subject-matter.[25]

The gap between form and content is here properly dialectical, in contrast with the transcendental gap whose point is that every content appears within an a priori formal frame, and we should always be aware of the invisible transcendental frame which "constitutes" the content we perceive—or, in structural terms, we should distinguish between elements and the formal places these elements occupy. We only attain the level of proper dialectical analysis of a form when we conceive of a certain formal procedure not as expressing a certain aspect of the (narrative) content, but as marking/signalling the part of the content that is excluded from the explicit narrative line, so that—therein resides the proper theoretical point—if we want to reconstruct "all" of the narrative content, we must reach beyond the explicit narrative content as such, and include some formal features which act as the stand-in for the "repressed" aspect of the content. To take the well-known elementary example from the analysis of melodramas: the emotional excess that cannot express itself directly in the narrative line finds its outlet in the ridiculously sentimental musical accompaniment or in other formal features. In this respect, melodramas are to be opposed to Lars von Trier's *Breaking the Waves*: in both cases, we are dealing with the tension between form and content, while in *Breaking the Waves* the excess is located in the content (the subdued pseudo-documentary form makes palpable the excessive content).[26]

However, insofar as we are dealing here with the properly dialectical mediation between form and content, we should not reduce primordial repression only to the form of a gap: something insists, a weird positivity of an excessive "content" not only impervious to negation but even produced by the very process of redoubled (self-relating) negation. Consequently, this something is not simply a remainder of the pre-symbolic real that resists symbolic negation, but a spectral X called by Lacan *objet a* or surplus-enjoyment. One should mobilize here Lacan's key distinction between pleasure (*Lust*, *plaisir*) and enjoyment (*Geniessen*, *jouissance*): what is "beyond the pleasure principle" is enjoyment itself, it is drive as such. The basic paradox of *jouissance* is that it is both impossible *and* unavoidable: it is never fully achieved, always missed, but, simultaneously, we never can get rid of it—every renunciation of enjoyment generates an enjoyment in renunciation, every obstacle to desire generates a desire for obstacle, etc. This reversal provides the minimal definition of the surplus-enjoyment: it involves the paradoxical "pleasure in pain." That is to say, when Lacan uses the term *plus-de-jouir*, one has to ask a naive, but crucial question: in what does this surplus consist? Is it merely a qualitative increase of ordinary pleasure? The ambiguity of the French expression is decisive here: it can mean "surplus of enjoyment" as well as "no enjoyment"—the surplus of enjoyment over mere pleasure is generated by the presence of the very opposite of pleasure, i.e. pain; it is the part of *jouissance* which resists being contained by the homeostasis, by the pleasure principle. Or, it is the excess of pleasure produced by "repression" itself, which is why we lose it if we abolish repression. This is what Herbert Marcuse, in his *Eros and Civilization*, misses when he proposes a distinction between "basic repression" ("the 'modifications' of the instincts necessary for the perpetuation of the human race in civilization") and "surplus-repression" ("the restrictions necessitated by social domination"):

> While any form of the reality principle demands a considerable degree and scope of repressive control over the instincts, the

> specific historical institutions of the reality principle and the specific interests of domination introduce additional controls over and above those indispensable for civilized human association. These additional controls arising from the specific institutions of domination are what we denote as surplus-repression.[27]

Marcuse enumerates as examples of surplus-repression "the modifications and deflections of instinctual energy necessitated by the perpetuation of the monogamic-patriarchal family, or by a hierarchical division of labor, or by public control over the individual's private existence."[28] Although he concedes that basic and surplus-repression are de facto inextricably intertwined, one should go a step further and render problematic their very conceptual distinction: it is the paradox of libidinal economy that surplus/excess is necessary for its very "basic" functioning—why? An ideological edifice "bribes" subjects to accept "repression"/renunciation by way of offering as surplus-enjoyment (Lacan's *plus-de-jouir*), and this surplus-enjoyment is an enjoyment generated by the very "excessive" renunciation to enjoyment—surplus-enjoyment is by definition enjoyment-in-pain. (Its paradigmatic case is the Fascist call "Renounce corrupt pleasures! Sacrifice yourself for your country!," a call which promises an obscene enjoyment brought about by this very renunciation.) One thus cannot have only "basic" repression without the surplus-repression, since it is the very enjoyment generated by the surplus-repression which renders the "basic" repression palpable to the subjects. The paradox is thus a kind of "less is more": "more" repression is less traumatic, more easily acceptable, than less. When repression is diminished, the lesser degree of repression is much more difficult to endure and provokes rebellion. (This may be one of the reasons why revolutions break out not when oppression is at its worst, but when it diminishes to a more "reasonable" and "rational" level—this diminishing deprives repression of the aura which makes it acceptable.)[29]

This is why we should also reject Marcuse's idea of a "non-repressive desublimation" as the goal of sexual emancipation. If we follow Lacan's precise definition of sublimation, then

Marcuse's idea of "liberated persons" who are able to experience "the non-repressive desublimation of resexualizing their polymorphously perverse bodies" is a utopian nonsense—why? For Lacan, "repressive desublimation" cannot be opposed to non-repressive desublimation because *desublimation is AS SUCH repressive*, which is why perversion in which the subject actualizes its dirtiest fantasies is, as Lacan pointed out, the hidden part of any oppressive power. For Lacan, sexual drive as such relies on sublimation: sublimation elevates an ordinary worldly object to the level of the impossible Thing—this is how sublimation sexualizes an ordinary object. So when Johnston claims that "Freudian sublimation is nothing other than the achievement of satisfaction in the face of aim-inhibition," we should NOT read this in the ordinary sense of replacing a direct sexual object or act by a desexualized activity. Lacan reads sublimation in the Kantian way: what is prohibited in sublimation is not the direct object but the impossible Thing—that's the basic paradox here: what is prohibited is already in itself impossible-to-reach. In sublimation, we shift from one to another object to catch the elusive Thing which eludes already the direct object.

To get the paradoxical logic of "less is more," it is crucial to distinguish symbolic castration from real castration (in which the penis—or testicles—is actually cut off) and imaginary castration in which the loss is just imagined (as in the case of a woman imagining she once had a penis and lost it). In symbolic castration, nothing happens in (bodily) reality, all that happens is that phallus itself (as the moment of bodily excess) becomes a signifier of "castration," of its lack/impotence. In this sense, social authority really is "phallic" insofar as it has the effect of symbolic castration on its bearer: if, say, I am a king, I have to accept that the ritual of investiture makes me a king, that my authority is embodied in the insignia I wear, so that my authority is in some sense external to me as a person in my miserable reality. As Lacan put it, only a psychotic is a king who thinks he is a king (or a father who is a father) by his nature, as he is, without the processes of symbolic investiture. This is why being-a-father is by definition a failure: no "empirical" father can live up to his symbolic function, to his title. How can I, if I am invested with such an authority, live with this gap without obfuscating it through the psychotic direct identification of my symbolic status with my reality?

And this is why, from the strict Freudian standpoint, human finitude (symbolic castration) and immortality (death drive) are two sides of the same operation, i.e., it's not that the substance of life, the immortal *Jouissance*-Thing, is "castrated" by the arrival of the symbolic order. As in the case of lack and excess, the structure is that of parallax: the undead Thing is the remainder of castration, it is generated by castration, and *vice versa*; there is no "pure" castration, castration itself is sustained by the immortal excess which eludes it. Castration and excess are not two different entities, but the front and the back of one and the same entity, that is, one and the same entity inscribed onto the two surfaces of a Möbius strip. The unity of limitation and immortality can now be clearly formulated: an entity finds its peace and completion in fitting its finite contours (form), so what pushes it beyond its finite form is the very fact that it cannot achieve it, that it cannot be what it is, that it is marked by an irreducible impossibility, thwarted in its core—it is on behalf of this immanent and constitutive obstacle that a thing persists beyond its "death." Recall Hamlet's father: why does he return as a ghost after his natural death? Because of the gap between his natural death and his symbolic death, i.e., because he died in the flower of his sins, unable to find peace in death, to enact his symbolic death (settlement of accounts).

The Failed Negation of Negation

This brings us back to the third form of the "negation of negation": one of the determinations of modernity is that, in it, a specific form of the negation of negation arises:[30] far from the triumphant reversal of negativity into a new positivity, this "negation of negation" means that even negation (our striving to reach the bottom, the zero-point) fails. Not only are we not immortal but we are not even mortal, we fail in that endeavour to disappear, we survive in the guise of the obscene immortality of the "undead" (living dead). Not only do we fail in our pursuit of happiness, we even fail in our pursuit of unhappiness, our attempts to ruin our life produce small unexpected bits of miserable happiness, of surplus-enjoyment. In old Yugoslavia, policemen were the butt of jokes as stupid and corrupted; in one of these jokes, a policeman returns home unexpectedly and finds his wife alone in bed, half-naked and aroused; he suspects a lover is hiding beneath the big bed, gets on his knees and looks beneath. After a couple of seconds, he rises up with a satisfied expression, just mumbling, "Everything OK, nobody is there!," while quickly pushing a couple of banknotes into the pocket of his trousers … This is how in our daily lives accepting failure is paid by the misery of some form of surplus-enjoyment.

The masterpiece of the failed suicidal negation remains Edith Wharton's *Ethan Frome* (1911), a short novel which takes place against a backdrop of the cold, grey, bleakness of a New England winter: in Starkfield (an invented small town), the narrator spots Ethan Frome, "the most striking figure in Starkfield," "the ruin of a man" with a "careless powerful look … in spite of a lameness checking each step like the jerk of a chain." The narrator gradually learns the whole story reaching decades into the past when Frome was an isolated farmer trying to scrape out a meagre living while also tending to his frigid, demanding and ungrateful wife, Zeena. A ray of hope enters Ethan's life of despair when, 24 years ago, his wife's cousin Mattie arrives to help. His life is transformed as he falls in love with Mattie who returns his love. Zeena suspects this and orders Mattie to leave. Since Ethan lacks money to escape with Mattie, he takes her to the train station. They stop at a hill upon which they had once planned to go sledding and decide to sled together as a way of delaying their sad parting, after which they anticipate never seeing each other again. After their first run, Mattie suggests a suicide pact: that they go down again, and steer the sled directly into a tree, so they will never be parted and so that they may spend their last moments together. Ethan first refuses to go through with the plan, but in his despair that mirrors Mattie's, he ultimately agrees, and they get on the sled, clutching each other. They crash headlong and at high speed into the elm tree. Ethan regains consciousness after the accident, but Mattie lies beside him, "cheeping" in pain like a small, wounded animal, while Ethan is left with a permanent limp … The epilogue returns to the present: while visiting Frome in his house, the narrator hears a complaining female voice, and it is easy to assume that it belongs to the never-happy Zeena, but it emerges that it is Mattie who now lives with the Fromes due to having been paralyzed in the accident. Her misery over her plight and dependence has embittered her, and, with roles reversed, Zeena is now forced to care for her as well as Ethan: she has now found the strength through the necessity to be the caregiver rather than being the invalid.[31] In an agonizing irony, the love couple Ethan and Mattie have gotten their wish to stay together, but in mutual unhappiness and discontent, with Zeena as a constant presence between the two of them—the ultimate case of Mladen Dolar's formula of being as a failed non-being …

Is then the attempted suicide an authentic act, and the couple's survival a pure contingent accident, or is there an inner truth to the survival that makes the suicide attempt a fake? No wonder that, in spite of the simplicity of its plot, *Ethan Frome* caused such confusion among its interpreters. At the level of genre, it was described as a work of brutal realism, a Gothic tale, or an adult fairy tale (the wicked witch wins and the lovers do not live happily ever after). With regard to the ethical stance implied by *Ethan Frome*, a long line of critics, from Frederic Taber Cooper, who wrote back in 1911 "It is hard to forgive Mrs. Wharton for the utter remorselessness of her latest volume […] Art for art's sake is the one justification of a piece of work as perfect in technique as it is relentless in substance,"[32] to Lionel Trilling, who wrote, "In the context of morality, there is nothing to say about Ethan Frome. It presents no moral issue at all,"[33] insist on its lack of moral substance, while Robert Ebert (in his review of the movie) characterizes the novel as a "cheerless morality tale" … Especially weird is the case of Trilling. In reply to a taunt by Richard Sennett, "You have no position; you are always in between," Trilling replied, "Between is the only honest place to be."[34] It sounds like those who, today, condemn Russia's attack on Ukraine, but show an understanding for Russia … In a stance which cannot hide its elitism, Trilling dismisses average people caught in the circle of habitude, as if only a small elite is able to act in a properly ethical way: he suggests that

> the story examines what happens to individuals who are hobbled by "the morality of inertia." The lovers lack both the courage and

the conviction to forge a new life for themselves, thanks to their subservience to community standards. Their fear dooms them to the routine, death-in-life existence that they so desperately yearned to transcend. The real moral of Ethan Frome is — follow the imperatives of your heart or risk losing your soul.[35]

Again, there is the opposite reading: "the ending turns *Ethan Frome* into a cautionary tale, a warning to the readers that not following your dreams can have serious negative consequences.[36] But is this really the case? Ethan abandons his plan to borrow money and escape with Mattie for moral reasons—he is a sensitive moral person. What brings him to self-destruction are class distinctions: the harsh poverty that deprives him of choices. In the pre-accident part of the story, Mattie and Ethan seem to think that the best they can hope for is to be able to continue living together with Zeena, seeing each other as often as possible. This plan comes true in a hideous way: they are forever together, but as two crippled living dead. Ethan and Mattie end up in a desperate situation because they were NOT ready to follow their dreams (and, say, escape together, or at least openly confront Zeena with the fact that they could not stay away from each other), i.e., in Lacanese, because they compromised their desire . . . but did they? Here enters the final twist of the story: in the very last pages, Mrs Ruth Hale tells the narrator something that changes everything:

> Mrs. Hale glanced at me tentatively, as though trying to see how much footing my conjectures gave her; and I guessed that if she had kept silence till now it was because she had been waiting, through all the years, for someone who should see what she alone had seen.
>
> I waited to let her trust in me gather strength before I said: "Yes, it's pretty bad, seeing all three of them there together."
>
> She drew her mild brows into a frown of pain. "It was just awful from the beginning. I was here in the house when they were carried up—they laid Mattie Silver in the room you're in. She and I were great friends, and she was to have been my bridesmaid in the spring . . . When she came to I went up to her and stayed all night. They gave her things to quiet her, and she didn't know much till to'rd morning, and then all of a sudden

> she woke up just like herself, and looked straight at me out of her big eyes, and said . . . Oh, I don't know why I'm telling you all this," Mrs. Hale broke off, crying.

What exactly did Mattie say to Ruth when she woke up after the accident? Why couldn't Ruth bear to repeat it to the narrator? Whatever it was, it, combined with the change (for the worse) in Mattie's personality (who now acts and even looks like Zeena 24 years ago), and leads Ruth to speak the novella's final lines:

> There was one day, about a week after the accident, when they all thought Mattie couldn't live. Well, I say it's a pity she did. I said it right out to our minister once, and he was shocked at me. Only he wasn't with me that morning when she first came to . . . And I say, if she'd ha' died, Ethan might ha' lived; and the way they are now, I don't see's there's much difference between the Fromes up at the farm and the Fromes down in the graveyard; 'cept that down there they're all quiet, and the women have got to hold their tongues.

Are these last words—"the women have got to hold their tongues"—really anti-feminine, resuscitating the old cliché that women chatter too much? Things are not so simple: to what exactly does "holding tongues" refer? *Not* to general rumours that circulate in a small town but quite specifically to Mattie's words when she awakened after the snow accident—and they were not mere gossip, they possessed almost testimonial value of the last words one says when one is not sure one will survive. Mrs Hale's last words can thus more appropriately be read as a defence of mere chatter: hold your tongue instead of saying something that is a matter of life and death . . . Although we never learn what these words were, we can safely presume that they concern what happened between Mattie and Ethan. Since it must have been something really shocking, it can only be that the two had sex and/or then tried to kill themselves.[37] The often advocated reading according to which the finally revealed truth of the attempted escape and suicide is the narrator's fiction into which he projects his own "shadow" (in the Jungian sense of the dark repressed part of his Self) should thus be flatly rejected:

> Within Ethan Frome the narrator lapses into a vision (the tale of Ethan which is, as we have seen, a terrified expression of the narrator's latent self) [...] The novel focuses on the narrator's problem, the tension between his public self and his shadow self, his terror of a seductive and enveloping void.[38]

Mrs Hales's final words add an additional twist, they confirm that the narrator's "fiction" did lay a hand on some traumatic Real which is too strong to be directly put into words. Echoing Lacan's dictum "truth has the structure of a fiction," the narrator's fiction touches the Real ... in short, Freud wins over Jung.[39]

The motif of failed negation can also be a part (or, rather, the final touch) of a more complex plot, as is the case with Tana French's *Broken Harbour*,[40] which depicts a perfect case of how the capitalist self-reproduction can drive those who blindly adhere to the predominant ethics to murderous madness. Every theorist who loses time with musings on the complex relationship between the "economic base" and subjective libidinal economy should read the novel; while the liberal-capitalist financial speculations and their brutal consequences for individual lives are its massive background presence of the novel, it focuses on the way the affected individuals react to their economic and social predicament, bringing out all their idiosyncrasies, their unique ways of doing what each of them considers the right thing to do. None of them is dishonest, they are all ready to sacrifice everything, including their own life, to set things straight, and the novel presents different ways of how "doing the right thing" can go wrong. Therein resides the sad lesson of the novel: it is not simply that the turmoil of global capitalism corrupts individuals, pushing them to betray their basic ethical stance; even when they try to follow their ethical stance, the system insidiously works to achieve the opposite effect.

Two young kids of the Spain family are found smothered in their beds, while their parents, Pat and Jenny, are stabbed in the kitchen downstairs—against the odds, the mother may survive. These multiple murders happen in "Brianstown," a Dublin suburb planned as a glamorous multi-purpose, all-inclusive community; things went wrong when the market collapsed in 2008, leaving most of the estate unfinished and uninhabited. Only four families remained on the property, prisoners of a housing market where they owed more than the houses were worth after the developers cut corners and cannot be located . . . and now the multiple murder of the Spains haunts the eerie location. (Empty apartments and whole apartment blocks are one of the key symptoms of today's global capitalism, they abound in all big cities from New York to Dubai; in China alone, there are today enough uninhabited apartments to locate the entire population of Germany and France.)

The murders are investigated by Mick "Scorcher" Kennedy, the Murder Squad's star detective whose fundamental belief is that if one toes the line and follows the rules, everything will turn out right. The Spains pose a challenge to this belief because they *did* everything "right," they invested deeply into the way people are "supposed" to live. The house was beautifully furnished and maintained, they themselves were lovely, they seemed to be doing everything they were supposed to. They met and married young, they adored each other, they had two beautiful children. Pat had a prestigious job that earned enough that Jenny could stay home with the children. They drove the right cars, had the right parties, wore the right clothes, invested in home ownership so they could get onto "the property ladder." Jenny made herself into the perfect housewife, even switching out scented candles with the seasons. Then the economy collapsed, Pat lost his job and couldn't find another one, and they ended up dead.

Since Pat was, like Scorcher, also a man who played by the rules, Scorcher resists the evidence that would implicate Pat as the murderer and insists on pinning the deaths on a loner, Conor, who had loved Jenny since they were teens. Conor had his own personal financial crisis and had taken to hiding in an empty building on the estate where he could watch Pat and Jenny enact the kind of perfect life he dreamed of for himself. Early on in the novel, he is arrested and confesses to the murders. However, even as Scorcher celebrates the solve, he can't stop questioning: there are too many loose ends—why were there holes cut into the walls all over the house? Why were there baby monitors scattered around? Who wiped the browser history from the computer and why? Why did the killer use a kitchen knife rather than bringing his own weapon?

At the end we discover it was neither Conor nor Pat who did the killings: it was Jenny who caved into the psychological pressure of watching her husband become unmoored. As the months go by, Pat stops searching for work and slowly falls into his own obsession. He becomes convinced that his own worth as a husband and father is inextricably bound up in capturing an animal who lives in the attic; although they have almost no money left, he starts buying electronic equipment to capture this animal. First, he wants to protect his family, but as the weeks go by with no physical evidence of the animal, he cuts holes and sets up video baby monitors hoping to catch sight of it. He buys live bait (a mouse from a pet store) that he sticks to a glue trap and then places in the attic with the trap door open … The beast haunting the house is a Real that is not part of reality: a pure embodiment of negativity/antagonism, an anamorphic stain, which "looked on as it is, is naught but shadows of what it is not" (as Shakespeare put it in *Richard II*).

Jenny never believed in this animal, she just indulged Pat's weird hobby, but when Emma, Pat and Jenny's daughter, returns home with a picture of her house and she has drawn a large black animal with glowing eyes in a tree in the yard, Jenny is pushed to act: she goes upstairs and smothers the children to save them from their father's madness. She then goes into the kitchen, where Pat has stuck his own hand into one of the holes he's cut into the walls, using himself as live bait; in his other hand, he has a large kitchen knife. Jenny takes the knife and kills him; however, she's too exhausted to finish the job, killing herself also. This is when Conor rushes in: he's seen the struggle from his hide-out and runs to the Spain's house to save them; Jenny doesn't want to live, and she asks him to finish her off. He loves her, so he tries, but he's not ruthless enough, and she survives. It is Conor who also tries to save Pat's posthumous reputation by wiping the computer history. His final act is to confess to the murders, to save Jenny from the horror of realizing what she has done when she awakens.

Curran finds in Conor's apartment a piece of evidence that seems to implicate Jenny, but he doesn't turn it in—he thinks that it might be better to let Pat be blamed for the deaths and leave Jenny free to take her own life. Because Curran got the evidence tainted, this is the end of his career as a detective. He wanted to act on his own cognizance, his own belief as to the "right" thing to do—but if you do this, the system collapses. Scorcher falls into the same trap:

over-identified with Pat as he is, he simply cannot allow Pat to be thought of as a murderer, even though Pat is dead, and it wouldn't matter to him to be considered a murderer. So Scorcher manufactures his own evidence in order to put the case back on what he considers the right path: he enlists Jenny's sister in the play of "discovering" a piece of Jenny's jewellery and "remembering" she had picked it up at the crime scene ... in this way, Scorcher also destroys his own career.

Broken Harbour thus tells the story of the repeated failure of people who desperately want to do the right thing. Pat's case is straightforward: the father-provider who just wants to maintain a safe haven for his family isolates himself from them and ends up in full paranoia. Conan, who loves Jenny and is ready to ruin his life to save her, bungles things further and enacts a meaningless sacrifice. Curran and Scorcher, the two detectives investigating the case, are both brought by their ethical commitment to violate the rules of police investigation ... Jenny's fate is the most desperate—her plan is to obliterate her entire family, but she fails to include herself in the series of corpses, so she survives as a miserable totally broken leftover, turning her intended tragic act into a ridiculous, almost comical, performance. We don't know what will happen when/if Jenny awakens from her coma: will she persist in her miserable depression, kill herself, awaken with no memory and thus become able to begin again, or somehow manage to go through the painful process of mourning? There is a totally crazy optimist potential at the margin of the story: what if she awakens and gets together with Conan who truly loves her?

But in our actual social life, such potentials are rare. Not only do most of us fail to achieve social success and slide slowly towards some form of proletarization, we even fail in this tendency towards the bottom of the social scale: instead of becoming full proletarians who have nothing (to lose but their chains), we somehow maintain a minimum of social status. Perhaps, therein resides the impasse of today's Western radical Leftists who, disappointed at the lack of a "true proletariat" in their own country, desperately search for an ersatz proletariat which will mobilize itself as a revolutionary agent instead of "our" corrupted and inert working class (the most popular candidate is lately nomadic immigrants). Is this weird "downward negation of negation" really what escapes Hegel in his obsession with the forward march of the spirit? What if this "downward negation of negation" is rather the true secret of the Hegelian dialectical process? It is along these lines that one should reread Hegel backwards, from the perspective of Samuel Beckett's late short texts and plays which all deal with the problem of how to go on when the game is over, when it has reached its end-point.[41] Hegel is not simply the thinker of closure, of the closed circle of the end of history in Absolute Knowing, but also the thinker of the terrible void of inertia when, after "the system is closed," nothing (that we can think) happens although "the time goes on."

But what if the choice between finitude and immortality is false? What if finitude and immortality, like lack and excess, also form a parallax couple, what if they are the same from a different point of view? What if immortality is an object that is a remainder/excess over finitude, what if finitude is an attempt to escape from the excess of immortality? What if Kierkegaard was right here, but for the wrong reason, when he also understood the claim that we, humans, are just mortal beings who disappear after their biological death as an easy way to escape the ethical responsibility that comes with the immortal soul? He was right for the wrong reason insofar as he equated immortality with the divine and ethical part of a human being—but there is another immortality. What Cantor did for infinity we should do for immortality, and assert the multiplicity of immortalities: the Badiouian noble immortality/infinity of the deployment of an Event (as opposed to the finitude of a human animal) comes after a more basic form of immortality which resides in what Lacan calls the Sadean fundamental fantasy: the fantasy of another, ethereal body of the victim, which can be tortured indefinitely and nonetheless magically retains its beauty (recall the Sadean figure of the young girl sustaining endless humiliations and mutilations from her depraved torturer and somehow mysteriously surviving it all intact, in the same way Tom and Jerry and other cartoon heroes survive all their ridiculous ordeals intact). In this form, the comical and the disgustingly terrifying (recall different versions of the "undead"—zombies, vampires, etc.—in popular culture) are inextricably connected. (Therein resides the point of proper burial, from *Antigone* to

Hamlet: to prevent the dead from returning in the guise of this obscene immortality . . .)[42]

So, again, the idea of the "negation of negation" as a failure is not strange to Hegel. In one of the most famous passages in his *Phenomenology*, the dialectic of master and servant, he imagines the confrontation of the two self-consciousnesses engaged in the struggle of life and death; each side is ready to go to the end in risking its life, but if they both persist to the end, there is no winner—one dies, the other survives but without another to recognize it. The whole history of freedom and recognition—in short, the whole of history *tout court*, the whole of human culture—can take place only with an original compromise: in the eye-to-eye confrontation, one side (the future servant) blinks, averts its gaze, is not ready to go to the end.

Back to Schelling and Hegel, for Hegel, the "indivisible remainder" of the dialectical process is the obscene undeadness, the outcome of the failed negation of negation, what survives the radical self-negation. It is the excess of this obscene undeadness which pulverizes from within all binary oppositions. To understand this key point, we have to recall Hegel's basic dialectic of identity and difference. For Hegel, identity is the most radical form of difference, difference brought to its self-reference, not just in the obvious sense that a thing's identity is defined by the difference from all other things but above all in the sense that "identity" names the difference of a thing with itself, a thing's difference from all its particular properties (each of which can be shared by other things): a thing "is" not its properties, it "is" a unique receptacle of its properties. This is why, for Hegel, identity and difference are moments of the logic of essence, reflexive determinations—this reflexive structure is absent in the logic of being, i.e., when we talk about, say, a quality, this quality does not have an "identity" in the described sense.[43]

However, we have to add another reversal here: not only is identity difference brought to its self-reference (or, rather, self-relating); difference itself (at its most radical, as an impossible-real that cannot be reduced to symbolic differentiality) also acquires its own identity as a separate entity which cannot be reduced to the difference between the two terms it differentiates. We thus have three elements at work in such a difference: the two opposed elements AND their difference "as such" existing apart from the two as a separate entity. Only in this sense can we properly understand the role of transgender individuals with regard to sexual difference. Sexual difference (for a Lacanian) and class difference (for a Marxist). Class difference (or its political expression, Left and Right) are "real" in the sense that every determination of the difference is already partial, "coloured" by one of the two sides—there is no "neutral" determination of class difference, and this is what Lacan means by "there is no meta-language": we cannot take a look at class difference from a neutral standpoint exempted from class difference. But—now comes the paradox we are aiming at—class struggle means precisely that a society is never clearly differentiated into two classes (the ruling one and the subordinated one): there is always "at least one," a third element, which does not fit this opposition ("middle classes," "rabble")—if there were just two classes, we would not have a struggle but just a stable co-existence of the two classes. (Or, a more problematic case, in anti-Semitism, the figure of the Jew stands for class antagonism as such: without the Jew, society would be a harmonious hierarchic order, and the Jew is the foreign intruder which triggers antagonism and class struggle—what anti-Semitism disavows is that social hierarchy is already in itself antagonistic.) This third element, in its very positive existence, works as a stand-in for difference as antagonistic, irreducible to symbolic differentiality—in short, there is no original plurality (multiple positions) which is then reduced to two fixed identities plus something that remains; what is primordial is the antagonism itself. In sexuality, this third element which gives body to sexual difference as such (as the real of an antagonism) are *trans-subjects*: they are not external to sexual difference, a remainder of some primordial polymorphous-perverse multiplicity; they are constitutive of sexual difference as such, the privileged point of its positive existence. This is the only sense in which we should fully assert "identity politics": when the "identity" in question is the identity which gives body to the real of the difference itself.

Appendices I

Appendix 1
Potestas versus Superdeterminism

Being involved in a decades-long debate with Adrian Johnston, I gladly accept his designation of our difference as one between layer cake and doughnut. Yes, my model is that of a doughnut, a twisted space that resembles the structure of the Moebius band: if we progress to the end on one side, making a full circle, we find ourselves on the opposite side, at our starting point. The process of notional mediation, of making-discovering a rational structure beneath the contingency of immediate reality can only be completed, brought to a conclusion (and Hegel's axiom is that to bring stability to a form of rationality it HAS to be brought to a conclusion), through a return to some figure of "brute immediacy" which actualizes (gives body to) the rational totality. THIS necessity of the return to immediacy is for Hegel the key feature of Reason that a mere Understanding cannot grasp. In Lacan's terms, every rational (symbolic) edifice has to be sustained by *le peu du réel*, a little piece of the contingent Real which acts as *la réponse du réel*, the "answer of the Real." Hegel was deeply aware of this paradox when he opposed ancient democracy to modern monarchy: it was precisely because the ancient Greeks did not have a figure of pure subjectivity (a king) at the summit of their state edifice that they needed to resort to "superstitious" practices—such as looking for signs in the flight-paths of birds or in the entrails of animals—to guide the *polis* in making crucial decisions. It was clear to Hegel that the modern world cannot dispense with this contingent Real and organize social life only through choices and decisions based on "objective" qualifications (the illusion of what Lacan later called the discourse of the University): there is always some aspect of ritual involved in being invested with a title, even if the conferring of the title follows automatically from certain "objective" criteria having been met. Another name for this final turn of the doughnut is "negation of negation," the return to immediacy, the cut that concludes the endless process of sublation/mediation. In clear contrast to this doughnut structure, the layer cake model stands for simple gradual progress, layer upon layer . . .

Furthermore, I admit that in some sense I do oscillate between Hegel and Schelling. While I fully endorse Hegel's critique of Schelling's early philosophy of identity, I find Hegel's reaction to Schelling's treatise on freedom (a brief note towards the end of his *History of Philosophy*) totally inadequate—Hegel simply misses the point there. Consequently, where I disagree with Johnston is his basic interpretive premise according to which Schelling's distinction between *Grund* and *Existenz* (from his treatise on freedom) is just a renaming of Spinoza's distinction between *natura naturans* and *natura naturata*. Schelling:

> begins with the fluid "ground" (*Grund*) of a primordial creative power (i.e., verb-like *natura naturans*) that then produces the fixed "existence" (*Existenz*) of stable entities (i.e., noun-like *natura naturata*). According to Schelling, human subjectivity, as the highest spiritual power, is nothing other than an irruption within the field of existence of the ground-zero substratum underlying and generating this field. In psychoanalytic terms, the subject is the return of repressed (Spinozistic) substance, the resurfacing of *natura naturans* within the domain of *natura naturata*. As such, reaching the highest Schellingian emergent layer amounts to reconnecting with the lowest one – hence a layer doughnut model.[1]

Johnston's critical point is that such a doughnut model "fails actually to explain the genesis of subjectivity": it either amounts to physicalist reductionism (discerning the basic structure of subjectivity already in the quantum reality) or to panpsychism (projecting into quantum reality the psychic structure of subjectivity). My view is that Johnston's layer cake model implies a simple gradual evolutionary progress which ignores the cuts and retroactivity that characterize a proper dialectical process.

What I find fascinating in Schelling's *Freiheitschrift* and in quantum physics is that, in both cases, the elementary ontological couple (*Grund-Existenz*, wave oscillations and their collapse in a single reality) precisely *cannot* be reduced to the opposition between a dynamic production process and its fixation in determinate fixed entities. How/why does the collapse/fixation occur? My point is that there has to be a tension/gap already in the Ground or in the wave oscillations: there is no "pure" flux of production, a gap or obstacle must already be inscribed into it. More precisely, if human beings, in their freedom, are "points of return for the darkness of *Grund* within the light of *Existenz*," this means that the darkness of the Ground is not the primordial fact: this "darkness" already presupposes the Void it envelops, and it is this (primordially repressed) Void that "returns" in human freedom.

So yes, Schelling is not reducible to Hegel, what he came up with in his *Freiheitsschrift* and *Weltalter* fragments is something breathtakingly new, in some sense a shock for himself, and he desperately tried to recuperate this shock, to reinscribe it into the frame of traditional metaphysics, in his late philosophy of revelation. It is easy to find superficial continuities in Schelling's thought, but they are, I think, his attempts to downplay the radicality of his break. In short, concerning the choice between Hegel and Schelling, I do find myself in a kind of parallax situation: while both are indispensable, there is no common language, the one cannot be reduced to the other.

It is interesting to note a homologous parallax in the very heart of quantum physics. Quantum physics inverts the common notion that there is a self-identical thing beneath appearances and that this thing appears differently to the objects with which it interacts (the ontological premise endorsed also by Harman): in quantum physics, particles do not just interact in the form of waves, particles also can be said to emerge at the point where the different waves cut into each other. So it is as if a thing is not the cause of how it appears in the interaction with other things, it is also something that emerges through the intersection of different appearances. Again, the parallax gap goes down to the bottom, it is irreducible. For this reason, we should be careful to avoid any attempt to reduce the difference between quantum wave fluctuations and their "collapse" into a single fixed reality to the difference between a multiple productive flux and fixed reality as its "reified" effect.

Dealing with this topic, Ricardo Sanín Restrepo[2] evokes Hugh Everett's "Many Worlds Interpretation" (MWI) of quantum physics:

> The fundamental tenet of the theory is that the worlds are infinite and increasingly complex as every possible outcome constitutes the need of a new universe. Everett is signaling the flaws of theories of quantum mechanics that depend on just one observer and therefore a single observation method in worlds riddled by a multiplicity of sets of observables.

In order to account for the passage from the contingent fluid space of wave oscillations to space of fixed identities, Restrepo proposes the term *potestas* as the basic feature of the latter: "Potestas is power as domination, it is the arrangement of solid systems of identity through the permanent construction of transcendent models (presuppositions) to define life and determine its exercise." Restrepo then goes on to construct a chain of equivalences between potestas (the power of domination) and identity (in contrast to difference), necessity (in contrast to contingency), actuality (in contrast to potentiality), sterile fixity (in contrast to the flux of change) and immaterial unreality (in contrast to the full actuality of contingent quantum oscillations):

> Potestas (power as domination, the denial of difference and this very world we live in) is the only world that is unreal, immaterial, and impossible. Precisely the most shocking and dire feature of potestas is that it has no reflection, no double side, it is a frozen state of identity and oppression. Potestas is thus the paradox of existence, a sheer simulacrum of world, the utter denial of difference and of multiplicity. The world of potestas (of the simulacrum of difference) is that which cannot exist outside itself, that which is not even different in itself. Every moment is its own actuality, as the "coming to be" in time is barred by the "given" perfection of what exists there in space.

As one could expect, this opposition is given an anti-Western spin: "Difference is always contingent, and thus any definition of it as necessity is its primal disavowal. Western philosophy's driving force is to negate negativity, to summon the 'some-thing', the being, in what actuality is, so it may dissolve the abomination of non-being, of no-thing, of contingency." But this celebration of contingency as "the unleashing of immanence, generation, transitions and creativity," as the "unbound multiplicity of becoming," is problematic at multiple levels. First, difference is by definition difference between identities, without identities the flow of differences becomes a chaotic flow, a formless One—the hierarchic order of identities is by definition the order of their differences. Second, the collapse of quantum wave oscillations into a single reality is in itself contingent (it cannot be predicted, one can just calculate its probability), so there is in some sense more contingency in reality than in quantum proto-reality—necessity (that reigns over reality) is in itself contingent. Third, power (in its social dimension of authority) is *always* potential, a not-fully-actualized threat—without this potential dimension, power loses its aura, which is a key moment of its efficiency (a father who fully uses his power and beats his child basically displays his weakness and impotence). So one should strictly distinguish between possibility in the sense of the openness of quantum wave oscillations and possibility in the sense of the possibility that pertains to reality itself. Fourth, the whole point of quantum mechanics is that waves prior to their collapse into (a single) reality are precisely not the true reality but a virtual domain of shadows, a weird proto-reality—if one proclaims this virtual domain the true reality, one misses the paradox of quantum physics. Here I also see a problem with Everett's MW interpretation: if there are infinite realities since all quantum possibilities are realized, each in its own world, then, again, there is no possibility, every option is realized. Fifth, if we celebrate contingent becoming as the space of creative freedom, then the key question remains unanswered: why does this flow of contingent collapse into a fixed reality, why does it not just go on in its happy fluctuation? There is only one consistent answer: the radical parallax between quantum oscillations and our reality. Not only is every reality the outcome of a collapse of wave oscillations the opposite also holds: the fact that we only can talk about quantum wave oscillations when we perform measurements with apparatuses in our reality is not only an epistemological necessity, but it also has ontological status. Restrepo rejects this version with horror—in such a universe, everything is detained, held at a stop in the necessity of *the* world that measures and compares the others. This would suppose the need of one actual world to create all others. This is nothing but subjugation, and at least ideally, would hinder the very possibility of the "alternate" and the "parallel" as uniquely different. There is a stabilization process that names "what is the case", a conduit that ordains the universes under the guise of one of them. Among the infinite possible worlds, there is one that serves as a kind of milieu for all the other worlds.

I think one should accept this conclusion: yes, there is one world (reality) that serves as a kind of milieu for all the other possible worlds which remain mere possibilities. Everett is right to emphasize that we should move to multiple observers, but we should reject the (falsely obvious) conclusion that multiple observers mean multiple realities since in each observation wave oscillations collapse in a different way. The way to proceed here would have been to introduce into quantum observations and measurements the dimension of intersubjectivity: it is not only empirically wrong but also theoretically misleading to conceive the observing scientist as a single individual—measurement is a socially mediated process. Bohr himself introduced this dimension when he defined scientific truth as a result that can be confirmed by repeated measurements in different circumstances and by different observers. In short, the big Other of a shared symbolic space is already at work in experimental science.

And the same goes for the attempts to ground our consciousness in quantum physics: where a possible analogy with quantum processes enters is not consciousness but the Unconscious. Roger Penrose tried to conceive the unconscious as the space of superposition of thoughts, and the passage to consciousness as the collapse of wave oscillations into a single reality: "Could thoughts exist in some sort of quantum superposition on an unconscious level only to become conscious when there is a specific selection—akin to a measurement of the electron's position?"[3] Although there seem to be good empirical reasons to reject the grounding of the psychic unconscious directly in quantum physics, the broad parallel which confers on the unconscious a pre-ontological status seems valid and productive, it was emphasized already by Lacan against Freud's occasional crude realism which conceives the Unconscious as a deeper vital reality of drives which precedes the superficial domain of consciousness and its illusions.

At the opposite end of Restrepo, we find the model of *superdeterminism*, an attempt to "renormalize" quantum mechanics, to get rid of the weirdness that makes it impossible to understand (to translate it in our ordinary notion of reality). Sabine Hossenfelder and Tim Palmer, today's main proponents of superdeterminism, advocate it as the only adequate way to resolve the problematic status of measurement that plagues quantum mechanics in its entire history: "Trouble is, no one knows why quantum effects disappear when one tries to measure them. This 'measurement problem' has bugged physicists ever since they thought up quantum mechanics."[4] In quantum mechanics, you

> can have a particle that is in two states at the same time. You can, for example, send it through a beam-splitter so that afterward it is going both left and right. Physicists say the particle is in a "superposition" of left and right. But you never observe a particle in a superposition of measurement outcomes. For such a superposition, the wave function of the particle will not let you predict what you measure; you can only predict the probability of what you measure.
>
> Sabine Hossenfelder and Tim Palmer, "How to Make Sense of Quantum Physics," *Nautilus*, (online 2020). https://nautil.us/how-to-make-sense-of-quantum-physics-237736/

For Hossenfelder and Palmer, this inexplicable passage from quantum superpositions to a single reality proves that "quantum mechanics cannot be how nature works on the most fundamental level; we have to move beyond it." Their solution is a return to old Einstein's reproach that, since God does not play dice, the image of a quantum universe of superpositions does not describe reality but projects into reality the limitation of our knowledge—there are in reality hidden variables ignored by quantum physics: "If quantum mechanics is not a fundamental theory, then the reason we cannot predict outcomes of quantum measurements is simply that we lack information. Quantum randomness, then, is no different from the randomness in, say, throwing a dice." In the same way, when we throw a dice, we cannot predict the outcome because we cannot know all the data that regulate its spinning around and fall, but in itself the final result is totally determined by the physical data; we cannot predict the measurement result because of the limitation of our knowledge. When we throw a dice, the dice spinning in the air is never in a state of superposition of six possible outcomes, the situation involves a probability only because of the observer's limitation, and the same holds for a particle prior to measurement . . . Are we dealing here with a return to old mechanistic materialism? It may sound like this: when Hossenfelder and Palmer formulate the "core idea" of superdeterminism—"everything in the universe is related to everything else because the laws of nature prohibit certain configurations of particles (or make them so unlikely that for all practical purposes they never occur)"—does this not sound like the first feature of dialectics in Stalin's systematization of dialectical materialism?

> This universal relatedness means in particular that if you want to measure the properties of a quantum particle, then this particle was never independent of the measurement apparatus. This is not because there is any interaction happening between the apparatus and the particle. The dependence between both is simply a property of nature.
>
> Sabine Hossenfelder and Tim Palmer, "How to Make Sense of Quantum Physics," *Nautilus*, (online 2020). https://nautil.us/how-to-make-sense-of-quantum-physics-237736/

This crucial specification sounds almost Hegelian, which is what makes it philosophically interesting: there are hidden variables, but not in the sense of a hidden Beyond that we cannot cover by measuring apparatus—what is hidden is the measuring itself, how the measuring is included in the measured reality. The hidden cause of the specific outcome (the "collapse" of the wave function) is our intervention into the observed reality through the measuring apparatus. As Hossenfelder likes to emphasize, "superdeterminism" is a misnomer since it just means determinism, inclusive of the negation of the free will (although her main argument does not directly involve the topic of free will). Her point is that, in the general interrelatedness of nature (reality), the measuring process is part of the same reality as the measured phenomena; however, quantum physics as a scientific practice is firmly grounded in our "ordinary" reality, it paints the fascinating pre-ontological realm of quantum waves, but this realm is never directly observed (no machine can register superpositions), it forever remains a theoretical construct that cannot be "schematized" in the Kantian sense (imagined as part of our spatio-temporal reality). While quantum mechanics can convincingly regress back from our ordinary reality to quantum waves as its presupposition, it can never fully explain the passage in the opposite direction, i.e., how/why wave oscillations collapse into our reality. Our reality is always-already here, presupposed as something that is external to the domain of quantum waves: we (observing scientists, our measurement machines and our conceptual apparatus).

The obvious way to get rid of the (subjective) observer is to claim that the collapse happens independently of it: collapse happens through measurement, and measurement is a relationship between two objects, the measured process and the measuring machine—the observing subject only takes note of the result which exists independently of being observed in our reality. However, such a solution leaves too many questions unanswered: the (re)description of the collapse as an objective process still doesn't explain the status of the observer.

Superdeterminism abolishes this ontological gap, reducing superpositions to an epistemological limitation and restoring the image of fully deterministic reality—although, as many commentators noticed, this solution remains an abstract principle which resolves the philosophical crisis unleashed by quantum physics without seriously affecting scientific work: the claim that in quantum measurement the observed phenomena and the measurement itself are part of some globally interconnected reality remains a philosophical intervention, a revenge of classical ontology on quantum physics. Do quantum computers nonetheless not provide a kind of proof of quantum reality? They use the properties of quantum physics to store data and perform computations which vastly outperform the best supercomputers:

> Classical computers, which include smartphones and laptops, encode information in binary "bits" that can either be 0s or 1s. In

a quantum computer, the basic unit of memory is a quantum bit or qubit. Qubits are made using physical systems, such as the spin of an electron or the orientation of a photon. These systems can be in many different arrangements all at once, a property known as quantum superposition. Qubits can also be inextricably linked together using a phenomenon called quantum entanglement. The result is that a series of qubits can represent different things simultaneously.[5]

Although I am not qualified to judge the strict scientific value of Hossenfelder's critique of quantum mechanics, do cases like this not indicate that the superdeterminist "renormalization" of quantum physics robs us of what is the most fascinating feature of the quantum revolution? Yes, the irreducible gap that separates quantum waves from ordinary reality brings with it a set of new problems, but our very dealing with these problems allows us to generate extraordinary insights.

Appendix 2
Sublation as Dislocation

A key feature of the Hegelian universality is that it is not just divided into its particular species but is itself caught into the process of division, acting as one of its own species—in short, it is again and again dislocated. Let's take a perhaps unexpected example: Bernard Herrmann's clarinet quintet "Souvenirs de voyage" (1967), which opens up with the same melodic line that he used a decade earlier in the beginning of the most famous piece ("Scene d'amour") from his score of Hitchcock's *Vertigo* (1958). We are dealing here with a nice case of dislocation, of tearing an element (a melodic line, in this case) out from its context and placing it into a different context in which it is subordinated to a space regulated by different logic. In our case, the same melodic line is first (in *Vertigo*) the opening moment of a movement that inexorably leads towards a Romantic crescendo, heavily relying on Wagner's *Tristan*, while its reprise in the quintet remains firmly within the pre-Wagnerian space of a theme and its variations. The surprising element here is the regressive direction of this shift: first a Romantic push towards a climactic crescendo, then the step back to a more classical space in which such crescendos are excluded.

Dislocation is a key dialectical concept whose proper understanding enables us to dispel some key misunderstandings that haunt Hegel's notion of *Aufhebung* (sublation). Let's take a different case from the sphere of politics. Rejecting the idea of the Haitian Revolution as the true consummation of the ideals of the French Revolution, Jean Casimir argues in his *The Haitians: A Decolonial History* that "Haiti dislocates rather than consummates the project of modernity."[1] Casimir's critique is directed at all those (me included) who see in the Haitian Revolution the universalization and radicalization of the French Revolution: only through its repetition in Haiti does the French Revolution really become a world-historical event with universal meaning. In this sense, the Haitian Revolution is the *Aufhebung* of the French Revolution: the full actualization of its potential, its repetition at a higher level. From the standpoint of the predominant post-colonial thought, such a view is all too "Eurocentric": if the Haitian Revolution is reduced to the deployment of the immanent potentials of the French Revolution, then—to put it in Hegelese—the French Revolution, a European phenomenon, is the over-reaching notion and the Haitian Revolution remains a subordinate moment of its self-deployment. Even if Haitians were "more French than the French themselves," even if they went further and were more consequent than the French, they were part of the European dynamic process.

Dislocation, on the contrary, means that elements are thoroughly re-contextualized, integrated into a new symbolic and social space which confers on them a new meaning unrelated to the original meaning—one can in no way "deduce" this new meaning from the original one. Let's take equality, a notion which originates in modern European thought. Although many advocates of equality worked to expand this notion also to women, other races, etc., such an expansion remains within the scope of the Western notion of equality. When a true other (Black slaves, exemplarily) appropriates equality, this notion is not just expanded but transposed in a different domain which radically affects its functioning—the unease with Black Lives Matter proves this abundantly. Furthermore, is the entire history of Marxism and Communist revolutions not a history of dislocations? In spite of Lenin's abundant quotes from Marx, Lenin effectively transposes Marx into a radically different historical situation in which the revolution was executed by a narrow party of professionals and won by addressing non-proletarian issues (land and peace). Mao Zedong did something even more radical: against Marx and Engels' vision, he moved from workers to farmers in the countryside as the revolutionary force—something unimaginable for Marx and Engels. Again, in each of these two cases, we are not talking about a continuous expansion but about a radical dislocation—no wonder that in both cases, orthodox Marxists opposed the reorientation (the basic reproach of Mensheviks to Lenin was that, in a non-Marxist way, he wants a revolution before the circumstances for it are ripe).

We should also bear in mind that capitalism as such involves a process of continuous dislocation. Capitalism originated in Europe but then gradually expanded into a global economic order, and this expansion was not continuous, it involved radical dislocations. Not only was capitalism from the very beginning linked to colonization and a new rise of slavery, but it also changed with the emergence of strong non-European capitalism in countries like Japan, India and now China. Incidentally, it is interesting to note how the same post-colonial Leftists who decry every expansion of equality and democracy as a dislocation and not a continuous development always insist that capitalism is "Eurocentric", attributed to Europe: even if it appears in China, India, etc., capitalism remains European. The underlying premise is clear: when a progressive idea like equality and democracy is expanded into a Third World, it involves a radical dislocation and is no longer European, but "bad" capitalism remains a foreign (European) intruder ... This mistake is serious because it misses the key fact that capitalism is actually universal, trans-cultural, indifferent towards particular cultures: it is not dislocated from one culture and then appropriated by another; rather, it stands for a universal dislocation from cultural space as such.

At this point, we can return to the relationship between Hegelian sublation and dislocation: the approach which opposes the two (as we have seen with Casimir apropos Haiti) misses a key feature of the Hegelian dialectical process, it reduces subject to a dynamized Substance. The critics dismiss the Hegelian notion of democracy-and-equality as an all-encompassing substantial entity which gradually actualizes its immanent potential, passing from one to another particular figure but remaining the same ground of the entire process. Say, the state goes through the stages of Asiatic despotic state, Ancient slave-owning democracies, feudal monarchies, modern authoritarian state, etc., but all these are particular formations which emerge as the immanent deployment of the same notion of State. But is this the case? If we remain at this abstract level, we have to add at least two points. First, for Hegel, the full consummation of an idea (when reality fits its idea) always implies the self-negation of this idea itself; say, the reality of states never fully fits the idea of state—when this happens, we no longer have a state, but we pass into a religious community. Second and more important, in a dialectical process predicate always passes into subject: what was at the beginning a subordinate particular moment of the process asserts itself as its subject and retroactively posits its presuppositions as its own moments ("predicates"). So, again, it is not the same Subject which goes from one to another particular figure, remaining the same agent which pulls the strings and controls the entire movement: what Hegel calls "Absolute" is the very process in which radical reversals happen and a predicate turns into a new Subject. Every dialectical passage is thus a form of dislocation: the previous Substance is dislocated into a new encompassing universality. It is not the same Universality which passes from one to another particular form—in each passage, Universality itself is dislocated, it is reduced to a subordinate moment of a new Universality. Let's take the passage from money to capital described by Marx: in pre-capitalist market exchange, money is a mediator of the exchange between producers which disappears in the final result (when I sell what I produced and buy what I need); with capitalism, however, money becomes capital, the subject (active agent) of the entire process. Although, from my individual standpoint, I produce (and sell) things so that I will get (other) things that I need (or desire) for my life, with capitalism, the true goal of the entire process is the expanded self-reproduction of capital itself—my needs and their satisfaction are just subordinated moments of capital's self-reproduction. In this sense, social production is radically dislocated, reduced to a subordinate moment of capital's reproduction.

Back to Haiti, what further complicates the picture is that the tension between imitating Europe and breaking out of European modernity is inscribed into the very heart of the revolutionary process itself. Toussaint l'Ouverture, the first leader of free Haiti, insisted on the equality of all races and rejected any privileging of the Blacks, plus, although he formally abolished slavery, he simultaneously imposed obligatory work (plantation workers had to remain at their posts so that production was ongoing). The two leaders who came after him, Dessalines and Christophe, enacted the anti-White turn (all non-Blacks with the exception of Poles who supported the revolution were massacred), but mandatory work remained, so that for ex-slaves things didn't change a lot. During Christophe's reign, Haiti was divided into two states: Christophe ruled as the emperor of the northern part and Alexandre Petion of the republic in the southern part. While the North turned into a half-feudal authoritarian imitation of a European modern state focused on boosting production and wealth (concentrated in the hands of the ruling Black elite), in the republic in the South land was distributed to small farmers who survived in a self-subsistent economy with low productivity. Although some commentators celebrate the South as an attempt to develop new communal forms of life as an alternate outside to European modernity, the experiment soon failed. A further paradox to be noted here is that the anti-White shift from equality of races to Black domination which occurred with Dessalines coincided with the rise of an authoritarian class structure with the Emperor at the top, which imitated the worst of European authoritarian modernity.

Similar paradoxes are already discernible in the case of Paraguay: before it was destroyed by the Spanish-Portugese intervention, Paraguay, under the domination of the Jesuit order which organized indigenous tribes into *reducciones* (missions), was not only an early form of Communism but was also much closer to cultural independence than Argentina or Brazil. Jesuits were already printing books in Guaraní language (which is even today spoken by the majority in Paraguay), so if the Jesuits were not thrown out, the history of Latin America would take a different turn, with the aboriginal language becoming one of the official state languages. Throughout modern history, Jesuits were as a rule much more progressive than Franciscans, although (or precisely because) Jesuits were organized as dogmatic fanatics while Franciscans emphasized poverty and spiritual inner life. Even today, Jesuits are the bastion of the Catholic Left while many Franciscans are neo-Fascists. Brecht was right to copy ("dislocate") Jesuitical sacred propaganda theatrical pieces in his Communist "learning plays."

There is an important paradox in the distinction between Guaraní spoken outside of the missions and the Jesuit Guaraní: Jesuits constructed new words in Guaraní to translate European notions while ordinary people simply incorporated hispanicisms:

> By and large, the Guaraní of the Jesuits shied away from direct phonological loans from Spanish. Instead, the missionaries relied on the agglutinative nature of the language to formulate calque terms from native morphemes. This process often led the Jesuits to employ complicated, highly synthetic terms to convey Western concepts. By contrast, the Guaraní spoken outside of the missions was characterized by a free, unregulated flow of hispanicisms; frequently, Spanish words and phrases were simply incorporated into Guaraní with minimal phonological adaptation. A good example of that phenomenon is found in the word "communion." The Jesuits, using their agglutinative strategy, rendered this word "Tupârahava," a calque based on the word "Tupâ," meaning God. In modern Paraguayan Guaraní, the same word is rendered "komuño."[2]

We encounter something similar in many of today's languages (the state protects their purity, prohibiting anglicisms, etc.), but in the Jesuit Paraguay, foreign colonizers themselves played this role.[3] Who was then in this case resisting the colonization of language, the colonizers themselves who wanted to maintain the purity of the indigenous language or the natives who easily incorporated foreign words? The answer is clear: the natives.

Appendix 3
Inventing Anna, Inventing Madeleine

In our permissive world, a consistent strategy to be free is difficult even to imagine—so how can we be free today? One of the answers is provided by the Netflix 2022 mini-series *Inventing Anna*, created and produced by Shonda Rhimes. The series is inspired by the story of Anna Sorokin and Jessica Pressler's article "How Anna Delvey Tricked New York's Party People" that appeared in *New York* magazine in 2018, telling the stranger-than-fiction story of a Russian-born twenty-something Anna Sorokin, a con artist who, through rebranding herself as Anna Delvey, a wealthy German heiress, had conned her way into an extravagant lifestyle, rubbing shoulders with the city's elite. Almost overnight, Sorokin had captured the internet's imagination, and after her prison sentence, she continues to fascinate the public media.

Most of the reviewers expressed their uneasiness at the mini-series: they find the portrayal of Anna unconvincing because it does not depict the real person beneath multiple masks … But what if this IS the truth, what if there is no self-aware manipulating subject behind pulling the strings? Anna does not just act following a Ponzi scheme, postponing paying debts, covering one debt with another, trying to convince people that the money she owes them is on the way, etc. In a crazy way, her subjective life itself functions as a Ponzi scheme: she doesn't just deceive others, she, as it were, borrows from herself, from her own imagined future. This is what makes her stance feminine, in clear contrast to Shimon Hayut, the con artist portrayed in the docu *Tinder Swindler* (one should note that *Tinder Swindler* is a documentary and *Inventing Anna* a fiction). Hayut travelled around Europe, presenting himself as the son of Russian-Israeli diamond mogul Lev Leviev. He used Tinder to contact women as Simon Leviev and tricked them into lending him money that he never repaid. He would charm women with lavish gifts and take them to dinners on private jets using money he borrowed from other women he had previously conned. He then asked his victims to help him financially due to the breach of "security," allegedly hindering his use of his credit cards and bank accounts; the women would often take out bank loans and new credit cards in order to help. His career ended quite appropriately: in late February 2022, he launched an NFT collection and merchandise with images seen and quotes heard in the film on him . . .

The obvious parallels between the two stories should not distract us from the crucial difference: Hayut is a swindler who coldly manipulates others, he has no project he really identifies with, he just abandons a woman he deceived and passes onto another woman, while Anna stays with a permanent circle of collaborators involved in the big plan to launch the Anna Delvey Foundation. What characterizes her is an unconditional fidelity to appearance: her friends often plead to her just to admit that she lied or cheated, but she *never* breaks down or lets the mask down. We watch again and again how she will find a way to save her face when she is confronted with the facts that prove her lies.

Anna is immoral but definitely ethical. When her lawyer defends her in his closing speech for the jury by claiming she just lived in her dream world and never came "dangerously close" to real success (getting the money for her big project), she feels betrayed and reacts furiously—she prefers to be punished much more heavily if this means that she will be perceived as somebody who almost succeeded, not as a ridiculous small dreamer.

It is this unconditional desire that makes her ethical—she literally obeys Lacan's formula "do not compromise your desire." This is why even some of those she swindled and are aware that she doesn't care for them continue to care for her. As Lacan said, "the hero can be betrayed without damage done to him"—Anna remains a hero to the end. That's why the usual psycho-social explanations fail: even her father is surprised by what she became.

To paraphrase a well-known line from one of the early novels about Hannibal Lecter, nothing happened *to* her, *she* happened to the world. Yes, her project is a ridiculous fake, but she nonetheless acts as a sublime figure because she elevated this ridiculous project into a Thing, a Cause for which she is ready to stake her entire life. Whatever she is, she is not cynical but utterly naive, and we need such naivete today for a precise reason: Anna is FREE in clear contrast to Hayut who just follows his egotistic need to manipulate others and profit from them. Freedom does not reside in a hidden core of my Self that eludes the grasp of others, a position from which I can manipulate others from a safe distance; freedom resides in my very unconditional identification with the role I decide to play for others. And we should read in the same way *The Testament of Judith Barton*,[1] a novel in which the unfortunate Judy Barton from Hitchcock's *Vertigo* tells the story from her own first-person standpoint:

> Initially, the flat, first-person narrative feels bogged down in the banality of Barton's pre-San Francisco existence. The years she spends growing up in America's heartland in a picture-perfect nuclear family carry the verisimilitude of tranquility, and tragedy is a foregone conclusion. It takes a while to escape it all (or is that merely subterfuge, à la Alfred?), and there are layers of chaos roiling just below the calm, much like the Hitchcock classic itself. Authors Powers and McLeod have a lot to say about the suppression of women during America's "Happy Days," and they do so quite deftly. The plot picks up in the final third of the book as Barton's date with the bell tower looms, and she's revealed as the most fantastic cipher – most tragically to herself, and all but oblivious to the deepening depths of her own anger and desolation. All of which, sadly, makes her the perfect pigeon for Gavin Elster's elaborate machinations to murder his wife and make it look like suicide.[2]

Are we then getting here the usual "feminist" reading of a well-known novel or movie, retelling the story from the woman's side and thus leaving behind her "objectivization"? The perhaps unsurpassable model is here *Wide Sargasso Sea* (Jean Rhys, 1966), a prequel to Charlotte Brontë's *Jane Eyre* describing the background to Mr Rochester's marriage from the point of view of his wife Antoinette Cosway, a Creole heiress. Antoinette is Rhys's version of

Brontë's devilish "madwoman in the attic," and her story is told from the time of her youth in Jamaica to her unhappy marriage to an English gentleman, Mr Rochester, who renames her Bertha, declares her mad, takes her to England, and isolates her from the rest of the world in his mansion.

But there is a big difference that separates *The Testament of Judith Barton* from *Wide Sargasso Sea*. Rhys's novel pursuits a clear feminist and anti-colonial agenda (re-subjectivizing the "mad woman in the attic" as the victim of oppression), while in *The Testament*, although we also get a first-person narrative of the woman, this narrative effectively objectivizes her *more* than the movie, in contrast to the authors' claim that

> most viewers [of the film] are satisfied, like Scottie, like the film itself, with objectifying Judy. As long as she looks the part, nobody on either side of the screen seems interested in who Judy really is and why she does what she does.[3]

The question to be raised here is a quite naive one but crucial for all fanatical Hitchcockians (like myself): the novel strives to be fully compatible with the movie, so should it be elevated to the same status, should it be considered *part of the same imagined universe*, in the strong sense that the novel simply describes what we don't see in the movie and that they both give a partial view of the same universe? I am ready to give to the novel a conditional YES, but with an important proviso. In telling her side of the story, the novel simply provides the "objective" background of her life story, and even the "subjective" elements merely provide the data on how she experienced her situation. In the movie, however, Judy displays authentic subjectivity in the evening scene in her Empire hotel room, where she returns with Scottie after dinner at Ernie's. We see Judy's profile, which is completely dark (in contrast to Madeleine's dazzling profile at Ernie's). From this shot, we pass to the front shot of her face, the left half completely dark, and the right half in a weird green (from the neon light outside the room). Instead of reading this shot as simply designating Judy's inner conflict, we should confer on it its full ontological ambiguity: as in some versions of gnosticism, Judy is depicted here as a proto-entity, not yet ontologically constituted in full (a greenish plasma plus darkness). It is as if, in order to fully exist, her dark half waits to be filled in with the ethereal image of Madeleine. In other words, we get here literally the other side of the magnificent profile-shot of Madeleine at Ernie's, its negative: the previously unseen dark half of Madeleine (the green anguished face of Judy), plus the dark half to be filled in by Madeleine's dazzling profile. And, at this very point at which Judy is reduced to less-than-an-object, to a formless pre-ontological stain, she is *subjectivized*—this anguished half-face, totally unsure of itself, designates the birth of the subject. Recall the proverbial imaginary resolution of Zeno's paradox of infinite divisibility: if we continue the division long enough, we will finally stumble upon a point at which a part will no longer be divided into smaller parts, but into a (smaller) part *and nothing*—this nothing "is" the subject.

The proper dimension of the subject is thus something much more radical than the display of a person's first-person "subjective" standpoint: the narrative that emerges in this way provides a continuous story which obfuscates the gap, the division, that defines subjectivity. And is this, exactly, not the division of Judy in the above-mentioned shot? We see half of her face, while the other half is a dark void.[4] The key thing to bear in mind here is that this division of her face (which makes her a subject) becomes visible *only* through her identification with "Madeleine": the dark half of her space is not only filled in with her identification with "Madeleine," it is in some sense even created by this identification.

As in the case of Anna, "Madeleine" is not just an alienated mask from which Judy has to liberate herself—she over-identifies with "Madeleine" and discovers/creates her authentic identity in playing this role. Yes, "Madeleine" was invented by the evil Gavin Elster and Judy was manipulated into playing this role, but she gets caught in it by falling in love with Scottie. *Vertigo* does not reduce Judy to a projection screen for male (Scottie's) deadly fantasy: her love for Scottie is the only real love in the movie. The novel just gives/tells the background which Judy was able to leave behind, and this act of transcending her "objective" situation is rendered in the movie. To put it in another way, the dark half of Madeleine's face is the space of her freedom—with her full space, she is just a product of her circumstances.

Freedom is thus a strange notion—although spontaneously experienced as a fact, the moment we reflect on it paradoxes and coincidences of opposites explode. For Kant, freedom hurts, it involves a painful renunciation to our spontaneous tendencies on behalf of duty, while at the same time, the deepest freedom is experienced as an inner necessity ("I have to do it, I just cannot not do it!"). Schelling further deployed this coincidence of opposites in his philosophy of art: in the process of creation, an artist is free in the deepest sense, while he just follows his inner drive which tells him what to do.

Appendix 4
The Political Implications of Non-representational Art

In his *Philosophy of History*, Hegel provided a wonderful characterization of Thucydides's book on the Peloponnesian war: "His immortal work is the absolute gain which humanity has derived from that contest."[1] One should read this judgment in all its naivete: in a way, from the standpoint of the world history, the Peloponnesian war took place so that Thucydides could write a book on it. What if something similar holds for the relationship between the explosion of modernism and the First World War, but in the opposite direction? The Great War was not the traumatic break that shattered late nineteenth-century progressism but a reaction to the *true* threat to the established order: the explosion of vanguard art, scientific and political which undermined the established world view (artistic modernism in literature—from Kafka to Joyce—, in music—Schoenberg and Stravinsky—, in painting—Picasso, Malevich, Kandinsky—, psychoanalysis, relativity theory and quantum physics, the rise of Social Democracy . . .). This rupture—condensed in 1913, the *annus mirabilis* of the artistic vanguard—was so shattering in its opening of new spaces that, in a speculative historiography, one is even tempted to claim that the outbreak of the Great War in 1914 was, from the "spiritual" standpoint, a reaction to this Event of rupture—or, to paraphrase Hegel, the horror of the World War I is the price humanity had to pay for waging the immortal artistic revolution of the years just prior to the war. In other words, one has to turn around the pseudo-deep insight on how Schoenberg and others prefigured the horrors of twentieth-century war: what if the true Event is 1913? It is crucial to focus on this intermediate explosive moment between the complacency of the late nineteenth-century and the catastrophe of WWI—1914 was not the awakening from slumber, but the forceful and violent return of the patriotic sleep destined to block the true awakening. The fact that Fascists and other patriots hated the vanguard *entartete Kunst* is not a marginal detail but a key feature of Fascism. It is against this background that we should approach the relationship between modern art and the horrors of the twentieth-century history.

In his *Concerning the Spiritual in Art* (1911), Wassily Kandinsky elaborates how every artwork influences the spectator not through its subject matter but through a certain choice of colours and forms.

In this sense, Kandinsky sees "high art" not as the thematization of a neutral medium which represents nothing but as having its own operational goal—the irrational, subconscious influence on the spectator, in which particular colours and forms influence the psyche of spectators and produce specific moods in them:

> Here the individual is placed not outside the artwork or in front of it but inside the artwork, and totally immersed in it. Such an artificial environment can create a powerful subconscious effect on the spectator, who becomes a visitor to, if not a prisoner of, the artwork . . . This approach to art does not propagate irrationality, it relies on an even more radical spiritualism: spiritual meaning is inscribed already into the form itself, not only into the content the work of art represents.[2]

However, a quite naive problem immediately arises here: if the specific form of a work of art produces moods of anxiety, discontent and disorientation, does it not deprive itself of any emancipatory dimension? Does it not propagate irrational pessimism and hopelessness? This is how abstract art (as well as atonal music and free-association writing) were perceived by both poles of the political spectrum in the 1930s. In 1938, during the Spanish Civil War, the French poet, artist, and architect of Slovene origins Alphonse Laurencic relied on Kandinsky's theories of colour and form to decorate cells at a prison in Barcelona where Republicans held captured Francoists. He designed each cell like an avant-garde art installation: the compositions of colour and form inside the cells were chosen with the goal of causing the prisoners to experience disorientation, depression, and deep sadness:

> During the trial Laurencic revealed he was inspired by modern artists, such as surrealist Salvador Dali and Bauhaus artist Wassily Kandinsky, to create the torture cells [. . .] Laurencic told the court the cells, in Barcelona, featured sloping beds at a 20-degree angle that were almost impossible to sleep on.
>
> They also had irregularly shaped bricks on the floor that prevented prisoners from walking backwards or forwards, the trial papers said. The walls in the 6ftx3ft cells were covered in surrealist patterns designed to make prisoners distressed and

> confused, the report continued, and lighting effects were used to make the artwork even more dizzying. Some of them had a stone seat designed to make occupants instantly slide to the floor, while other cells were painted in tar and became stiflingly hot in the summer.[3]

Indeed later, the prisoners held in these so-called "psychotechnic" cells did report extreme negative moods and psychological suffering due to their visual environment. Here the mood becomes the message—the message that coincides with the medium. The power of this message is shown in Himmler's reaction to the cells: he visited the psychotechnic cells after Barcelona was taken by the Fascists and said that the cells showed the "cruelty of Communism." They looked like Bauhaus installations and, thus, Himmler understood them as a manifestation of *Kulturbolschevismus* (cultural Bolshevism). No wonder Laurencic was put on trial and executed in 1939.

But the paradox is that orthodox Stalinist Marxism advocated the same thesis, just in the opposite direction. In the 1930s, writing in Moscow, Georg Lukács diagnosed expressionist "activism" as a precursor to National Socialism: he stressed the "irrational" aspects of expressionism that later, according to his analysis, culminated in Nazi ideology.[4] Along the same lines, Ilya Ehrenburg wrote at that time about the surrealists: "For them a woman means conformism. They preach onanism, pederasty, fetishism, exhibitionism, and even sodomy."[5] As late as 1963, in a famous pamphlet called *Why I Am Not a Modernist*, the Soviet art critic Mikhail Lifshitz (a close friend and collaborator of Lukács in the 1930s) repeated the same point: modernism is cultural fascism because it celebrates irrationality and anti-humanism. He wrote:

> So, why am I not a modernist? Why does the slightest hint of such ideas in art and philosophy provoke my innermost protest? Because in my eyes modernism is linked to the darkest psychological facts of our time. Among them are a cult of power, a joy at destruction, a love for brutality, a thirst for a thoughtless life and blind obedience [. . .] The conventional collaborationism of academics and writers with the reactionary policies of imperialist states is nothing compared to the gospel of new

> barbarity implicit in even the most heartfelt and innocent modernist pursuits. The former is like an official church, based on the observance of traditional rites. The latter is a social movement of voluntary obscurantism and modern mysticism. There can be no two opinions as to which of the two poses a greater public danger.[6]

In short, modernism is a much greater danger than Fascism ... While modernism is Fascist for Soviet Marxism, it is Communist for the Fascists. (There are, of course, exceptions on both sides, of course: futurism was appropriated by Italian Fascism as well as by Soviet art in the 1920s.) On the opposite side, the realism of representation is "totalitarian" for Western modernists who see in anti-representational modern art the liberation of the medium from the message it is supposed to transmit: the message is (in) the medium itself, not in what the medium represents ...[7] But the truly surprising fact is that today, some cognitivists propagate the same anti-modernist stance, claiming that good traditional taste for beauty as a source of pleasure is grounded in our nature, so that we should trust people's taste—here is what Steven Pinker wrote:

> The dominant theories of elite art and criticism in the 20th century grew out of a militant denial of human nature. One legacy is ugly, baffling, and insulting art. The other is pretentious and unintelligible scholarship. And they're surprised that people are staying away in droves?[8]

Such a stance is not just expanding among some theoreticians, it is also spreading among Rightist populists—in Slovenia, the Rightists are elevating national folk music into the emblem of being a true Slovene, and are attacking its critics as traitors to Slovene nationhood ... The proponents of the idea that the sense of artistic beauty and pleasure is grounded in our nature denounces the modernist "desire to destroy beauty" as an ideological moment of the elitist-globalist elite. In a quite naive sense, they are making a valuable point: modern art reproduces the horror, anxiety and dissonances which characterize our social being. The question we should ask here is: so why is reproducing anxiety and horror in art subversive, not just imitating and thereby sustaining the existing alienated social life? The answer is simple: just as bringing out anxieties and dissonances in art is in itself an act of liberation, it enables us to regain a distance towards the existing order. To see this, we have to accept the Hegelian position of Adorno: art is not about pleasure or the experience of beauty, art is a medium of truth, the truth of our human condition in a given historical epoch—and in our epoch, after the modernist break, sticking to the tradition of tonal music or realist painting is as such a fake.

Why? Let's return to Hegel, to his notion of the end of art. Hegel's fateful limitation was that his notion of art remained within the confines of classical representational art: he was unable to consider the possibility of what we call abstract (nonfigurative) art (or atonal music, or literature which reflexively focuses on its own process of writing, etc.). The truly interesting question here is in what way this limitation—remaining within the constraints of the classical notion of representational art—is linked to what Robert Pippin detects as Hegel's other limitation, his inability to detect the alienation/antagonism which persists even in a modern rational society where individuals attain their formal freedom and mutual recognition. In what way—and *why*—can this persisting unfreedom, uneasiness, dislocation in a modern free society be properly articulated, brought to light, only in an art which is no longer constrained to the representational model? Is it that the modern uneasiness, unfreedom in the very form of formal freedom, servitude in the very form of autonomy, and, more fundamentally, the anxiety and perplexity caused by that very autonomy, reaches so deep into the very ontological foundations of our being that it can be expressed only in an art form which destabilizes and denaturalizes the most elementary coordinates of our sense of reality? So, for Pippin, Hegel's "greatest failure" is that he

> never seemed very concerned about [the] potential instability in the modern world, about citizens of the same ethical commonwealth potentially losing so much common ground and common confidence that a general irresolvability of any of these possible conflicts becomes ever more apparent, the kind of high challenge and low expectations we see in all those vacant looks . . . He does not worry much because his general theory

> about the gradual actual historical achievement of some mutual recognitive status, a historical claim that has come to look like the least plausible aspect of Hegel's account and that is connected with our resistance to his proclamations about art as a thing of the past.[9]

And Pippin himself designates as the core of this new dissatisfaction class division and struggle (here, of course, class is to be opposed to castes, estates, and other hierarchies). A fundamental ambiguity thus characterizes the disturbing and disorienting effect of Manet's painting: yes, they indicate the "alienation" of modern individuals who lack a proper place within a society traversed by radical antagonisms, individuals deprived of the intersubjective space of collective mutual recognition and understanding; however, they simultaneously generate and reflect a liberating effect (the individuals they depict appear as no longer bound to a specific place in the social hierarchy).

Pippin is right to point out that, in his proclamation of the end of art (as the highest expression of the absolute), Hegel is paradoxically *not idealist enough*. What Hegel doesn't see is not simply some post-Hegelian dimension totally outside his grasp, but *the very "Hegelian" dimension of the analysed phenomenon*. The same goes for economy: what Marx demonstrated in his *Capital* is how the self-reproduction of capital obeys the logic of the Hegelian dialectical process of a substance-subject which retroactively posits its own presuppositions. However, Hegel himself missed this dimension—his notion of industrial revolution was the Adam Smith-type manufacture where the work process is still that of combined individuals using tools, not yet the factory in which the machinery sets the rhythm and individual workers are de facto reduced to organs serving the machinery, to its appendices. This is why Hegel could not yet imagine the way abstraction rules in developed capitalism: this abstraction is not only in our (financial speculator's) misperception of social reality, but is "real" in the precise sense of determining the structure of the very material social processes: the fate of whole strata of population and sometimes of whole countries can be decided by the "solipsistic" speculative dance of capital, which pursues its goal of profitability in a blessed indifference to how its movement will affect social reality. Therein resides the fundamental systemic violence of capitalism, much more uncanny than the direct pre-capitalist socio-ideological violence: this violence is no longer attributable to concrete individuals and their "evil" intentions, but purely "objective," systemic, anonymous.

And in exact homology to this reign of abstraction in capitalism, Hegel was paradoxically not idealist enough to imagine the reign of abstraction in art. That is to say, in the same way that, in the domain of economy, he wasn't able to discern the self-mediating Notion which structures the economic reality of production, distribution, exchange, and consumption, he wasn't able to discern the Notional content of a painting which mediates and regulates its form (shapes, colours) at a level which is more basic than the content represented (pictured) by a painting—"abstract painting" mediates/reflects sensuality at a non-representational level.[10]

Human Freedom

4
Marx Invented Not Only Symptom But Also Drive

Instead Of . . .

They Do it with Mirrors (the title of one of Agatha Christie's Miss Marple novels) is a slang term for the illusions of magicians and of a stage set—and we should shamelessly link this to Lacan's mirror-stage. However, in the Freudian unconscious as well as in Marx's interaction between the economic base and its superstructures, they mostly and principally *don't do it with mirrors*, which means that ideology can in no way be reduced to an effect of imaginary misrecognition or reversal of actual life process. Marx himself gets caught here in a fatal ambiguity. Although he clearly discerned the abstraction that mediates the self-movement of capital clearly and saw that capital self-reproduces itself like a Hegelian notion, i.e., that Hegel's dialectical self-mediation of a notion is a speculative-mystified expression of the self-reproduction of capital, he ultimately tends to reduce this speculative movement to the ideological inversion of actual life.

The symptom of this reduction is the rhetorical figure "instead of" to which Marx regularly resorts, especially in his youthful texts. His implicit (and sometimes explicit) line of reasoning begins with "instead of . . ." (which stands for the alleged "normal" state of things), and then he goes on to describe the alienated inversion of this "normal" state: instead of being the realization of the worker, labour appears as the loss of his realization; instead of appearing as what it is, the appropriation of the object through labour appears as its estrangement; instead of possessing what he produces, the more the worker produces the less he possesses; instead of civilizing himself through producing civilized objects, the more civilized his object, the more barbarous becomes the worker; etc., etc. The implication of this figure is that the revolution should somehow return things to normal: labour should be the realization of the worker who should civilize himself through work, etc.—and we should question precisely this restoration of normality, as does Marx himself in his late work. Even when the mature Marx returns to this figure from time to time, he gives it a specific spin, as in the following passage from *Capital*:

> This *inversion* (*Verkehrung*) by which the sensibly-concrete counts only as the form of appearance of the abstractly general and not, on the contrary, the abstractly general as property of the concrete, characterizes the expression of value. At the same time, it makes understanding it difficult. If I say: Roman Law and German Law are both laws, that is obvious. But if I say: Law (*Das Recht*), this abstraction (*Abstraktum*) *realizes itself* in Roman Law and in German Law, in these concrete laws, the interconnection becoming mystical.[1]

In this case, however, one should be very careful: Marx is not simply criticizing the "inversion" that characterizes Hegelian idealism (in the style of his youthful writings, especially *German Ideology*)—his point is not that, while "effectively" Roman Law and German Law are two kinds of law, in idealist dialectics the Law itself is the active agent—the subject of the entire process—which "realizes itself" in Roman Law and German Law; Marx's thesis is not only that this "inversion" characterizes capitalist social reality itself but above all that *both positions—the alienated inversion as well as the presupposed "normal" state of things—belong to the space of ideological mystification*. That is to say, the "normal" character of the state of things in which Roman Law and German Law are both laws (i.e., in which a worker possesses what he produces, in which the more powerful labour becomes, the more powerful becomes the worker, in which the more civilized his object, the more civilized becomes the worker, etc.) is effectively the everyday form of appearance of alienated society, the "normal" form of appearance of its speculative truth. The desire to fully actualize this "normal" state is therefore ideology at its purest and cannot but end in a catastrophe.

The lesson is thus that we should reject any reference to positive Life as the ground which is perverted in alienation (as Marx often does): there is no actual life external to alienation which serves as its positive foundation. The true fetish is not the fetishist reversal of the "natural" hierarchy (instead of actual productive life serving as the foundation of the spectral life of capital, actual life itself is reduced to a subordinate moment of the mad dance of speculative capital); *the true fetish is the very notion of direct positive life preceding alienation, an organic life whose balance was destroyed by capitalist alienation*. Such a notion is a fetish since it disavows the antagonisms that traverse the very heart of actual life.

But what makes this figure of "instead of" really interesting is that it should be put into a series with two other similar figures. When the mature Marx analyses the figure of the hoarder, he resorts to a similar rhetorical reversal, but with an added castrative dimension:

> Our hoarder is a martyr to exchange-value, a holy ascetic seated at the top of a metal column. He cares for wealth only in its social form, and accordingly he hides it away from society. He wants commodities in a form in which they can always circulate and he therefore withdraws them from circulation. He adores exchange-value and he consequently refrains from exchange. The liquid form of wealth and its petrification, the elixir of life and the philosopher's stone are wildly mixed together like an alchemist's apparitions. His imaginary boundless thirst for enjoyment causes him to renounce all enjoyment. Because he desires to satisfy all social requirements, he scarcely satisfies the most urgent physical wants.[2]

Or, as Marx puts it in *Theories of Surplus-Value*, "the industrial capitalist becomes more or less unable to fulfill his function as soon as he personifies the enjoyment of wealth, as soon as he wants the accumulation of pleasures instead of the pleasure of accumulation."[3] Here a Hegelian reversal takes place: when, instead of the accumulation of pleasures, we get the pleasure of accumulation, this second pleasure becomes *jouissance* on behalf of its castrative dimension described by Marx (the capitalist's "imaginary boundless thirst for enjoyment causes him to renounce all enjoyment")—it is not just a symmetrical reversal since Marx brings out the castrative dimension of this reversal. (Freud similarly talks about the repression of desire turning into a desire of repression, talking about pleasure turning into the pleasure of talking . . .) So if the first "instead of" reversal is imaginary (the second "abnormal" version, the symmetrical reversal, the mirror-image, of the first "normal" one), the second reversal is symbolic due to the castration implied by universalization.

There is yet another, third, figure of "instead of" which is found in Marx's *Poverty of Philosophy* (1847), his critical analysis of Proudhon's "philosophy of poverty" (so a reversal is already in the title itself): "Instead of the ordinary individual with his ordinary manner of speaking and thinking we have nothing but this ordinary manner in itself—without the individual."[4] Although this passage is a rather cheap stab at (Proudhon and) Hegel, it fits Pippin's description of what Hegel is doing in his logic: Hegel deploys the basic forms of argumentative thinking in its independence of who is thinking—whenever and wherever there is thinking, these forms are operative:

> If someone simply persists in asking what we were asking above: "But *where* is all this thinking and explaining happening?" all one can reply is "wherever there is thinking." This is not to say that there is not always a thinker or subject of thought; it is to say that thought that can be truth-bearing is constituted by what is necessary for truth-bearing, by any being of whatever sort capable of objective (possibly true or false) judgment.[5]

In this sense, Hegel's logic is *the logic of the Real*: precisely where it appears to be at its most idealist (analysing pure thinking in its independence from any positive bearer of thinking, i.e., ignoring the material and psychic conditions of thinking, ignoring what Marx always adds: "But thinking is actually always an activity performed by individuals who live, interact and produce in a material social reality, it is as aspect of human social practice!"), Hegel's logic touches the Real. And, as Adrian Johnston amply demonstrates, does Marx not do the same in his analysis of capital's drive? Capitalism's

> fundamental driving force, the unshakable thirst for surplus-value (i.e., M-C-M′ as the core logic of capital), is a strange selfless greed. This motivating structural dynamic is an acephalous and anonymous prosthetic drive, an impersonal template implanted into those subjected to capitalism. [. . .] This *Wiederholungszwang* of capital's self-valorization through the boundless accumulation of quantified surplus-value is an acephalous kinetic configuration disregarding and overriding any and every other interest. The latter include even the (self-) interests of those human beings who, as capitalists, are this drive's personifications/bearers.[6]

So if "the only subject who truly enjoys capitalism is anonymous Capital itself as the idiotic, acephalous repetition of M-C-M′, as a drive without a driver," does this description not directly echo Lacan's description of drive as idiotic acephalous push? Lacan is, of course, well aware that drive is always related to individual human and social bodies—the same as Hegel, who is well aware that thinking appears, comes to exist "for itself," only in bodily human beings (he develops how this happens in his "Anthropology" at the beginning of the philosophy of Spirit, the third part of *Encyclopaedia*). But what Marx also knows is that, in order to grasp how capitalism functions, one has to describe it "counterfactually" as the Real of an acephalous mechanism. This Real is, of course, purely virtual, with no actual existence in itself—but it has to be presupposed by individuals as an In-itself if capitalism is to function.

There are thus three forms of the "instead of" reversal: imaginary, symbolic, and real. And we can add even some further complications here—is it not that Freudian "infantile sexuality" can also be described as a specific form of "instead of"? Its imaginary formula would be something like: "Instead of fully satisfying adult sex" (what Lacan describes as "big fat *jouissance*, plain *jouissance*, *jouissance* that is realized in copulation in the raw"), "we just get stupid infantile fantasies." Its symbolic formula would be: "Instead of just a 'copulation in the raw,' we need fantasies to supplant it—without them real sex gets desexualized." And its real formula would be: "Instead of conceiving real sex as always a disappointment with regard to what we fantasized we will get out of it, a truly intense sex can also function as the traumatic real of an unbearable enjoyment that shatters our complacency, something so powerful that we are not able to translate it into the (symbolic) coordinates of our reality, so that we experience in it what Freud called *Realitaetsverlust*, a momentary loss of reality."

Progress and Apathy

The key premise of Adrian Johnston's path-breaking reading of Hegel's political thought is that both Hegel and Marx deployed the historical process as a dynamic progression towards freedom, even if this progress involves many crises, reversals and violent ruptures; what they both missed (or neglected, at least) are the opposite moments of stasis and regression. A true dialectical thinking of history should be

> capable of comprehending non-dynamism (as blockage, defeat, exhaustion, impasse, regression, stagnation, etc.) as thoroughly as it comprehends dynamism. Both Hegelianism and Marxism require the ability to explain not only examples of progress in social history, but also instances of the failure of social history to make any progress, instances of what could be dubbed socio-historical "stuck-ness." Only with this explanatory ability can either or both of these theoretical orientations serve as a contemporary Owl of Minerva sufficiently wise to grasp the course of actual events from Hegel's time to today, a course exhibiting at least as much, if not more, anti-progress than progress – as well as exhibiting hefty doses of jarring contingent occurrences defying any purported predictive power or description in terms of any theodicy, however secularized.[7]

As a rule, one tries to soften Hegel's notion of history by claiming that, although he prohibits any visions of how the future should be, he nonetheless remains a thinker of progress (the entirety of history is the gradual actualization of the notion of freedom), and makes it clear that every moment of history involves not only its own specific vision of the entire past but also a specific vision of a possible future, a specific tendency which signals how things should go on. It is, however, precisely because of this that the future of human history is impenetrable: each vision of the future, each tendency (good or bad) inscribed into a particular situation, is limited by this situation itself, and it is this situation which is transformed in a real change. This is why, when a radical change occurs, things necessarily go wrong—the very situation which gave birth to a vision of the future disappears. This is the Hegelian view of the entirety of modern history: the French Revolution had to end in terror, the peaceful progress of the second half of the nineteenth century was cut short by the carnage of the Great War, the authentic emancipatory potential of the October Revolution gave birth to Stalinism, and the Fukuyamaist dream of the end of history turned into the mess we are in now.

The paradox of today's global capitalism is that stuckness and the failure of progress generate immense dynamic progress in production, consummation, even in ethics (Politically Correct moralism)—we are hyper-active so that things do not change. This is why Peter Coffin was right in pointing out how "cancel culture" reproduces in ideology market relations, in the same way that the elevating of consent into a key moment of sexual intercourse echoes the role of consent in a "free" market transaction:

> When people get cancelled, they get taken off the market. A cancel campaign is a collective of small-time buyers at the consumer level committing to revoke their buying power [...] "cancel culture" is a set of dynamics which developed out of neoliberal capitalist society that mirror a subscription model and have power relative to all involved parties' capital. [...] Cancel Culture is real. But it's not simply "a modern form of ostracism in which someone is thrust out of social or professional circles." It's capitalism itself ideologically manifesting in our social relationships.[8]

No wonder that, even among its partisans, Cancel Culture evokes no joyful enthusiasm but a bitter resentment which just feeds our apathy—to "cancel" someone is a non-act in the form of a pseudo-act. There is no affirmative stance in it, just a desperate attempt to make 90 percent of the people feel guilty for the fact that they are "binary heterosexuals," and to profit from being a minority by one or another form of affirmative action. This inability to act means that today's permissive liberal capitalism is melancholic: we are losing the desire for what we know it has to be done. By contrast, nationalist populism mobilizes mourning (for the true popular capitalism and its way of life threatened by corporate globalization). James Godley evokes here Byung-chul han's observation that

> one of the things that has made the pandemic particularly difficult for people is not just that it is harder to participate in mass gatherings, but that we no longer even know what such rituals are for. Neoliberal capitalism's valorization of innovative "disruption" and its myopic focus on finding ever new resources for surplus value have pathologized these rituals which build a collective, replacing them with neurotic "private" ceremonials and confessional experiences. This has led to stigmatizing structures of collectivity as antiquated or even potentially harmful to the social fabric. Thus despite, or even because of, the current cultural emphasis on openness and interpersonal communication, a subjectivist discourse of psychologization has rerouted concern with objective social structures to the mental health of individuals. As a result, what has been forgotten, Han observes, is that "ritual acts also include feelings, but the bearer of these feelings is not the isolated individual" but the community. We have forgotten, for example, how rituals of mourning deal not with individual emotionality but with what Han describes as "an objective feeling, a collective feeling [which] imposes mourning" on everyone collectively and thereby "consolidate[s] a community."[9]

In short, proper mourning is only possible when a figure of the big Other is here doing it for us—one can accept the loss of an object only when this loss is inscribed into the big Other. We should recall here the notion of interpassivity (in the authentic sense of this term developed by Robert Pfaller[10]). Lacan evokes the common situation of people at a theatre enjoying the performance of a Greek tragedy, but his reading of it makes it clear that something strange is going on: it is as if some figure of the other (in this case, the Chorus) can take over from us and experience for us our innermost and most spontaneous feelings and attitudes, inclusive of crying and laughing. In some societies, the same role is played by so-called "weepers" (women hired to cry at funerals): they can carry out the spectacle of mourning for us, relatives of the deceived, who can dedicate their time to more profitable endeavours (like taking care of how to split the inheritance). (There is also a more authentic way to rely on weepers: a grief-stricken person is too traumatized to externalize his/her pain into a proper ritual, so that s/he can only do it through another.[11]) And what about the Tibetan praying wheels? I put a piece of paper with a prayer written on it into the wheel, I mechanically turn it around (or, even more practically, I let the wind turn it around), and the wheel is praying for me—as the Stalinists would have put it, "objectively," I am praying, even if my thoughts are occupied with the most obscene sexual fantasies. And to dispel the illusion that such things can only happen in "primitive" societies, think about the so-called "canned laughter" on a TV screen (the reaction of laughter to a comic scene which is included in the soundtrack itself): even if I do not laugh, but simply stare at the screen, tired after a hard day's work, I nonetheless feel relieved after the show, as if the TV did the laughing for me ... Instead of dismissing interpassivity as an alienated "non-authentic" procedure, we should note that it sustains the space for our activity: if we are not able to transfer our passive experience onto an Other, we end up being passivized ourselves, even if we appear to be caught in permanent hyper-activity—I can only be truly active through the passivity of the Other, and this is what no longer functions today.

In order to see what has gone wrong, we should introduce the difference between melancholy and mourning. The melancholic is not primarily the subject fixated on the lost object, unable to perform the work of mourning on it, but rather the subject who possesses the object and has lost its desire for it, because the cause which made it desire this object lost its efficiency. In this sense, melancholy precedes prohibition: what makes melancholy so deadening is that objects are here, available, the subject just no longer desires them. The function of prohibition is to shatter the subject out of its melancholic lethargy and set its desire alight. The wager of prohibition is that, by depriving the subject of the object, it will resuscitate the cause of desire. Is, then, some kind of new prohibition (say, ecologically grounded) what we need? Adrian Johnston characterized today's geo-political situation as

> a situation in which the world's societies and humanity as a whole are facing multiple acute crises (a global pandemic, environmental disasters, massive inequality, ballooning poverty, potentially devastating wars, etc.), yet seem unable to take the (admittedly radical or revolutionary) measures necessary to resolve these crises. We know things are broken. We know what needs fixing. We even sometimes have ideas about how to fix them. But, nevertheless, we keep doing nothing either to mend damage already done or to prevent further easily foreseeable damage.[12]

A phrase uttered in one of the episodes of *House*—"Even your actions lie"—offers a correct rebuttal to the standard wisdom: "Your words lie, your actions (what you really do) tell the truth." Sometimes, our words tell the truth but our actions lie, not just in the sense that they don't fit our words (we say one thing, we do another), but in the more radical sense that our actions are in themselves false, undermining their immanent goal—or, as John Vidal put it in a comment: "Floods, storms and heatwaves are a direct product of the climate crisis—that's a fact, so where is the action?"[13] Where does this passivity come from? Today's global capitalism generates apathy precisely because it demands from us permanent hyper-activity, constant engagement in its devastating dynamic—are we aware how thoroughly our lives have changed in the last decades? So to open up the path for a real change, we have first to put a brake on the mad rhythm of continuous change. We are never given a moment of respite to think. Apathy is thus the other side of extreme dynamism: things change all the time to make sure that nothing that matters will really change. It's a little bit like the compulsive neurotic—like me—who talks and gesticulates all the time not to achieve something but because he is afraid that, if he stops for a moment, others will notice the worthlessness of what he is doing and may raise a question that really matters.

This stuckness sustained by hyper-activity also allows us to explain how today's capitalism succeeds in neutralizing threats and critical voices to a degree unthinkable for Marx: "This neutralization is one of the keys to accounting for capitalism's surprising longevity, including in the face of repeated predictions of its imminent implosion made by Hegel, Marx, and many others."[14] How? Today, ideology functions less and less like a symptom and more and more like a fetish. The symptomal functioning makes ideology vulnerable to the usual ideologico-critical procedure: in the classic Enlightenment way, when an individual caught in ideology understands the hidden mechanism of ideological deception, the symptom disappears, the spell of ideology is broken. In the fetishist functioning, ideology works in a cynical mode, it includes a distance towards itself—or, to repeat Sloterdijk's old formula of cynical reason: "I know what I am doing, but I am nonetheless doing it."[15]

As Alenka Zupančič wrote, in a cynical mode, the fetishist disavowal "I know very well, but ... (I don't really believe it)" is raised to a higher reflexive level: fetish is not the element to which I hold so that I can act ignoring what I know—fetish is *this knowledge itself*.[16] The cynical reasoning is: "I know very well what I am doing, so you cannot reproach me that I don't know what I am doing." This is how in today's capitalism the hegemonic ideology includes (and thereby neutralizes the efficiency of) critical knowledge: critical distance towards the social order is the very medium through which this order reproduces itself. Just think about today's explosion of art biennales (Venice, Kassel ...): although they usually present themselves as a form of resistance towards global capitalism and its commodification of everything, they are in their mode of organization the ultimate form of art as a moment of capitalist self-reproduction.

We have to go a step further here. In her analysis of *Don't Look Up!*, Zupančič proposed the thesis that conspiracy theorists (about the pandemic or global warming) in a way *give body to the "unconscious" of the "rational" liberal establishment itself*.[17] The truth is exactly the opposite of the conspiracy-theory claim that the forces of establishment don't really believe in the danger and stage the danger as a conspiracy to control people: the forces of establishment know reality but they ultimately don't believe in it—they are the true deniers. The lesson of Boris Johnson's garden parties at the time of strict lockdown tells us a lot here: although he knew well of the reality of Covid (he almost died of it), his activity (like partying) demonstrates that he didn't really believe in it, that he perceived himself (and the circle around him) as somehow exempted from it. When, in the movie *Don't Look Up!*, the president (played by Meryl Street) asks worriedly, "But will the comet hitting the earth prevent the Super Bowl?," she perfectly renders this stance: as if the end of life on Earth doesn't render this question meaningless . . . That's why the true target of our critique should not be the deniers but the false "rationalism" of the establishment itself.

One should be careful not to confuse here the function of the subject-supposed-to-know with another's knowledge (i.e., with another subject who simply knows). Relying on others' knowledge is unavoidable in our lives: scientists know things that the majority of us are not able to grasp (just think quantum mechanics); there *are* authentic experts, we simply have to trust them up to a point—the idea that we should be able to check every piece of knowledge before we trust in it ends up in endless googling where we fall for ridiculous idiosyncrasies. But in interpassive non-knowledge, *the other DOESN'T know for me*—I comfortably dwell in my knowledge, ignoring this knowledge through an Other. This is what happens with today's liberal establishment: as in *Don't Look Up!*, they know how things stand (that catastrophe is impending), but they do not act upon this knowledge and transfer their ignorance onto the other (of actual deniers).[18]

In Agatha Christie's *The Hollow* (1946), the eccentric Lucy Angkatell has invited the Christows (John, a top Harley street doctor, and his wife Gerda), along with other members of her extended family, to her estate for the weekend. Poirot (who is staying nearby in his country cottage) is also invited to dinner; the next morning he witnesses a scene that seems strangely staged: Gerda Christow stands with a gun in her hand next to John's body, as it bleeds into the swimming pool. Lucy, Henrietta (John's lover) and Edward (a cousin of Lucy's and a second cousin of Henrietta) are also present at the scene. John utters a final urgent appeal, "Henrietta," and dies. It seems obvious that Gerda is the murderer. Henrietta steps forward to take the revolver from her hand, but apparently fumbles and drops it into the swimming pool, destroying the evidence (Gerda's fingerprints on the revolver). Poirot realizes that the dying man's "Henrietta" was a call to his lover to protect his wife from imprisonment for his own death—without a conscious plan, the entire family joined the plot and deliberately misdirected Poirot, as they each know Gerda is the murderer, and are attempting to save her …

The reversal of the standard formula (a murder is committed, there is a group of suspects who had interest and opportunity to do it, and even if the murderer seems obvious the detective discovers clues which belie the scene of the murder staged by the true murderer to cover his tracks) is turned around even more than in *Murder at the Orient Express* (the entire group of suspects is guilty, and this makes the victim the true criminal) in *And Then There Were None* (the entire isolated group of suspects, murderer included, is murdered), or in *Curtain* (where Poirot himself is the murderer since this is the only way to stop the "bad guy" who knows how to bring others to commit murders without doing anything illegal himself): the group of suspects make clues pointing to themselves to cover up the fact that the true murderer *is* the obvious one who was caught at the scene of the murder with a gun in her hand. So the scene of the crime is staged, but in a reflexive way: the deception resides in the very fact that it appears artificially staged, i.e., truth masks itself as an artificial appearance, so that the true fake is the "clues" themselves—or, as Jane Marple says in Christie's *They Do It With Mirrors*: "Never underestimate the power of the obvious."

And does ideology not often function like this, today especially? It presents itself as something mysterious, pointing towards a hidden behind, to cover up the crime that it is committing (or legitimizing) openly—or, in Freudian terms, it invites us to read it as a symptom while it functions like a fetish. The favoured expression that announces such double mystification is "the situation is more complex": an obvious fact—let's say, a brutal military aggression—is relativized by evoking a "much more complex situation in the background" (which, as expected, makes the aggression an act of defence). Which is why, at some level, one should ignore the hidden "complexity" of the situation and trust simple numbers. David Wallace-Wells, the author of *Uninhabitable Earth* (2019), made the case for climate reparations in which rich countries would pay to ameliorate the damage they have caused by burning fossil fuels. His argument is based on the extraordinary inequality in historical emissions of the greenhouse gases causing global warming:

> All of sub-Saharan Africa, where there are more than a billion people living today, is responsible for about 1 percent of all historical emissions. The U.S., one country whose total population is about a third of all of sub-Saharan Africa, is responsible for 20 percent of all historical emissions.[19]

All this is obvious, we know it, but the apathy persists—where does it come from? We should note that there is not an external opposition between dialectical process and stuckness, i.e., there is no smooth dialectical process which is then occasionally side-tracked or interrupted. When things run smoothly, following their "logical" course, the movement is flat, nothing really new emerges. Things only really change when their "normal" progress gets stuck, so that the entire constellation has to be changed to re-establish a new "normal" run. Like a revolution, a dialectical change never occurs "at its proper time," it always comes too late (when things get stuck) or too early (as did the October Revolution for the orthodox Marxists). This is why, when a radical change happens, its outcome is as a rule always the opposite of what was expected—the October Revolution turned into Stalinism.

The Big Four (1927), one of the two craziest Agatha Christie novels (the other being *Passenger to Frankfurt*, 1970), reacts to the trauma of the October Revolution, and Christie's claim is that Lenin and Trotsky were just puppets in the hands of a secret world-wide organization whose aim is "to destroy the existing social order, and to replace it with an anarchy in which they would reign as dictators" (as Poirot says in the novel). The kernel of truth in this otherwise rather lunatic theory is that the anarchic mobilization of the crowds can often finish in a dictatorship of a new elite. Hegel himself had the same presentiment: in his last published text, the 1831 essay "On the English Reform Bill," he cautions about a possible socio-historical turn for the worse, at least in Britain; it is usually perceived as Hegel's anti-democratic warning against the widening of the franchise for parliamentary elections, against the shift from corporate order in which individuals participate in the social totality only through their role in a particular estate, with the direct access of individuals in the universal order. However, as Adrian Johnston pointed out, a closer look allows us to propose a different reading—Hegel "depicts a rich rabble of English landowners as having dispossessed the subsistence-farming peasantry":

> While the "English Reform Bill" of the title of Hegel's essay promises democratic gains through the widening of the franchise for British Parliamentary elections, the just-mentioned dispossession process creates a situation in which this "reform" makes it likely that a wealthy *Pöbel* will manipulate a gullible impoverished populace whose poverty leaves them vulnerable to demagoguery and the like. Thus, seeming progress towards greater democracy, through a bad cunning of reason, probably will lead to actual tyranny in the guise of mob rule by a mob itself ruled by the socially irresponsible rich. Hegel ends this essay predicting that this particular piece of English legislation will lead not to a desirable and peaceful reform but to an undesirable and bloody revolution.[20]

Hegel was not yet able to think the capitalist class struggle in its contrast to the division of a society into estates; but Johnston is nonetheless right in reading Hegel backwards (from our experience of Rightist populism): although Hegel's doubt about the English Reform Bill is motivated by his vision of a state divided in estates and thus opposed to liberal egalitarianism (each individual can participate in the universal political sphere only through his/her belonging to a specific estate, s/he should have no direct participation in the universality that by-passes the hierarchic order of estates), he foresaw the anti-egalitarian corruption of the universal right to vote which occurs when the "rich rabble" manipulates the poor, as is the case in today's nationalist populism . . . And in a similar way, we are witnessing today the turn from the anarchic project of cryptocurrencies to new forms of domination.

The so-called oligarchs in Russia and other post-Communist countries are another case of "rich rabble"; they are not even an authentic creative bourgeoisie, they are a bourgeois counterpart to what Marx called lumpen-proletariat: *lumpen-bourgeoisie*. It was the lumpen-bourgeoisie which exploded in post-Communist countries from the late 1980s on, through wild "privatizations," etc. In Slovenia, the exemplary case of a lumpen-bourgeois is the "independent tax advisor" Rok Snežič, a collaborator and friend of the Rightist ex-PM of Slovenia Janez Janša. He advises Slovene companies on how to move their seat to Republika Srpska (the Serb part of Bosnia) where taxes are much lower than in Slovenia, but he is prohibited to enter the territory of Bosnia because of criminal investigations against him (he is the main suspect in the police investigation of an international money laundering network). While he has declared bankruptcy, has no private possessions and successfully avoids paying millions of Euros of tax, he drives around in luxury new cars and pays for jumbo road posters. He has no bank account and is officially employed at a company owned by his wife, with a monthly salary of 373.62 Euros delivered in cash . . . But is such a trend towards lumpen-bourgeoisie not a global trend of today's "normal" capitalism? Are figures like Donald Trump and Elon Musk also not lumpen-billionaires?

Dialectical Materialism? Yes, But . . .

Johnston seems to avoid the radical implications of his insight because, to paraphrase for the nth time the Groucho Marx one-line joke, he talks and argues like a dialectical materialist, but this shouldn't deceive us, he ultimately really *is* a "dialectical materialist" in the traditional Marxist sense of overall dynamic interconnectedness, thereby ignoring the philosophical absurdity and nothingness of "diamat." That is to say, does Johnston's vision of the gradual evolution of nature not miss what I dare to call the proper madness of the Hegelian dialectics? In his book, he openly endorses "the phrase 'dialectical materialism' in its standard sense as designating the extension of the models of historical materialism, developed through analyses of societies and social history, to cover pre- and non-human realities (first and foremost, objective nature as per the natural sciences)," ignoring the fact that the term was NEVER used by Marx and Engels. Even in his manuscripts edited in the mid-1920s under the title *Dialectics of Nature*, Engels NEVER uses the term "dialectics of nature"—the closest he gets to it is when he only once speaks of "dialectics so to say (*sozusagen*) in nature." The term "dialectical materialism" was introduced by Georgi Plekhanov who fatefully defined it as "dynamized Spinozism," and the idea that dialectical materialism is a general ontology and historical materialism its application to human history was elaborated by Stalin.

What is missing in dialectical materialism "in its standard sense" is the transcendental dimension, the properly Hegelian dialectical mediation of subject and object, so it is not clear why Johnston himself calls his thought "transcendental materialism." The point of the young Lukács is not the denigration of the economic base to just one of the "factors" of social totality but its elevation into a transcendental status—transcendental in the sense that the structure of the economic base (described by Marx in his critique of political economy) provides a formal model for all other social relations, inclusive of politics, ideology and even science (recall that Darwinism itself arose after Darwin read Malthus's description of the fight for survival in contemporary societies). While Johnston is well aware of this key role of the economic base, he reduces it to another version of economic reductionism. But Lukács's point is not that only society is properly dialectical while nature is mechanistic; his point is that social praxis is the ultimate horizon of our approach to reality, nature included, so that our image of nature is always mediated by society. Reductionist mechanist materialism does not provide a correct description of nature, it is mediated by the reduction/reification operative in social life; today, nature is perceived as a self-reproducing process of genetic information, echoing the key role of digitalization in our lives.

Johnston detects an antinomy in Lukács: the total reification and commodification in social life versus the freedom of self-conscious proletariat. But there is no antinomy here: it is the very reification that empties subjectivity of all positive content, reducing it to "empty" subject, to what Marx called *substanzlose Subjektivitaet*, and thus opens up the space for freedom—Johnston himself quotes Shlomo Avineri's remarks, "When the worker comprehends that under capitalist production he is degraded to the status of a mere object, of a commodity, he ceases to be a commodity, an object, and becomes a subject."[21] In short, Lukács is no Romantic follower of *Lebensphilosophie* who bemoans the reification of life in modern industrial society, he knows that free subjectivity only arises through total reification.

In this sense, Johnston and Pippin, the two great opponents, seem to be the two Hegelian embodiments of the basic opposition between the general-ontological reading of Hegel as providing the dialectical view of reality and the transcendental reading of Hegel as providing the basic structure of thinking as such. My position is a third one: the two options form a parallax, and the zero-level of the "night of the world" is our only contact with the Real. What this means, among other things, is that Johnston ultimately endorses the idea of basic material positive reality, "weak" as it is, ignoring the fact that this reality is not a starting point but already in itself the outcome of a radical negation (of logic releasing nature out of itself in Hegel, of quantum waves in physics . . .).

Johnston's "dialectical materialism" relies on his (problematic, for me) distinction between the transhistorical universal anthropological structure of drive and its specific historic exemplifications: drive in premodern societies, capitalist drive, Communist drive . . . Although Johnston applies here the Hegelian distinction between drive in itself (an anthropological constant) and the "coming-out" of drive, the open display of its paradox, drive for itself, in capitalism, in my view drive as an anthropological constant remains too much an abstract universal not really caught in the concrete mutations. One should never forget Hegel's lesson that the conflict between particular versions of a universality is a conflict immanent to universality itself. The endlessly self-reproducing capitalist drive to generate a surplus is not just a particular case of an anthropological constant, it gives a unique twist to this constant itself, elevating into a central position what was until then a marginal deviation. Capitalism not only provides the key to universal history—without the contingent rise of capitalism the very basic structure of universal history would have been different, in the same sense that, if the anatomy of man offers the key to the anatomy of the ape this doesn't mean that, if humans were not to evolve accidentally out of apes the anatomy of apes would be missing its key—more precisely, this key would be different, it would emerge retroactively out of a different process of evolutionary change.[22]

How Marx Invented Drive?

Johnston's basic premise runs against the standard Freudo-Marxist idea that the explanation of the subjective features of individuals living in today's capitalism (why do millions act and vote against their obvious interests?, why can they be mobilized for nationalist, religious and military struggles which pose a threat to their very lives?) in the terms of their determination by the economic base is insufficient—to explain such phenomena, Marxist economic analysis has to be supplemented by psychoanalytic research into collective libidinal investments. While Johnston agrees that Marxism needs psychoanalysis, he convincingly argues that these unconscious libidinal mechanisms are at work already in the very heart of the "economic base": we just have to read Marx closely to see that the individuals caught in capitalist reproduction do not really follow their egotist interests—they act as the instruments of the capital's drive to ever-expanding reproduction, ready to renounce many of life's pleasures: "Maybe Marx ought to be credited not only with inventing the psychoanalytic concept of the symptom *avant la lettre*, as Lacan proposes, but also with inventing the analytic idea of the drive prior to Freud." Johnston, of course, does not ignore the complexity of the interaction between the reproduction of capital and the subjective life of capital's agents who are also "psychical subjects of enjoyments having to do with socio-symbolic secondary gains exuded from the pure accumulation of capital"—just think about the esteem gained by the charities of today's ultra-wealthy neo-feudal masters.

The very difference between the economic base and its political and ideological superstructure is not simply a universal feature of human history: it is actualized as such only in capitalist society in which economic life does not rely on direct (non-economic) relations of domination (in the same sense in which, for Marx, although all history until now is the history of class struggles, the bourgeoisie is the first class "for itself"—before capitalism, class differences were obfuscated by estate hierarchies). However, the obverse of this emergence of the economic base in its autonomy, outside of its links with the political and ideological superstructure, is that, at the same time, in capitalism economy itself is more than ever "theologized," i.e., that theology, the highest and most spiritual form of ideology, directly structures economy—as Walter Benjamin pointed out, capitalism is a mode of secularized religion, the world of commodities is impregnated by "theological niceties," with capital itself as an obscene self-moving divinity.

The homology between capitalism and the Unconscious is evoked already by Freud: in order to explain the distinction between the (conscious) wish encoded in a dream and the dream's unconscious desire, he compares the wish to a contractor (manager, entrepreneur) and the unconscious to the capital that finances (covers the libidinal expenses of) the translation of this wish into a dream:

> To speak figuratively, it is quite possible that a day thought plays the part of the contractor (*entrepreneur*) in the dream. But it is known that no matter what idea the contractor may have in mind, and how desirous he may be of putting it into operation, he can do nothing without capital; he must depend upon a capitalist to defray the necessary expenses, and this capitalist, who supplies the psychic expenditure for the dream, is invariably and indisputably *a wish from the unconscious*, no matter what the nature of the waking thought maybe.[23]

Clear as it is, this metaphor lends itself to a superficial reading which totally misses its point. That is to say, it may appear that the work proper (dream-work) is just a mediator between the conscious wish and the unconscious capital: the contractor (conscious wish) borrows from the unconscious capital to finance its translation into the dream-language. Here, however, we have to take into account Freud's insistence on how the unconscious desire "infects" the dream *only through the dream-work*: the exclusive source of the unconscious desire is the work of encoding/masking of the dream thoughts, it does not have a substantial being outside this work. This primacy of form over content also accounts for the paradox of perversion in the Freudian theoretical edifice: perversion demonstrates the insufficiency of the simple logic of transgression. The standard wisdom tells us that perverts practice (do) what hysterics only dream about (doing), i.e., "everything is allowed" in perversion, a perversion openly actualizes all repressed content—and nonetheless, as Freud emphasizes, *nowhere is repression as strong as in perversion*, a fact more than confirmed by our late-capitalist reality in which total sexual permissiveness causes anxiety and impotence or frigidity instead of liberation. Lacan's reading of this "metaphor" of Freud is instructive here:

> These are things that look like they are a metaphor. Isn't it amusing to see how this takes on a different value after what I have been telling you concerning the relationship between capitalism and the function of the master—concerning the altogether distinct nature of what can be done with the process of accumulation in the presence of surplus *jouissance*—in the very presence of this surplus *jouissance*, to the exclusion of the big fat *jouissance*, plain *jouissance*, *jouissance* that is realized in copulation in the raw? Isn't this precisely where infantile desire gets its force from, its force of accumulation with respect to this object that constitutes the cause of desire, namely that which is accumulated as libido capital by virtue, precisely, of infantile non-maturity, the exclusion of *jouissance* that others will call normal? There you have what suddenly gives Freud's metaphor its proper connotation when he refers to the capitalist.[24]

Or, as Johnston puts it in a succinctly-brutal way: "Analysis is not about teaching neurotics how to fuck." It is about making them abandon the fantasy of a full normal fuck, about making them identify with their "symptom," with the fragile arrangement of the figures of enjoyment that enable them to go on living without too much suffering and pain. The point of Lacan's reading of Freud's metaphor of capitalism is very precise here, it reaches beyond the mechanism of dreams into sexual life itself: in the same way, the capitalist who wants to start an enterprise has to borrow the capital from a bank or another pre-existing fund, a subject who wants to engage in a "normal" sexual activity has to mobilize "that which is accumulated as libido capital by virtue, precisely, of infantile non-maturity"—in short, when we are engaged in "normal" mature sex ("*jouissance* that is realized in copulation in the raw"), we can do this only if our activity is sustained by pre-mature infantile sexual fantasies. The promise that, at some point, we will reach the "big fat" full *jouissance* at its purest, leaving behind infantile fantasies, is in itself the ultimate fantasy—to quote Johnston, if a subject were to throw itself without restraint into the abyss of impossible full *jouissance*,

> the whole unconscious economy orbiting around the (absent) center of *jouissance* would grind to a halt and come crashing down. There would be a psychical market collapse causing the libidinal economy to sink into the depression of "subjective destitution." The primal repression concealing from the libidinal investor the truth that the economy he/she participates in is, in a sense, one giant Ponzi scheme erected on nothing more than empty promises of "big fat *jouissance*, plain *jouissance*, *jouissance* that is realized in copulation in the raw" (as per the already-quoted Lacan of *Seminar XVII*) would be lifted and the jig would be up. A libidinal investor who would go to King Oedipus's bitter end and try to cash out for good would end up empty handed or, perhaps worse still, with a handful of delivered shit in place of promised gold.[25]

I have two problems with this passage. First, an actual sexual encounter is not just lacking with regard to what we expected: lack is also always supplemented by excess. Instead of conceiving real sex as always a disappointment with regard to what we fantasized we will get out of it, truly intense sex can also function as the traumatic real of an unbearable enjoyment that shatters our complacency, something so powerful that we are not able to translate it into the (symbolic) coordinates of our reality, so that we experience in it what Freud called *Realitaetsverlust*, a momentary loss of reality. Second, in the quoted passage, Johnston uses the term "subjective destitution" in the rather common sense of a fall into depression, of the subject's psychic collapse which disables its ability to desire. However, I think Lacan's "subjective destitution" rather refers to: a form of self-erasure without any reliance on the survival in posterity through my work, but which in no way incapacitates my full engagement. This subjective stance is perfectly rendered by Vladimir Mayakovsky, THE poet of the October Revolution: "Die / die, my verse / like any rank and file / like those of us / who fought and fell anonymous." What makes this stance unique is that it does not involve any false modesty—Mayakovsky quite often refers to himself in a quite cocky way: "I am not like everyone else – I am Mayakovsky. / I sit and eat my horse steak." It is precisely this uniqueness that he is ready to sacrifice.[26]

For Lacan (who uses this term only twice, as far as I know), "subjective destitution" designates the "traversing of fantasy" as the concluding moment of the psychoanalytic process; there is no catastrophic depression that explodes at this moment (although Freud and Lacan also evoke the possibility of a suicidal "negative therapeutic reaction"). Analysts who are expected to pass through subjective destitution certainly do not lose their ability to desire—Lacan regularly talks about the analyst's desire. The status of *objet petit a* as the object-cause of desire is not limited to its role in fantasy, which is why our libidinal life is not caught in the debilitating alternative: either we are caught into the fantasy of chasing the forever-elusive full *jouissance*, or, if we rip up the veil of fantasy and confront the void of the Thing, we fall into suicidal depression. The first solution is obvious: subjective destitution brings about the shift from desire to drive, and in drive, enjoyment is not forever postponed but always-already won since what we enjoy is the very repeated failure of our attempt to reach the Thing. And is, as Johnston demonstrated in his reading of Marx, drive also not the basic libidinal component of the capitalist expanded self-reproduction condensed in the formula of M-C-M′, from money to more money (with ′, surplus-value, added to it)?

If, then, capitalism involves the infinitization of desire, forever postponing its full gratification, the temptation here is to conceive the exit from capitalism as a return to a new version of the premodern/precapitalist "closed economy" in which we renounce the expansion as a self-goal and enjoy a modest self-satisfied life. This vision was totally strange to Marx: his idea of Communism is firmly entrenched in the idea of humans enjoying and exploiting the fruits of the earth as the ground of their being, and he always emphasizes the liberating aspect of capitalism and claims that *capitalism is in itself already liberation*. Communism involves the infinite plasticity of needs and the expanding of production as its own goal, and Marx sees in capitalist infinite greed also a precursor of Communism as infinite expansion of human productivity. The passage from capitalism to Communism is thus the passage *within* the horizon of endlessly expanding drive. In capitalism, the true goal of production is the expanded self-reproduction of capital while workers work for survival, to satisfy their needs. In a post-capitalist society, workers will not work for the satisfaction of their needs but for the pleasure of expanded production itself.

This is why debts are today a key instrument in guaranteeing that even people who cannot afford it will go on consuming and that they will remain disciplined workers in the cog of capital's reproduction. That's why debts are never meant to be fully repaid—although, simultaneously, the fiction that at some future point they will be repaid is what keeps the economic machine running. Johnston perspicuously links today's economy of debt to Kant's ethical postulates like the one on immortal soul:

> one needs an immortal soul in order to: have enough time to pay off all the credit cards, student loans, medical bills, and mortgages; put away money for a university education that still will plunge one's own children into staggering debt themselves; save for a viable retirement in which one would not be reduced to eating canned dog food . . .[27]

How to account for the dynamic of endless expansion shared by capitalism and Communism? Johnston follows here a series of thinkers from Hegel and Marx to Lacan and Althusser, whom all locate the key feature that pushes the (to-be-human) animal into labour and social relations: the helplessness of the newborn baby who needs much more parental care for a much longer time than other mammals; to this helplessness, he adds plasticity—human nature is not ready-made, it doesn't provide humans with a preordained set of properties that would enable them to survive, so that humans have to construct a complex network of work and social patterns:

> For both Marx and this relatively unfamiliar Althusser, bio-material being makes it such that humans are thrown into

> existence destined for sociality and labor as their entwined twin fates [. . .] initial helplessness, at the ontogenetic level, contributes to human nature leading naturally into the dominance of nurture over nature [. . .] sociality is an inevitable basic feature of human nature (as naturally social) [. . .] human beings are both helpless and plastic. What is more, *Hilflosigkeit* and *Plastizität* conspire so as to result in human nature amounting to a nature that necessarily inclines itself towards (self-) denaturalization via social laboring.[28]

Two points should be added here. Lacan is all too easily reduced to a poet of lack, of a central void the subject endlessly tries to fill with stand-ins, fantasies and other imaginary supplements. But there is also the opposite of lack, excess, a too-muchness—lack is the other side of excess. The problem with formulas like "LGBT+" is: is + just a stand-in for the missing positions (like "and others"), or can one be directly a +? The properly dialectical answer is: yes, the subject is inscribed into a series of its possible identities precisely as a +, as an excess that eludes every identification. What this means is that subject is a + and simultaneously a –, a lack in the signifying chain: it is the excess itself which functions as a lack. So when Johnston writes when "desiring and divided subjectivity ($), in aiming at the fantasized heavenly ecstasy of angelic '*jouissance* expected,' ends up getting instead the actualized hellish agony of beastly '*jouissance* obtained,'" we should add that this passage from gold to shit is also its opposite: an intense experience of *jouissance* can erupt when we are engaged in what we perceive as an ordinary activity from which we expect nothing special. As Jean Laplanche repeatedly asserted, the primordial experience of sexuality is not that of a lack but that of a too-muchness, of intrusive density of an Other's desire of which the Other itself is not aware.

The second more important point is that upon a closer look, helplessness and plasticity in themselves are not enough to account for the emergence of the symbolic universe, sociality and labour. Johnston is aware that helplessness alone is not enough, and neither is plasticity alone; but I think their combination also does not account for the emergence of the symbolic universe. Such an explanation of the rise of the symbolic universe is clearly circular:

helplessness and plasticity appear as such—as pointing towards the social order of discipline and cooperation—only retroactively, i.e., once the socio-symbolic order is already here. The only consistent materialist solution is that—true, against the background of helplessness and plasticity—something unexpected emerged, but it did not emerge as a way to cope with helplessness, to promote social cooperation and labour. What we have to reject is the instrumental view of the emergence of social order: newborn babies are helpless, humans need a better way to survive, so, due to their plasticity, they invent social cooperation and labour ... A Freudian counter-claim is that the actual break with animal life occurs in sexuality: the instinctual rhythm of coupling is broken, sexuality turns into a domain of failure (we never get That, the full enjoyment) and obsession with an absolute (again, the full enjoyment). This moment is critical: our initial organic helplessness—failure to survive relying on our instincts—is overcome by being supplanted by much more radical helplessness, helplessness with regard to the sexual Thing that eludes us but to which we are fixed, condemned to trying to reach it repetitively. Such a libidinal economy can take place only in a symbolic universe: the loss of the Thing is what Freud calls "primordial repression" and what Lacan calls "symbolic castration." This rise of the spectre of the impossible Thing serves nothing: the primordial function of language is *not* to enable better cooperation. Language emerged out of some meaningless malfunctioning of our organs, it is not a case of adaptation but a case of what evolutionary theorists call "ex-aptation": some ridiculous deadlock was ex-apted, and language itself also served nothing—its use for social cooperation and labour was the secondary use of a primordial meaningless excess.

5
The Path to Anarcho-feudalism

The Blue Pill Called Metaverse

Lacan's key name for the Real is *jouissance*, and this is why the symbolic matrix in which we dwell needs us, humans: to appropriate from us the *jouissance* by means of which it can fill in (or, rather, cover up) its inconsistencies and antagonisms. Recall the cult movie *Matrix*: its unique impact resides in its central image of the millions of human beings leading a claustrophobic life in water-filled cradles, kept alive in order to generate the energy for the Matrix. So when (some of the) people "awaken" from their immersion into the Matrix-controlled virtual reality, this awakening is not the opening into the wide space of the external reality, but first the horrible realization of this enclosure, where each of us is effectively just a foetus-like organism, immersed in pre-natal fluid ... This utter passivity is the foreclosed fantasy that sustains our conscious experience as active, self-positing subjects—it is the ultimate *perverse* fantasy, the notion that we are ultimately *instruments* of the Other's (Matrix's) *jouissance*, sucked out of our life-substance like batteries. But it is the fantasy that stages the Real of our situation: the horror of our utter submission to the Matrix, the Real sustaining our false freedom to circulate in different realities regulated by the Matrix. Therein resides the key difference: the Real is not the external reality into which some of us awaken, the Real is the matrix itself and our position of servitude to it, our reduction to its source of energy.

Now we can see clearly what *The Matrix* (the movie) gets wrong: it presumes that the Matrix is an object in the world (in reality) controlled by a mega-subjectivity (artificial intelligence). However, although such an idea is a paranoiac dream, today we are getting closer and closer to realizing this dream and constructing Matrixes, manufactured machines which promise to play a transcendental role, i.e., to provide a virtual universe into which we can enter (or which controls us against our will). China's Academy of Military Medical Sciences pursues what it calls the "intelligentization" of warfare: "War has started to shift from the pursuit of destroying bodies to paralyzing and controlling the opponent."[1] We can be sure that the West is doing the same—the only difference will be (maybe) that if it goes public about it, there will be a humanitarian twist ("we are not killing humans, we are just for a brief moment diverting their minds . . ."). To use the language of *Matrix*, one of the names of "taking the blue pill" is Zuckerberg's project of "metaverse": we take the blue pill by registering in the metaverse in which the limitations, tensions and frustrations of ordinary reality are magically left behind—but we have to pay a big price for it: "Mark Zuckerberg 'has unilateral control over 3 billion people' due to his unassailable position at the top of Facebook, the whistleblower Frances Haugen told the British MPs as she called for urgent external regulation to rein in the tech company's management and reduce the harm being done to society."[2] The big achievement of modernity, the public space, is thus disappearing. Days after the Haugen revelations, Zuckerberg announced that his company will change its name from "Facebook" to "Meta," and outlined his vision of "metaverse" in a speech that is a true *neo-feudal manifesto*:

> Zuckerberg wants the metaverse to ultimately encompass the rest of our reality—connecting bits of real space here to real space there, while totally subsuming what we think of as the real world. In the virtual and augmented future Facebook has planned for us, it's not that Zuckerberg's simulations will rise to the level of reality, it's that our behaviors and interactions will become so standardized and mechanical that it won't even matter. Instead of making human facial expressions, our avatars can make iconic thumbs-up gestures. Instead of sharing air and space together, we can collaborate on a digital document. We learn to downgrade our experience of being together with another human being to seeing their projection overlaid into the room like an augmented reality Pokemon figure.[3]

Metaverse will act as a virtual space beyond (meta) our fractured and hurtful reality, a virtual space in which we will smoothly interact through our avatars, with elements of augmented reality (reality overlaid with digital signs). It will thus be nothing less than meta-physics actualized: a meta-physical space fully subsuming reality which will be allowed to enter it in fragments only insofar as it will be overlaid by digital guidelines manipulating our perception and intervention. And the catch is that we will get a commons which is privately owned, with a private feudal Lord overseeing and regulating our interaction—since the standard form of these commons is a digital "cloud" storing all the data, Yanis Varoufakis is right in talking about "the rise of a new cloud-based ruling class."[4]

Apropos his offer to purchase Twitter, Elon Musk said that he sees this acquisition as nothing less than a turning point for civilization—his goal is to ensure that Twitter remains a trusted platform for democracy: "My strong intuitive sense is that having a public platform that is maximally trusted and broadly inclusive is extremely important to the future of civilization." He railed against what he saw as a lack of free speech on Twitter, and explained that his test for whether a platform adheres to free speech principles is simple: "Is someone you don't like allowed to say something you don't like? And if that is the case, then we have free speech." The question is, again, what kind of world we live in in which only a private property (by a single individual, in this case) of one of the main commons can guarantee freedom and democracy—in short, a world in which neo-feudalism presents itself as the safeguard of freedoms. One should also note that Musk defines "free speech" in terms of *like / don't like*, i.e., in terms of opinions which should be all treated as equal. What about truths which concern basic human rights, education, healthcare?

What we should always bear in mind here is that, no matter how automated they become, machines will still need humans—they need us not for our intelligence and conscious planning but at a more elementary level of libidinal economy. The idea that machines could reproduce without humans is similar to the dream of a market economy reproducing itself without humans. Some analysts have recently proposed the idea that, with the explosive growth of robotization of production and of artificial intelligence which will more and more play the managerial role of organizing production, capitalism will gradually morph into a self-reproducing monster, a network of digital and production machines with less and less need for humans. (In June 2022 it was reported that humans only make up 38.5% of internet traffic; the other 61.5% is non-human—bots, hacking tools, etc.) Property and stocks will remain, but competition on stock exchanges will be done automatically, just to optimize profit and productivity. So for whom or what will things be produced? Will humans not remain as consumers? Ideally, we can even imagine machines just feeding each other, producing machined parts, energy . . . Perversely attractive as it is, this prospect is an ideological fantasy: capital is not an objective fact like a mountain or a machine which will remain even if all the people around it disappear, it exists only as a virtual Other of a society, a "reified" form of a social relationship, in the same way that values of stocks are the outcome of the interaction of thousands of individuals but appear to each of them as something objectively given.

But this idea is worth exploring if we draw a parallel with the relationship between individual bodies and genes (or memes): the idea of capital turning into a self-reproducing monster with no need for humans is similar to the idea—developed by Richard Dawkins—that we, humans, do not just reproduce ourselves through genes but can also be considered as an instrument of the self-reproduction of genes. Marx described this shift in clear terms: people produce and exchange commodities to satisfy their needs, but, with capitalism, people satisfying their needs is just an instrument of the self-reproduction of capital itself. But what is the exact status of the "will" of capital, i.e., in what sense can we say that we impute to capital an intentional stance of its own and treat it as an entity with a will of its own? At the level of genes (and memes), Dawkins, of course, never goes to the extreme of imagining just genes directly reproducing themselves, by-passing living individual organisms. The reason is a certain limitation in the very idea of individual organisms as instruments of the self-reproduction of genes—or, applied to the topic of memes, the idea that our conscious minds are just instruments in the reproduction of memes (elementary elements of our minds). It may appear that, with artificial intelligence and the direct communication between digital machines, we can also imagine memes interacting and multiplying directly, by-passing human individuals. The problem arises with Dawkins's premise that the reproduction of genes and memes works like a natural selection in which the "better" genes and memes survive—Daniel Dennett was quite right to provide Dawkins's account with a critical comment in his usual acerbic style:[5]

> When you examine the reasons for the spread of scientific memes, Dawkins assures us, "you find they are good ones." This, the standard, official position of science, is undeniable in its own terms, but question-begging to the mullah and the nun—and Rorty, who would quite appropriately ask Dawkins: "Where is your demonstration that these 'virtues' are good virtues? You note that people evaluate these memes and pass them on—but if Dennett is right, people [. . .] are themselves in large measure the creation of memes [. . .]. How clever of some memes to team together to create meme-evaluators that favour them! Where, then, is the Archimedan point from which you can deliver your benediction on science?"[6]

So what is the dimension that machines are missing? Not intelligence, of course, but *jouissance* at its most stupid. A Slovene actor Blaž Popovski said in an interview on February 6, 2022: "You have to enjoy—even if you don't agree!"[7] Although he refers to playing a role on stage, his remark should be universalized. Novelodge is offering "50 Difficult Songs To Get Out Of Your Head," with the explanation:

> On some days, having a song stuck in your head is a pleasant experience, as you hum along and carry on cheerfully with your day. However, the last thing you want is for your head to be filled with an annoyingly repetitive track. This is particularly true if you are stressed or have a lot going on. Our list includes 50 of the most vexing songs of all time, which you should avoid at all costs if you don't want to spend the remainder of the day humming.[8]

All of us know this feeling of being haunted by a musical fragment which we find even disgusting—what haunts us certainly brings no pleasure, so the pressure we experience is that of enjoyment. Enjoyment is a superego injunction you have to follow even if you don't agree with it. Victims themselves have to enjoy: the more humans enjoy, the more surplus-enjoyment can be drawn from them—Lacan's parallel between surplus-value and surplus-enjoyment is again confirmed here. Lacan is fully aware that *jouissance* is a political factor: "the intrusion into the political can only be made by recognizing that the only discourse there is [. . .] the discourse of *jouissance*."[9] In short, ideology and politics can be explained neither by crude reference to actual class interests nor by discourse-analysis which focuses on the competitive game for discursive hegemony, for which ideology will provide the dominant cognitive mapping of the situation. Even a brief look at racism and sexism suffices to see how, for an ideology to really take hold of us, it has to mobilize the dimension of *jouissance*. Oppression of women is sustained by the fear that, if not controlled, women will explode in excessive pleasures. Racism envies the Other's enjoyments in perceiving this Other as a threat to the enjoyments that form our way of life . . . All such passionate ideological investments are traversed by sadism, masochism and all their perverted combinations like enjoying one's own humiliation.

The extreme case of *jouissance* today is, of course, the prospect of apocalypse in all its versions (pandemic, ecological catastrophes, nuclear war, dissolution of social order . . .), inclusive of total knowledge itself: wouldn't it be properly apocalyptic to gain direct access to another's stream of thoughts? Lorenzo Chiesa deftly points out that this desire is "manifestly witnessed by our current fascination with virological, ecological, and technological figures of the Apocalypse. Adopting the terminology of *Seminar XX*, we could also call it a desire to be One in order to absolutely enjoy through and in (sexual) knowledge, a desire which instead leads to maximal entropy."[10] Just think about a snuff movie (a pornographic film that shows the actual torture and murder of one of the performers during the sexual interaction)—really, as Lacan put it in a concise way, "everyone is dying to know what would happen if things went really bad."[11] This is why we are so fascinated by the precise features of a dystopian reality, from *The Handmaid's Tale* and stories about European daily life if Hitler won the war up to the future life on a devastated earth. "Dying to know" should be taken here in its ambiguity: it means that I would really like to know it and that this knowledge would bring me to death.

What the notion of fully knowing a catastrophe misses is the fact that, when we get too close to a catastrophe, the distance necessary for knowledge breaks down. We cannot combine the real of a full catastrophe with the safe distance of knowledge (like the idea of entering the sun or a black hole and registering what goes down there). The lesson of Hegel's absolute knowing is exactly the opposite: it is a knowing which includes its own incompleteness. Knowledge is non-all in the Lacanian sense: it is not that something a priori eludes it, there is nothing that eludes it, but for this very reason it cannot be totalized. G.K.Chesterton wrote that Christianity acknowledges one big mystery (God) as the exception which allows a Christian to perceive and understand all other reality as completely rational and knowable. For a materialist, the situation is exactly the opposite: there is no exception, which is why all reality is full of mysteries (just think of the mysteries of quantum physics). We can say that, in the same sense, anti-Semitism is the stupid man's anti-capitalism, the full knowledge of an apocalypse is the stupid man's version of Hegel's absolute knowing.

From Cultural Capitalism to Cryptocurrencies

The Real of *jouissance* is not part of our reality, its status is thoroughly virtual—only in a full apocalypse would the Real of *jouissance* fall into reality. There is a well-known anecdote of a guy who enjoys the smell of roasted meat in front of a restaurant kitchen; the owner approaches him and says: you smell it, so you have also to pay for it. The guy replies by shaking some coins in his hand which make a sound—an empty smell for an empty sound . . . This is how we are exploited in the commodification of experiences: in buying jeans, we pay (with real money) not just for the jeans but for the "smell" of the way of life embodied in jeans . . . This, however, is only the beginning, something that was present already in the early stages of commodification; now we are more and more directly buying just the experience—Jeremy Rifkin designated this new stage of commodification as "cultural capitalism."[12] In "cultural capitalism," the relationship between an object and its symbol-image is turned around: the image does not represent the product, but, rather, the product represents the image.[13] We buy a product—say, an organic apple—because it represents the image of a healthy life style.

As the example of buying an organic apple indicates, the very ecological protest against the capitalist ruthless exploitation of natural resources is already caught in the commodification of experiences: although ecology perceives itself as the protest against the digitalization/virtualization of our daily lives and advocates the return to the direct experience of sensual material reality in all its unpredictable fragility and inertia, ecology itself is branded as a new life style—what we are effectively buying when we are buying "organic food," etc., is already a certain cultural experience, the experience of a "healthy ecological life style." And the same goes for every return to "reality". A recent publicity spot widely broadcast on all main US TV stations shows a group of ordinary people engaged in a barbecue picnic with country music and dancing, with the accompanying message: "Beef. Real food for real people." The irony is that the beef offered here as the symbol of a certain life style (the "real" grass root working-class Americans) is much more chemically and genetically manipulated than the "organic" food consumed by "artificial" millennials.

Ultimately, nation itself is turning into an experiential commodity: we buy things which enable us to experience ourselves as participating in a Nationhood ... And one is tempted to risk even a step further, following Benedict Anderson's thesis on nations as "imagined communities":[14] what if nations were from the very outset "artificial" formations? Is not the rise of modern nations (as opposed to premodern "organic" communities) co-dependent with the rise of capitalism, i.e., of the commodity production? Is not "nation" the undead spectre of a Community which starts to haunt us after the market economy kills the "living" organic communities? Nation is an "imagined community" not only in the sense that its material base is the mass media (press) not the direct mutual acquaintance of its members; it is "imagined" also in a more radical sense of an "imaginary supplement" to the social reality of disintegration and irresolvable antagonisms. Nation thus from the very beginning functioned as a fetish: the point is not to believe in the National Cause, but to use this belief as a prop which enables us to engage in our egotistic pursuits ("we are really doing it for our nation"). What we are witnessing today, the defining feature of "postmodern" capitalism, is the direct commodification of our experience itself: what we are buying on the market are fewer and fewer products (material objects) which we want to own, and more and more life-experiences—experiences of sex, eating, communicating, cultural consumption, participating in a life style. Material objects are more and more here just to serve as props for this experience, which is more and more offered for free to seduce us into buying the true "experiential commodity,"[15] like the free cellular phones we get if we sign a one-year contract:

> As cultural production comes to dominate the economy, goods increasingly take on the qualities of props. They become mere platforms or settings around which elaborate cultural meanings are acted out. They lose their material importance and take on symbolic importance. They become less objects and more tools to help facilitate the performance of lived experiences.[16]

Or, to quote the succinct formula of Mark Slouka: "As more of the hours of our days are spent in synthetic environments [...] life itself is turned into a commodity. Someone makes it for us; we buy it from them. We become the consumers of our own lives."[17] The logic of the market exchange is here brought to a kind of Hegelian self-relating identity: we no longer buy objects, we ultimately buy (the time of) our own life. Michel Foucault's notion of turning one's Self itself into a work of art thus gets an unexpected confirmation: I buy my bodily fitness by way of visiting fitness clubs; I buy my spiritual enlightenment by way of enrolling in courses on transcendental meditation; I buy my public persona by way of going to restaurants visited by people I want to be associated with ...

Although this shift may appear as a break with the capitalist market economy, one can argue that it brings its logic to its consequent climax. The industrial market economy involves the temporal gap between the purchasing of a commodity and its consumption: from the standpoint of the seller, the affair is over the moment he sells his commodity—what happens afterwards (what the purchaser does with it, the direct consumption of the commodity) does not concern him; in the commodification of experience, this gap is closed, *the consumption itself is the commodity bought*. However, the possibility of closing this gap is inscribed in the very nominalist logic of the modern society and its community. That is to say, since the purchaser buys a commodity for its use-value, and since this use-value can be decomposed into its components (when I buy a Land Rover, I do this in order to drive myself and other people around, plus to signal my participation in a certain life style associated with the Land Rover), there is a logical next step towards commodifying and selling directly these components (leasing a car instead of buying it, etc.). At the end of the road is thus the solipsistic fact of subjective experience: since the subjective experience of individual consumption is the ultimate goal of the entire production, it is logical to by-pass the object and to commodify and sell directly this experience. And, perhaps, instead of interpreting this commodification of experiences as the result of the shift in the predominant mode of subjectivity (from the classical bourgeois subject focused on possessing objects to the "postmodern" Protean subject focused on the wealth of his experiences), one should rather conceive this Protean subject itself as the effect of the commodification of experiences.[18]

But with buying experiences, we have not yet reached the end of the road—Non-Fungible Tokens (NFT) take a step further, they return to possessing (or participating in the possession of) an object, but this possession itself is itself purely virtual, we pay for the *experience of possessing* without effectively possessing anything. The underlying absurdity became palpable in a curious incident reported on January 8, 2022, on Yahoo. A reality star who says she made $200K from selling her farts in Mason jars is pivoting to selling them as NFTs:

> Stephanie Matto said she made $200,000 by selling her farts in Mason jars. After a hospital visit, doctors told her that the excessive wind-breaking was taking a toll on her body. She has since pivoted to selling the fart jars as NFTs. They sell for 0.05 Ethereum. Now, Matto is hoping to carve out a space in the NFT

> world with her "unique" fart art. "There's space for everybody," she said during a phone call with Insider. A customer of hers, who asked to only be referred to as John, told Insider why the product was so appealing to him. The 43-year-old financier, who said he spent $1,000 on two fart jars, explained that it helped him feel a sense of "closeness" to Matto. "I have a lot of fetishes and one of them is that I like the smell of a woman," he said. "I like all of the smells."[19]

But while one can see a *raison d'etre*, weird as it is, in buying a bottle with a smell as a "little piece of the real" that bears witness to another human being, this "little piece of the real" disappears once we buy it as a NFT—how did we arrive at this point, not only with regard to objects sold but above all with regard to how finances work today?

This distasteful story exemplifies the weird world we live in, a world in which lack and excess, new poverty and the excess of money, are the two sides of the same coin since money (cash, especially) no longer really matters—as none other than Steve Bannon put it in one of his podcasts, today, "money is for jerks." We are afloat in virtual money, (many) people quite literally don't know what to do with money (as the case of Matto demonstrates), but this affluence is like a house of cards which can collapse at any moment (as it almost did in the 2008 financial meltdown). Hegel was the first to describe this paradox when he pointed out that, in a capitalist society, there is not enough money because there is too much of it, and this imbalance is structural, with no chance of rebalancing it (taking from the rich and giving to the poor). In the famous § 245 of his *Philosophy of Right*, Hegel produces the exact formula of this paradoxical relationship between lack and surplus apropos the notion of "rabble":

> When the masses begin to decline into poverty, (a) the burden of maintaining them at their ordinary standard of living might be directly laid on the wealthier classes, or they might receive the means of livelihood directly from other public sources of wealth (e.g. from the endowments of rich hospitals, monasteries, and other foundations). In either case, however, the needy would receive subsistence directly, not by means of their work, and this

> would violate the principle of civil society and the feeling of individual independence and self-respect in its individual members. (b) As an alternative, they might be given subsistence indirectly through being given work, i.e. the opportunity to work. In this event the volume of production would be increased, but the evil consists precisely in an excess of production and in the lack of a proportionate number of consumers who are themselves also producers, and thus it is simply intensified by both of the methods (a) and (b) by which it is sought to alleviate it. It hence becomes apparent that despite an excess of wealth civil society is not rich enough, i.e. its own resources are insufficient to check excessive poverty and the creation of a penurious rabble.[20]

It is thus the very surplus that (re)creates the lack it is supposed to fill in, so that we should even radicalize Hegel's formulation: it is not only that "despite an excess of wealth civil society is not rich enough," *it is the very excess of wealth that makes it not rich enough* (to get rid of poverty). In other words, the key question is: if there is a surplus (excessive wealth) on the one side and a lack (poverty) on the other side, why can't we re-establish the balance by simple redistribution (taking the wealth from those excessively rich and giving it to the poor)? The formal answer is: because lack and surplus are not located within the same surface where they are just unequally distributed (some people lack things, others have too much). The paradox of wealth resides in the fact that the more you have the more you feel the lack—it's again the superego paradox (the more you follow the injunction, the more guilty you are), discernible also in the paradox of anti-Semitism (the more Jews are destroyed, the more powerful is the remainder).

The new phase of global economy also implies a different functioning of the financial sphere. Yanis Varoufakis[21] noted a weird fact that took place in the Spring of 2020: on the same day that state statistics in the US and the UK registered a breath-taking fall of the GDP, comparable to the fall at the time of the Great Recession, stock markets registered a gigantic rise. In short, although "real" economy is stagnating or even decreasing, stock markets go up—an indication that fictitious financial capital is caught in its own circle, decoupled from the "real" economy. This is where the financial measures justified by the pandemic entered the game: they in a way turn around the traditional Keynesian procedure, i.e., their aim was not to help the "real" economy but to invest enormous amounts of money into the financial sphere (to prevent a financial collapse like the one of 2008) while making sure that most of this money will *not* flow into "real" economy (this could cause hyperinflation).

The best indication of the change that affects our financial system is the rise of two new interrelated phenomena: first bitcoin, then NFT ("NFT" was proclaimed by Collins as the word of the year for 2021). The feature that unites them is that they both emerged out of a libertarian idea to by-pass state apparatuses and establish a direct communication between concerned parties. In both cases, we see how the idea turned into its opposite: bitcoins and NFT have their own 1% which dominates and manipulates the field. Here we should avoid both extremes: neither praising bitcoins and NFT as a new space of freedom nor dismissing them as the latest speculative capitalist madness.

First, bitcoin (where we should bear in mind that bitcoin is just the most popular of the cryptocurrencies—there are already almost 20,000 of them). In our usual experience of money, its payment value is guaranteed by some state authority like the central bank, and the state can also misuse its authority (printing money and causing inflation, etc.). In the case of bitcoin, its value is not guaranteed by any public institution of authority, it is determined by what people will pay for it, and they are ready to pay for it if they believe in it, if they trust it. Here, in the domain of cold and ruthless financial speculations, belief and trust enter the stage: bitcoin is like an ideological Cause which exists as a real force only if enough people believe in it—without individuals who believe in the Communist cause there is no Communism . . . There's a similarity to how stocks are priced, but the difference is that, in principle, at least, the value of stocks is not purely self-referential, it refers to investments which are expected to generate profit from "real" production. If one wants the price of a stock to fall, one spreads false news about the company which issues the stock doing badly, but there is no such reference with bitcoins. This doesn't mean that the amount of bitcoins is limitless: the protocol established by the bitcoin founder Satoshi Nakamoto dictates that only 21 million bitcoins can ever be mined (almost 19 million have been mined so far), so there is a limited supply, like with gold and other precious metals, but no intrinsic "real value." How can this be? Bitcoins have to be registered in blockchains which are

> essentially decentralized ledgers. They're a "place" to store information, and crucially, because they are decentralized, cannot be edited without the knowledge of other users on the blockchain. The idea is that blockchains are able to store records of information without the need for third parties (e.g., banks and financial institutions), so that the system is essentially self-sufficient and self-regulating. As a digital infrastructure, an added benefit is that huge legal fees added by third parties are avoided.[22]

Here we stumble upon the tension that defines blockchains: precisely because there is no third party, because the system is essentially self-sufficient and self-regulating, every registration/inscription of a new bitcoin involves a tremendous amount of work through which the new bitcoin will be brought to "the knowledge of other users on the blockchain"—since there is no third party to which every bitcoin owner could refer, each new owner has to elaborate a complex texture of algorithms and codes which guarantees that the specific identity of the new bitcoin will be clearly perceived by all others without turning it into something that can be appropriated by others. Blockchain as a non-alienated big Other needs a lot of work to produce it by an alienated third party, making the bitcoin "miners" who do this work the "proletarians" of this new domain—we pass from old miners (who do their difficult work deep beneath in the earth) as the nineteenth-century proletarians *kat' exochen* to bitcoin miners who work to construct and secure the space for a bitcoin in the digital big Other. The paradox here is that the miners do not work to produce new use values (which then they could sell for money), they work to directly create new exchange value—to guarantee that bitcoins do not need a legal external authority and the accompanying legal fees, a work which takes a lot of time and uses so much energy (electricity) that it is a heavy ecological burden—an individual who does bitcoin mining pollutes our environment more than a miner digging coal. (Ideas are floating that, in the near future, it will be possible to minimize this expense.)

The potentially progressive idea of bitcoin as global, independent of particular state apparatuses, thus actualizes itself in a form which undermines its premises, and it is similar to NFTs, which were also invented as a decentralized, anti-State libertarian attempt to save the autonomy of artists from institutional clutches—the price we pay for this idea is that "the creation of an NFT is an attempt to create artificial scarcity where there is none. Anyone can create an NFT for a digital asset, even if there's no actual asset behind it!"[23] The paradox of NFTs is that they introduce scarcity into a domain in which items are accessible to everyone for free—for this reason, NFTs compel us to rethink the notion of property, of owning something in a digital space:

> Through subscription services, we have temporary access, but never own a thing. In some quite important sense we might ask, were we to own something, what would it be? An original master of a film or music? Perhaps. But in reality what we can say is ours is either the temporary access, or a download. The download is likely to be absolutely identical to every other download that exists. In other words, our owning it doesn't preclude others from owning it. This is why even the thought of owning a piece of art online has a tinge of absurdity about it. If the song exists as a file, it can exist identically in an infinite number of digital spaces. But NFTs provide a kind of 'solution': artificial scarcity. They give us digital collectibles in a world where duplication has zero costs.[24]

What is intriguing about NFTs is the idea of taking a digital asset that anyone can copy and claiming ownership of it: a NFT has almost no use value (maybe it brings some social prestige to owners), what sustains it is its potential future exchange value. It is a copy with a price, an item of purely symbolic ownership that can bring profit. The key Hegelian insight here (as well as in the case of bitcoins) is that, although bitcoins and NFT appear as an anomaly, as a pathological deviation of the "normal" functioning of money and commodities, the two effectively actualize a potentiality that is already contained in the very notion of commodity and money. Exemplary here is the figure of Peter Thiel for whom "AI is communist and crypto is libertarian"—why? Because with AI, "you're sort of going to have the big eye of Sauron watching you at all times, in all places":

> The main AI applications that people seem to talk about are using large data to sort of monitor people, know more about people than they know about themselves [. . .] where you can know enough about people that you know more about them than they know about themselves, and you can sort of enable communism to work, maybe not so much as an economic theory, but at least as a political theory. So it is definitely a Leninist thing. And then, it is literally communist because China loves AI.[25]

Sounds evident and convincing—however, as Thom Dunn duly noted:

> Thiel's big critique here does seem to be about the authoritarian use of data and surveillance. Which, okay, cool, I agree, that's a valid concern. I don't know what that has to do a revolutionary vanguard party forming a transitional state in order to establish a classless and leaderless society, but, um, sure. China does technically call itself a government. So I think I get what he's putting down here. But just so we're clear: this is the guy who helped found Palantir. Like, the big data analytics company that literally ICE [employs a user-identified ID] to organize its authoritarian tactics. Which is the same Peter Thiel who also founded the Anduril surveillance company, and used his billions to destroy a successful news organization for criticizing him. And he's afraid of AI because of . . . communism?[26]

Impossible to miss the irony here: the libertarian anti-Leninist Thiel relies on the very "Leninist" AI mechanisms he deplores—and the same goes for Steve Bannon who—yet another irony—openly declares himself to be the Rightist "Leninist for the twenty-first century":

> Bannon's White House adventure was only one stage of a long journey—the migration of revolutionary-populist language,

tactics, and strategies from the left to the right. Bannon has reportedly said: "I'm a Leninist. Lenin . . . wanted to destroy the state, and that's my goal too. I want to bring everything crashing down, and destroy all of today's establishment."[27]

This same Bannon rambling against big corporations which, together with apparatuses of state, control and exploiting ordinary working Americans, had no problem using the most sophisticated AI means of control to secure Trump's victory in 2015—how? One of the true heroes of our time is Christopher Wylie, a gay Canadian vegan who, at 24, came up with an idea that led to the foundation of Cambridge Analytica, a data analytics firm—he was a key figure in digital operations during Donald Trump's election campaign, creating Steve Bannon's psychological warfare tool. Wylie's plan was to break into Facebook and harvest the Facebook profiles of millions of people in the United States and use their private and personal information to create sophisticated psychological and political profiles, and then target them with political ads designed to work on their particular psychological makeup. At a certain point, Wylie was genuinely freaked out: "It's insane. The company has created psychological profiles of 230 million Americans. And now they want to work with the Pentagon? It's like Nixon on steroids."[28] What makes this story so fascinating is that it combines elements which we usually perceive as opposites. The alt-Right presents itself as a movement that addresses the concerns of ordinary white, hard-working, deeply religious people who stand for simple traditional values and abhor corrupted eccentrics like homosexuals and vegans, but also digital nerds—and now we learn that their electoral triumphs were masterminded and orchestrated precisely by such a nerd who stands for all they oppose . . . There is more than an anecdotal value in this fact: it clearly signals the vacuity of alt-Right populism which has to rely on the latest technological advances to maintain its popular redneck appeal.

There is no contradiction between Thiel's anti-Leninism and Bannon's Leninism: if we understand under "Leninism" the practice of total digital control over the population, they both practice it while maintaining a libertarian face. The difference resides only in the fact that, for Bannon, "Leninism" means the destruction of the state and its apparatuses (without, of course, really intending it). Here we have to go to the end: digital control and manipulation are not an anomaly of or a deviation from today's libertarian project, they are its necessary frame, its formal condition of possibility. The system can afford the appearance of freedom only under the conditions of digital and other modes of control that regulate our freedom—for the system to function, we HAVE to remain formally free and perceive ourselves as free.

Dan Olson provided a clear view of this oppressive aspect of cryptocurrencies in his interview with Amanda Marcotte:[29]

> With crypto, there isn't a line between who is running a pump and dump, who is starting a legitimate well-intentioned project, who is just a buyer, who is a speculator, who's an investor, who's a collector. It gets very vague. Similar to the structure and flow of multi-level marketing, everybody sort of exists in this nebulous state of being both a buyer and a seller.

This vagueness, this exploding non-transparency, is the obverse of the fake "egalitarianism" of the crypto-universe in which the lines get blurred "between the victim and the victimizer, because in order to succeed, particularly the further down the line you are, the more aggressive you need to become. You need to become a victimizer yourself in order to get your head back above water." What this non-transparency obfuscates is the extreme class division of the crypto-universe: a minority of millionaires versus the majority of the participants from lower classes who see in crypto-universe a chance to turn their luck around. This is why, as Olson points out, the crypto-universe is literally a materialized ideology, it is

> an ecosystem that exists entirely in the language of stories. That's the main thing that's being sold here. Crypto isn't functional. It doesn't do what the builders claimed it was being built to do. It has succeeded at very few of its public-facing goals. But it still transacts based on those stories, based on what it could become, based on what it intends to do, based on what it, in theory, might do in the future. It's a cultural moment that intersects with entertainment and the business of entertainment and the business of culture in a way that is just unavoidable.

So how to limit the nefarious consequences of cryptocurrencies? Olson provides a straight answer:

> Minimum wage corrected to inflation, public housing, equitable public housing policies, student debt forgiveness. We need fundamental changes to our economic policies and to our social policies that remove or that mitigate the desperation that allows schemes like this to take root.

Savage Verticality versus Uncontrollable Horizontality

To avoid a fatal misunderstanding, our reproach to cryptocurrencies and NFT is not that they ignore the way every ideal/virtual movement remains rooted in "real life" but, on the contrary, that they don't accept the basic alienation that comes with the socio-symbolic order: they try to re-introduce into it the transparency of direct exchange without a third element that sustains its place. This denial of basic alienation is also the fatal flaw of the so-called crypto-anarchism in which some Leftists see a new emancipatory potential. Catherine Malabou[30] justified her principled support for cryptocurrencies by pointing out that they offer "the reliability of the algorithm, which thereby takes the place of human confidence." Satoshi Nakamoto, bitcoin's enigmatic creator, already mentioned the disappearance of the notion of confidence: "The electronic payment system [is] based on cryptographic proof instead of trust." This reliability of the algorithm allows value to return in the form of transparency—we don't have to trust any higher authority (state, bank) which guarantees the value of a currency: "We have proposed a system for electronic transactions without relying on trust." (A passing remark: how then to account for the gigantic oscillations in the price of bitcoins? Do they also not depend on the trust of the public in bitcoin?) The idea of a cryptocurrency is "the circulation of a currency that is produced just like any other commodity. This is the function of 'mining.'" (A passing remark, again: but money is precisely NOT like any other commodity, which is why its reduction to a commodity among others necessarily leads to its opposite, to non-transparent chaotic multiplicities.)

So where does anarchism enter here? Malabou sees cryptocurrencies as an aspect of the change in capitalism itself, which "is beginning its anarchist turn": "How else are we to describe such phenomena as decentralized currencies, the end of the state's monopoly, the obsolescence of the mediating role played by banks, and the decentralization of exchanges and transactions?" Sounds nice, but, as Malabou immediately points out, "the semantics of anarchism that give ultra-capitalism its new tonality changes nothing as regards the logic of profit, which ultra-capitalism only expresses in a different form." With the gradual disappearance of the state's monopoly, the limits to the ruthless exploitation and domination imposed by the state also disappear. In this way, Malabou (and other proponents of cryptocurrencies) conceives the space of cryptocurrencies as a battlefield between a libertarian-anarchist tendency and a liberal-oppressive countertendency, as a field of struggle whose outcome is open; I as a Hegelian see this tension as an immanent deployment of negative implications: in the same way that liberalism ends up in market slavery or Fascism, that absolute freedom ends up in terror, that authentic fidelity ends up in flattery, etc., the original idea of cryptocurrencies as a new space of freedom without the external control of some authority ends up in what Malabou herself calls "the combination—at once senseless, monstrous, and unprecedented—of savage verticality and uncontrollable horizontality." Anarcho-capitalism aims at transparency, but the paradox of a discourse of transparency is that it "simultaneously authorizes the large-scale but opaque use of data, the dark web, and the fabrication of information." To prevent this descent into chaos, savage verticality

> also takes the form of the fascistic evolution of so many of today's governments' policies, with the excessive security and military build-up that goes along with it. Such phenomena do not contradict a drive towards anarchism. Rather, they indicate precisely the disappearance of the state, which, once its social function has been removed, expresses the obsolescence of its force through the use of violence. Ultra-nationalism thus signals the death agony of national authority.

As we have already seen, in cryptocurrencies, "automated confidence is in the process of becoming the substitute for a social bond"—and the rise of savage verticality signals precisely the failure of the algorithm as a substitute for a social bond, plus the failure of the concomitant utopia that the digital space will give a new boost to the dream of hippie communities outside the space of state authorities from 1960—Malabou quotes here Simon Brunfaut:

> "the former hippy communes of the 1960s, having failed to realize their utopian visions, will progressively [...] be reincarnated through the constitution of alternative communities based in cybernetics. An extraordinary encounter has thus taken place between notorious visionaries, artists, hackers, scientists and left-wing activists." We thus come full circle, back to liberatory anarchism. But not for long, as it is now a matter of anarcho-capitalism: "But this libertarian ideology, which is fundamentally left-wing, will progressively enter into alliance with right-wing libertarianism, that is, hyper-liberalism."[31]

The inevitability of this "progress" is what should interest us—progress in what direction? One should combine here the notion of anarcho-capitalism with the notion of today's epoch as techno-feudalism: although the two may appear to be opposed (isn't feudalism, the direct social domination, the very opposite of anarchic freedom?), their link is easy to see, it is indicated by Malabou herself when she writes that anarchist uncontrollable horizontality leads to savage verticality. The anarchist turn of capitalism dissolves the unity of the state which regulates social interaction, and, as in the Dark Middle Ages, the impenetrable chaos that thus emerges gets supplemented by feudal islands of domination, so what we are gradually approaching is anarcho-feudalism. So when Malabou writes about "capitalism's conflict with itself," which conflict does she have in mind? The one between uncontrollable horizontality and savage verticality, or the one between a new form of capitalist domination and a new form of liberation? Malabou sees in cryptocurrencies the possibility of "an anti-capitalism that will wrench a liberatory anarchism from the grip of its counter-model, libertarian anarchism." This brings us back to Rifkin's notion of the "internet of things" and of a Collaborative Commons:

> Without going so far as to use the word 'anarchism', [Rifkin] insists on the change of paradigm that capitalism is currently going through: 'A new economic paradigm—the Collaborative Commons—is rising [. . .] that will transform our way of life. We are already witnessing the emergence of a hybrid economy, part capitalist market and part Collaborative Commons. [. . .] Between these two rival paradigms, the struggle will be long and implacable.[32]

Rifkin's basic thesis is that, for the first time in human history, a path of overcoming capitalism is discernible as an actual tendency in social production and exchange (the growth of cooperative commons), so that the end of capitalism is on the horizon. "Collaborative commons" (CC) designates a new mode of production and exchange which leaves behind private property and market exchange: in CC, individuals are giving their products free into circulation. This emancipatory dimension of CC should, of course, be located in the context of the rise of the so-called "internet of things (IoT)," combined with another result of today's development of productive forces, the explosive rise of "zero marginal costs" (more and more products, not only information, can be reproduced for no additional costs). The internet of things (IoT) is the network of physical devices, vehicles, buildings and other items embedded with electronics, software, sensors, actuators, and network connectivity that enable these objects to collect and exchange data; it allows objects to be sensed and controlled remotely across the existing network infrastructure, creating opportunities for more direct integration of the physical world into computer-based systems, and resulting in improved efficiency, accuracy and economic benefit. When IoT is augmented with sensors and actuators, the technology becomes an instance of the more general class of cyber-physical systems, which also encompasses technologies such as smart grids, smart homes, intelligent transportation and smart cities; each thing is uniquely identifiable through its embedded computing system and is able to interoperate within the existing internet infrastructure. The interconnection of these embedded devices (including smart objects) is expected to usher in automation in nearly all fields, while also enabling advanced applications like a smart grid, and expanding to such areas as smart cities. "Things" can also refer to a wide variety of devices such as heart monitoring implants, biochip transponders on farm animals, electric clams in coastal waters, automobiles with built-in sensors, and DNA analysis devices for environmental/food/pathogen monitoring; these devices collect useful data with the help of various existing technologies and then autonomously flow the data between other devices. Human individuals are also "things" whose states and activities are continuously registered and transmitted without their knowledge: their physical movements, their financial transactions, their health, their eating and drinking habits, what they buy and sell, what they read, listen to and watch is all collected in digital networks which know them better than they know themselves. Malabou emphasizes the role of blockchains in IoT:

> Objects, connected to the internet and linked to the blockchain by a cryptocurrency protocol, are able to contract a service or validate a transaction all by themselves. A washing machine capable of calculating its own consumption, an electric heater that can enter into an appropriate contract, a rental car that can sign a contract directly with a driver—all of these are examples that give another twist to the new law of exchanges, with objects now contracting with and between one another. Not only are currencies becoming delinked from nations or territories, not only are they escaping the hands of the state, the human actors of exchange are themselves in some sense disappearing behind the horizontal autonomy of objects contracting with other objects with the help of currencies that are themselves objects connected to one another and to other commodities.

If, however, "the human actors of exchange are themselves in some sense disappearing behind the horizontal autonomy of objects contracting with other objects," and if we remain within the market economy, does this not imply that human actors are reduced to moments in an opaque totality of interacting objects? In what, then, does the emancipatory potential of the IoT consist? Rifkin is quite clear here: the capitalist market and Collaborative Commons are "two rival paradigms," and the struggle between the two "will be long and implacable"—and it is easy to see why: for Rifkin, CC means precisely free distribution and reproduction, while bitcoins and NFT introduce scarcity into this domain. In other words, CC is opposed to market, in deadly struggle with it, while for the partisans of bitcoin, bitcoins are the unity of market and anarchy.

6
The State and Counter-Revolution

When the Social Link Disintegrates

We can learn a lot about our global predicament from how, in January 2022, the ending of David Fincher's classic *Fight Club* was changed for the Chinese video release. In the 1999 original, the nameless Narrator (played by Edward Norton) kills off his imagined ideal ego Tyler Durden (Brad Pitt) before watching buildings burst into flames in apparent confirmation that his plan to destroy modern civilization is being executed. The version now playing on China's largest video streamer stops before the buildings explode; the final action is instead replaced with an English-language title card explaining that the anarchic plot was foiled by the authorities: "The police rapidly figured out the whole plan and arrested all criminals, successfully preventing the bomb from exploding. After the trial, Tyler was sent to a lunatic asylum receiving psychological treatment. He was discharged from the hospital in 2012."[1] One cannot but note the neoconservative tone of this change: it sustains unconditional solidarity with power, even if the power is in this case that of the American state. Plus the disturbance is not treated as a political revolt but as a case of mental illness to be cured. It is an irony that the Chinese ending comes closer to the ending of the novel on which the movie is based. The Narrator finds redemption at the end of the film by getting rid of Tyler Durden as his ego ideal (shooting at himself so that the bullet passes through his cheek), and assuming full personal responsibility for the violent revolutionary act that was planned (exploding buildings of banks which hold files on credit cards). There is no hint of pathology here—on the contrary, at this point, he becomes "normal," so there is no longer any need for him to beat himself up, his destructive energy can be directed outwards, at social reality. However, in the novel, the Narrator is placed in a mental institution, as in the Chinese version of the movie. The novel can still be read as a tale of reaching maturity, the fact that he is placed into a mental institution being merely a sign that our society which misrecognizes maturity as madness is in itself mad. This in no way holds for the Chinese version in which the Narrator's story is dismissed as a pathological case and social order is perceived as something normal.[2] What this should make us think is the weird fact that China, a country which legitimizes itself as a Socialist alternative to Western liberalism, changes the ending of a film which is highly critical of Western liberal society, disqualifying its critical stance as an expression of madness which should be cured in a mental institution . . .

Why is China doing this? There is only one consistent answer. In mid-October 2019, Chinese media launched an offensive promoting the claim that "demonstrations in Europe and South America are the direct result of Western tolerance of Hong Kong unrest." In a commentary published in *Beijing News*, former Chinese diplomat Wang Zhen wrote that "the disastrous impact of a 'chaotic Hong Kong' has begun to influence the Western world," i.e., that demonstrators in Chile and Spain were taking their cues from Hong Kong. Along the same lines, we could read in an editorial in *Global Times* that "there are many problems in the West and all kinds of undercurrents of dissatisfaction. Many of them will eventually manifest in the way the Hong Kong protests did."[3] The Communist China discreetly plays on the solidarity of those in power all around the world against the rebellious populace, warning the West not to underestimate the dissatisfaction in their own countries—as if, beneath all ideological and geo-political tensions, they all share the same basic interest in holding onto power . . .

To cope with this threat, China is ready to fully embrace new technological modes of control and regulation. They have already started to plant small chips into the bodies of individuals, not for the control of pandemic but with the general purpose of controlling the whereabouts and characteristics of individuals. However, "surveillance capitalism" involves much more than the passive registration and control of what individuals are/do/want—it is above all about regulating and manipulating their very opinions and desires (through choices offered, etc.). Digital control ultimately aims at relieving us of the very burden of desire, of deciding what we desire—it is as if a digital machine is desiring for us so that we can relax, thus acquiring a weird freedom: we are no longer desiring beings under siege by machines which want to penetrate the secret of our desire, our very desiring ability is already regulated . . . The paradox is that the prospect of such a direct regulation of our inner lives undermines the function of transference in our social interactions: the Other, the subject-supposed-to-know, is precisely the subject who is supposed to know what I really desire (which is why, at the end of the analytic process, the analysand steps out of transference because s/he learns him/herself what s/he desires). To explain this function, Lacan mentions the role of a good waiter in a restaurant: when we look perplexed at the list of items on the menu, not knowing what to choose, and we ask the waiter for advice—our basic demand to him/her is: "Can you please tell me what I want?" With digitalization, the subject-supposed-to-know disappears: I no longer need an Other as the subject of transference, I think I am making the choice myself, since I am manipulated at a deeper level—the very frame of choices presented to me is already rigged.

When this happens, the very base of our social link—transference onto a subject supposed to . . . (know, believe)—is threatened. In transference, we relate to persons in whom we are expected to (act as if we) believe although we know they don't really exist. The solution is not a return to fake naivete: to leave behind our knowledge and regain or maintain belief—our knowledge was never a threat to belief. Problems arise when we *transpose our knowledge onto these persons* themselves and surmise that they somehow know they don't exist. A recent caricature in a Slovene daily makes this point clearly: a broken Santa Claus goes to a psychiatrist who tells him: "You have to have more trust and belief in yourself!" Does something like that not happen to Christ himself who, dying on a cross, for a moment doesn't believe in himself, in his divinity ("Father, why have you abandoned me?")? Do we—the community of believers—not play the role of the psychiatrist from the caricature, is our message to Christ not "Don't be desperate, we will restore your own trust in yourself, you will return to life in our community!"?

We are not preaching here a return to belief but a belief grounded in despair: yes, we are doomed, there is no clear way out, but we should always bear in mind that the global capitalist system is even more doomed, approaching its apocalyptic end. The hopelessness is not ours when we experience ourselves at the mercy of a global always winning capitalist machine; the hopelessness is in the very heart of this machine—it ultimately means that there is no hope for us within the coordinates of the existing global system. We have to begin to think in terms of radical change. As he denounced the insufficiency of the latest wave of sanctions against Russia in June 2022, the Ukrainian president Zelensky said that "Western countries are more concerned with the economic impact of rising energy prices than with the deaths of innocent Ukrainians."[4] Well, it took Zelensky a long time to get how global capitalism and democracy really work, with Russian gas still flowing to Europe through Ukraine. To put it brutally, there is only one serious solution: our states will have to act beyond the reliance on market mechanisms and directly organize the production and distribution of certain basic products and services. The paradox is that only such War Communist measures can save our freedoms, not the capitalist market—the same market that allows Russian gas to still flow to Europe through the Ukraine while the war is raging.

The Limit of Spontaneous Order

We should of course resist the temptation of glorifying war as an authentic experience against our complacent apathy. But our answer to this complacency should be an even stronger mobilization for causes which reach well beyond armed conflicts. With regard to the dangers that confront humanity today, military passion is itself a cowardly escape from the abyss we are gradually approaching. What role will the state play in this mobilization? As a dedicated partisan of a strong state, I must confess I enjoyed immensely Graeber's and Wengrow's case for a new anarchism.[5] What makes the book so convincing is that they do not just argue that today we are moving in that direction; in a broad overview, they return to the very dawn of civilization, demonstrating that the passage to civilization with cities and complex social structures did not necessarily involve state domination:

> For generations, our remote ancestors have been cast as primitive and childlike—either free and equal innocents, or thuggish and warlike. Civilization, we are told, could be achieved only by sacrificing those original freedoms or, alternatively, by taming our baser instincts. But such theories first emerged in the eighteenth century as a conservative reaction to powerful critiques of European society posed by indigenous observers and intellectuals. Revisiting this encounter has startling implications for how we make sense of human history today, including the origins of farming, property, cities, democracy, slavery, and civilization itself. History becomes a far more interesting place once we learn to throw off our conceptual shackles and perceive what's really there. If humans did not spend 95 percent of their evolutionary past in tiny bands of hunter-gatherers, what were they doing all that time? If agriculture, and cities, did not mean a plunge into hierarchy and domination, then what kinds of social and economic organization did they lead to? The answers are often unexpected, and suggest that the course of human history may be less set in stone, and more full of playful, hopeful possibilities, than we tend to assume.[6]

What we get here is the anarchist alternate vision of the entirety of human history, with the ancient Incas as the supreme example: the Inca community was not just a hierarchic empire practicing human sacrifices but also an alternate model of cooperation, including housing for the poor—a complex social network with no higher state authority, far from oriental despotism. Graeber and Wengrow even locate the origin of modern European Enlightenment with the first contacts of European colonizers with aboriginal wise thinkers: their culture of dialogue and cooperation shattered medieval authoritarianism and gave the impetus to Enlightenment which simultaneously reasserted European primacy, reducing the non-European past to primitive despotism:

> To give just a sense of how different the emerging picture is: it is clear now that human societies before the advent of farming were not confined to small, egalitarian bands. On the contrary, the world of hunter-gatherers as it existed before the coming of

> agriculture was one of bold social experiments, resembling a carnival parade of political forms, far more than it does the drab abstractions of evolutionary theory. Agriculture, in turn, did not mean the inception of private property, nor did it mark an irreversible step towards inequality. In fact, many of the first farming communities were relatively free of ranks and hierarchies. And far from setting class differences in stone, a surprising number of the world's earliest cities were organized on robustly egalitarian lines, with no need for authoritarian rulers, ambitious warrior-politicians, or even bossy administrators.[7]

We can clearly see here how empty and inconsistent Marx's notion of the Asiatic Mode of Production is: it just puts into the same basket elements the unity of which is purely negative—they don't fit Marx's basic scheme of modes of production. However, although Graeber and Wengrow are correct in rejecting the linear progressive development of history, the attraction of their model secretly relies on projecting into the past the anti-authoritarian features that belong to modernity: the "robustly egalitarian lines, with no need for authoritarian rulers," of the earliest cities obviously do not include the modern sense of individual liberty whose space is paradoxically sustained by the state authority elevated above civil society and in this sense "alienated." Freedom in civil society is defined by the distance towards state authority, not by the absence of state authority. None other than Friedrich Hayek saw this clearly, and that's why Simon Griffiths (see "What can the Left learn from Friedrich Hayek?"[8]) is right in arguing that Hayek offers the Left three important insights. First, the limits of knowledge:

> Socialism, which Hayek understood largely as central economic planning, requires planners to make use of information which, because it exists in our heads only fleetingly and is never fully articulated, simply cannot be collected. For Hayek, only the market can make use of this diffused knowledge: state planning is bound to fail. However, for some on the left, Hayek's account of knowledge has very different implications. For example, Hilary Wainwright /.../ argues that Hayek mistakenly treats knowledge as "an individual attribute, rather than as a social

> product." Understood socially, knowledge can be shared by people taking action to overcome the limits of their individual perspectives. Wainwright's work is full of examples of organizations—trade unions, women's groups and co-ops—that have come together to pool knowledge in order to solve collective problems that cannot be solved by the market or by remote bureaucrats. Hayek's argument over the dispersed nature of knowledge can be used to support a form of radical social movement politics, not simply a scepticism about socialist planning.[9]
>
> Second, the idea of the spontaneous order: "some 'orders' emerge 'as a result of human action, but not of human design': language, common law, morality and markets are all examples. To Hayek, the state's role should be largely limited to protecting the spontaneous orders on which civilization is based." Third, markets as a space of freedom: markets allow greater freedom of choice over purchases; when and where to work; and freedom of expression. However,
>
> while Hayek was right about the importance of these freedoms, his views are incomplete because he never explained why freedom is valuable to us. This must be because of our desire to act autonomously. In order to do this, we need certain resources—food, shelter, and education, for example. The state is crucial in providing these. Market freedoms are important, but so is the autonomy needed to pursue them. Hayek's argument for freedom can end, not simply with a case for the free market, but with an account of those resources needed to make freedom valuable to us.[10]

Hayek's "spontaneous order" points towards the same thing as Lacan's "big Other," something that has no "objective" existence in itself but persists as a presupposition posited by the activity of subjects. Hayek here wisely insists on the irreducibility of alienation: his point is not anarchist individualism but the necessity for the "spontaneous" interaction of individuals to be perceived as related to a transcendent "objective" order. And Hayek's critique of Marx is justified insofar as Marx neglects this dimension in his vision of Communism, conceiving it as a social process regulated by a self-transparent singular Subject. Production will remain caught in fetishist alienation "until it becomes production by freely socialized men, and stands under their conscious and planned control"[11]—this tells us a lot about Marx's vision of Communism . . . However, the problem is here (among others) the ecological crisis which we cannot confront with the "spontaneous" interaction of individuals and local communities: the "spontaneous order" of today's global market is leading towards global catastrophe, and only a well-planned and coordinated action can (maybe) stop our drift into catastrophe.

There is thus a fundamental difference between the subject's alienation in the symbolic order and the worker's alienation in capitalist social relation. We have to avoid the two symmetrical traps which open up if we insist on the homology between the two alienations: the idea that capitalist social alienation is irreducible since the signifying alienation is constitutive of subjectivity, as well as the opposite idea that the signifying alienation could be abolished in the same way Marx imagined the overcoming of capitalist alienation. The point is not just that the signifying alienation is more fundamental and will persist even if we abolish the capitalist alienation—it is a more refined one. The very figure of a subject that would overcome the signifying alienation and become a free agent who is master of the symbolic universe, i.e., who is no longer embedded in a symbolic substance, can only arise within the space of capitalist alienation, the space in which free individuals interact.

The State is Here to Stay!

The dimension of the state that makes it indispensable in a market economy is exactly its alienation, the fact that it is a power elevated above the social chaos, not a direct expression of social forces. Although, of course, the state and its apparatuses always represent certain social forces—the classic lesson of Marxism—the minimal distance towards these forces allows it to play a mediating role. Álvaro Garcia Linera was the first who, from a radical Leftist stance, pointed out this positive role of the state: he did it when he approached the question "Why did, at the pandemic outburst, billions unquestionably accepted the severe limitation of their daily freedoms?" outside the predominant blahblah on state powers using the pandemic as the pretext to strengthen their control over the population and discipline it.[12] The main representative of this blahblah is unfortunately Giorgio Agamben—Eric Santner characterized Agamben's texts on the pandemic as the transformation, performed by himself, of his theory into ideology:

> The thrust of Agamben's interventions over the course of the pandemic comes down to the claim that the people ... have allowed themselves to be cast into just such a state of nature, to be cast as so many specimens of bare life that must be treated and governed. For Agamben, it would seem, as soon as health becomes *public health*—a species of what was once referred to in German as *Polizeiwissenschaft*—we are for all intents and purposes caught in the snares of, captured and captivated by, a state of exception that has become the norm. As soon as the state gets involved in monitoring and maintaining the *homeostasis*, the regulation of the life of its citizens, those citizens have consigned themselves to the edge of a *stasis* barely held in check by the state.[13]

Reacting to this view, Santner points out that in the US,

> the problem was not so much an excess of biopolitical administration but rather its lack. We might say that in the United States the state did not so much deploy as hinder those "plague doctors" from doing their work of "treating and governing." And indeed, it was Trump himself who, instead of declaring a state of emergency, seemed to push toward a true civil war; he was the one who has, since his departure from office and by way of his continued imposture of unbroken sovereignty, only come closer to its realization. Here the "multitude" appears not in the guise of those who submit to what Agamben, along with Ron DeSantos, Steve Bannon, Tucker Carlson, among others, have characterized, in a kind of caricature of Foucault's thought, as the regime of a biopolitical security state but rather as the ostensible resistance to it.[14]

Taking into account this paradox, Linera begins by pointing out that we were witnessing something absolutely unique—a kind of planetary general strike which hit also the circulation of capital:

> For the first time in human history, vast numbers of people across the world have agreed to abandon their paid activities, to stop attending public gatherings, and confine themselves in their homes for weeks and months. We are living in a kind of general planetary strike which has paralyzed most of the transport, commerce, production, and services. People have accepted confinement when asked to do so by their state institutions which justify the measure as a way to stop the spread of the coronavirus.[15]

So why did people not only accept this but sometimes even demand it? (In the UK, the public at some point demanded *harsher* measures than those enacted by the government.) Linera does not describe this unique situation in order to give rise to our horror in the style of "how could people be so manipulated that they voluntarily demand control and servitude?"—on the contrary, he refers here to the positive function of state: state is not just an agency of oppression and class domination but also the institutional representative of the common interest of the entire population, it is sustained by

> a common belief in the protection of everybody through public resource. Before, it meant the expectation of collective protection against wars, invasions, violent death, and also the hope of a safeguard against collective misfortunes, economic catastrophes, losing positions. At this moment, the State represents the promise of protection against the risk of death from the virus. It is in collective responses to constitutive fears where we can find decisive clues about the origins and functioning of States. But the State is not the same as fear. The fear of invasions, misery, the loss of possessions, the plague, allows a community of affected people to become a political community when everyone decides to accept a common way of organizing resources that allows to stop, mitigate, defeat imminent or perceived primary fears.[16]

And Linera's point is that, with the pandemic, this role of the state as the ultimate protector of the common good grew stronger than ever—markets were helpless, international cooperation failed, only the state remained:

> The pandemic has revealed the basic composition of the state relations by presenting it as the only and last social space of protection against the risk of death and economic catastrophe. International organizations and global markets have abdicated their prerogatives in relation to the State; globalized production is collapsing and companies are lining up to take refuge in public debt. The institutions that once drew on the creation of globalization over the State are now extending their hands in search of government benefits.[17]

In such an extraordinary situation, we became aware of what the state is at its most basic: state authority appears and functions as a neutral space above particular groups; this neutrality is illusory, of course, but it is a "real illusion" embodied in a series of material social and ideological apparatuses, from education to health. In short, the state is

> not only a belief of collective goods for the common protection; it is also a material reality of organizing a form of management of the common (government, parliament, ministries, legal apparatus, permanent coercive apparatuses); it is a material reality of having resources and common goods for protection (initially taxes, then public goods, services, savings, among others), consequently, it is a way of directing the common; and it is also discursive ways of territorially delimiting the community of beliefs (school system, national identity, recognition systems, state legitimacies).... It is an illusion, but it is a well-founded illusion objectively sustained by the persistence of these common goods.

The status of this "illusion" is not just objective (it is embodied in a series of material institutions and procedures) but also subjective: in some sense, a state exists only insofar as its subjects believe in it, "take it seriously" even when they oppose it or denounce it as a tyranny. That's why state decrees have a performative dimension: they do what they say, they are pronounced from the position of big Other—there is an invisible gap which separates pronouncements and declarations of even very influential individuals from state declarations.

As a Marxist, Linera is, of course, well aware of how the role of the state as representative and protector of all its citizen is always given a specific spin (privileging the rich, a certain religion or ethnic group, oppression of women, etc.), where this spin is (mis)represented as something done for the good of all (rich people are productive and give work to the poor, etc.). However, as he points out, in times of crisis, the state is compelled to privilege its function as the protector of the universal interest of its citizens at the expense of its privileged strata—how far the state is ready to go in this direction depends on the constellation of social struggles and on the popular mobilization. That's why it is crucial not just to dismiss the state as the instrument of domination but to assume state power when possible and use it for universal welfare—this is what the Bolivian state was doing when Linera was its vice president. In the situations of natural and health catastrophes, social unrests, etc., it is thus absolutely crucial for the progressive forces to try to grab state power and fully use it, not only in order to adequately react to the fears of ordinary people but also to fight against fears which were artificially created in order to keep the population in check (racist and sexist fears, etc.).

The standard Marxist point is that the state as an institution is not just biased in the empirical sense of serving particular interests, but that it is biased in its very form as an institution, independently of which group holds power—again, not just in the sense that state institutions obey their own immanent interests of domination, but also in the sense that the very form in which they "represent" all of society is not really neutral. So when progressive powers occupy the state, they as it were operate in enemy territory—however, this very fact is a unique chance to beat the enemy from within. We should also bear in mind that exploitation and domination are not linked to the state: already in the Neolithic period, there were patriarchy and social hierarchy, and since today's civil society is also immanently antagonistic, it is often a fact that civil society resists the state's progressive measures (anti-racism and anti-sexism). So when we are witnessing a rightist populist rebellion, there is no excuse for not ruthlessly using state mechanisms of repression—when the Capitol was invaded by the Trump mob on January 6, 2021, the police should have intervened with all force.

We should be ready to go to the end in this direction—where can or should we look for the solution in the ongoing ideological cold war within a single nation-state (as is the case in the US where Trump has a real chance to win again the 2024 elections)?[18] On Saturday June 19, 2022, meeting at their first in-person convention since 2018, Texas Republicans approved measures declaring that President Joe Biden "was not legitimately elected" and rebuking Sen. John Cornyn for taking part in bipartisan gun talks. They also voted on a platform that declares homosexuality "an abnormal lifestyle choice" and calls for Texas schoolchildren "to learn about the humanity of the preborn child."[19] The first measure—declaring that President Joe Biden "was not legitimately elected"—is a clear step in the direction of the "cold" civil war in the US: it delegitimizes the existing political order. If we combine this and other signs that the Republican party is more than ever controlled by Trump with the Ukraine war fatigue, a dark prospect opens up: what if Trump wins the next elections and enforces a pact with Russia, abandoning Ukrainians in the same way he did with the Kurds?

One should here be absolutely without any prejudice: when the social big Other is disintegrating, when society cannot come to terms with itself, even the army can play a positive role. The intervention of the army is not necessarily reactionary or Fascist, it can also be progressive, as was the case in Portugal when the army overthrew the Salazar regime, or in some Latin American countries. It is all the matter of the ideological situation in the armed forces, not so much in the top echelons but more among the mid-level officers. Even the US Army gave hints in this direction, making it clear that it will not tolerate Trump's manipulations to remain president after his electoral defeat. We should apply Linera's insights also in this domain: the "spontaneous ideology" of the armed forces is to perceive themselves as the ultimate safeguard of society, defending it against all threats including natural disasters (where the army is often called upon to protect the population), and the specific spin of this stance depends on the ideological struggle in specific conditions. Although, for various reasons, the US armed forces cannot be expected to play such a progressive role, it is nice to imagine a *coup d'etat* saving the US as a civilized state . . .

Before we dismiss such ideas as dangerous speculations, we should recall how our political space is already changing. The main shift in the structure of our political space was that the opposition between centre-Left and centre-Right parties as the main axis of our political space was replaced by the opposition between a big technocratic party (standing for expert knowledge) and its populist opponent with its anti-corporate and anti-financial motifs. However, this shift itself underwent another surprising turn: Bickerton and Accetti have shown convincingly that what we are witnessing lately is something one cannot but determine as *techno-populism*: a political movement with clear populist appeal (working for the people as such, for their "real interests," "neither Left nor Right"), promising to take care of the people through rational expert politics, a matter-of-fact approach, without mobilizing low passions and resorting to demagogic slogans. To quote Bickerton and Accetti:

> Technocratic appeals to expertise and populist invocations of "the people" have become mainstays of political competition in established democracies. This development is best understood as the emergence of technopopulism—a new political logic that is being superimposed on the traditional struggle between left and right. Political movements and actors combine technocratic and populist appeals in a variety of ways, as do more established parties that are adapting to the particular set of incentives and constraints implicit in this new, unmediated form of politics.[20]

What seemed the ultimate antagonism of today's politics, the big struggle which persists, is miraculously transformed into a peaceful coexistence—are we dealing here with some kind of "dialectical synthesis" of the opposites? No, because the opposites are reconciled through the exclusion of the third term: political antagonism, i.e., the political dimension as such. The unsurpassed model is here Mario Draghi in Italy, endorsed as the "neutral" and efficient prime minister by the entire political spectrum (with the significant exception of the extreme Rightist neo-Fascists who are saving the honour of politics), but elements of techno-populism are clearly recognizable also in Emmanuel Macron and even in Angela Merkel.

To overcome the prospect of techno-populism, the change that is required is not just subjective but a global social change. Even the populist right is taking note of this tendency, although in a negative way. *2025* (Wesely Bros 2021, Joshua and Simon Wesely, reported budget $10,000) is the latest example of a new genre: Christian-fundamentalist movies made on a very limited budget. As the title indicates, it takes place in 2025, and since the outbreak of the coronavirus in 2020, the world has not been the same: a Communist system with a single world government has been established, English has been chosen as the world language, contacts have been reduced to a minimum, Christianity has been banned completely—and the plot? In Germany, a small group of young Christians start an underground revolution to reunite Christians and regain freedom . . . In spite of its ridiculousness, the power of the movie resides in the fact that it got right the Communist potential of the pandemic, as well as the fact that the new fundamentalist Right is successfully re-appropriating the way to produce movies which was until recently the preserve of the marginal Left, mostly in Third World countries.

This reconfiguration puts (whatever remains of) the authentic Left into a difficult position: while being fully aware that techno-populism is the very form of today's counter-revolution, of the apolitical "neutralization" of political antagonisms, it should nonetheless sometimes strategically support it as a lesser evil when immediate catastrophes are posing a threat. With regard to the 2024 US presidential elections: should the Left support Biden (or whoever the Democratic candidate will be) against the fatal danger posed by Trump's return to power, or should we refuse to get caught in this liberal blackmail?[21] It is clear that this game cannot be played endlessly—a more radical change will impose itself.

Many people laughed at my mention of the Communist prospect: capitalism not only contained the crisis but even exploited it to strengthen itself . . . I still think I was right: in the last years, global capitalism has changed so radically that some (like Yanis Varoufakis and Jodi Dean[22]) even no longer call the new emerging order capitalism but corporate neo-feudalism. The pandemic gave a boost to this new corporate order, with new feudal lords like Bill Gates or Mark Zuckerberg more and more controlling our common spaces of communication and exchange . . . The danger we are courting here is, of course, the danger of abstract exaggeration, i.e., of extrapolating from a particular tendency to a general characteristic of the capitalist system: does "corporate neo-feudalism" not designate just a couple of big corporations each dominating a specific field, while the large majority of investments still take place outside these corporations? This critique misses a crucial point of "corporate neo-feudalism": the key structural role of the privatization of commons. The first big privatization of commons happened during the so-called primordial accumulation in England, but here commons (land, forests) were privatized in the sense of divided into private properties so that they were no longer commons, while today commons *remain* commons and are *as such* privatized. So although corporate neo-feudalists are a minority, they act as a common space through which a large part of other ("ordinary" capitalist) activities takes place.

One should complicate even further the picture here: it is not just that the privatized commons is the space within which exchange and communication takes place—the ideal counterpart of neo-feudal privatized commons are precarious workers who can experience themselves as free entrepreneurs since they as a rule own their own means of production (the PC of a programmer, the car of an Uber driver . . .). Precarious workers, although still a minority, are gradually becoming the specific case of work which confers its colour on the entire field of work—they are today workers *kat' exochen*. Precarious work has a double advantage for the predominant ideology: it allows you to experience yourself as an independent small capitalist selling your work freely, not a wage slave, plus since you compete with other precarious workers it makes organizing solidarity between precarious workers very difficult. So the ideal we are approaching today is a multitude of precarious workers interacting in a commons controlled by a neo-feudal lord. The mystification is thus complete: workers are free entrepreneurs, and their feudal lord is just providing the social space for their "free" activity.

The pessimistic conclusion that imposes itself is that even stronger shocks and crises will be needed to awaken us. Neoliberal capitalism is already dying, so the forthcoming battle will not be the one between neoliberalism and its beyond but the one between two forms of this beyond: corporate neo-feudalism which promises protective bubbles against the threats (like Zuckerberg's "metaverse"), bubbles in which we can continue to dream, and the rude awakening which will compel us to invent new forms of solidarity. How should the existing state be transformed in order to serve these new forms?

Do Not Give Up on Your Communist Desire!

In an old Soviet joke, a new arrival to the Gulag condemned to ten years is asked by prisoners: "What were you given ten years for?" "For nothing!" "Don't lie to us! Everybody knows here that for nothing you get three years."[23] There is a profound wisdom in this joke: in every social community, there is no neutral nothing, every "nothing" has a price determined by those in power, which means that we are all a priori guilty and that you have to work hard to get rid of this guilt and be given "nothing." In the old Communist regimes, there were moments of relative liberalization, and its sign was usually that the message of those in power to the people was the one Janos Kadar publicly announced as the head of the new Soviet-puppet government after the Soviet army crushed the Hungarian rebellion of 1956: "Those who are not against us are for us." But even this statement was ultimately a fake: "not being against" meant that you nonetheless had to participate minimally in official ideological rituals (you just didn't have to attend big official public events), to obey official prohibitions, etc. Under harsh Stalinism, the price for getting nothing (not being condemned or at least not arbitrarily accused) was to be active in, say, denouncing colleagues—in the Stalinist Soviet Union, there was a law which made it a criminal act just to know/hear about an "oppositional" activity (like making critical remarks about the regime) and not reporting it to the police.

But instead of repeating these old stories about totalitarian repression, we should focus on the growing "price of nothing" in our "permissive" liberal democracies in which, instead of the good old explicit "totalitarian" prohibitions and injunctions, more subtle forms of unwritten (hidden) censorship are exploding lately. What happens in revolutionary breaks when the violent intrusion of abstract freedom enables the change from one to another form of concrete freedom is precisely that the "price for nothing" (the price we have to pay to be "innocent" members of our society) is renegotiated. We are in the middle of such a process. The title of a song by the Slovene band Zaklonišče (Shelter) "Samo da prodje demokratija! [Just let democracy pass away!]" caused a violent reaction among the nationalist Rightists who accused the band of "anti-constitutional propaganda"; however, far from being a provocation, this title is simply correct—with the forthcoming crises the time of democracy as we know it (the multiparty parliamentary system) has passed. Claudia Chwalisz surveys the wave of experiments in this "new, non-electoral understanding of democratic representation" washing over the West: "The current democratic system for taking public decisions—anchored in the short-termism of elections and the inward-looking logic of political parties—has perverse incentives that are preventing action, exacerbating polarization and fueling distrust." For Chwalisz, the alternative path to forging a governing consensus would be

> widespread citizens' assemblies, such as we've seen in Ireland on abortion or in France on climate action. Instead of standing for elected office, citizens are selected through a random process that reflects the profile of the body politic at large, much like a jury, to address issues elected legislatures are too mired in immediacy or too riven by partisanship to resolve.[24]

Are we thereby back at anarchism? Things get much more complex here. In her stupendous *Yesterday's Tomorrow*,[25] Bini Adamczak provides nothing less than the definitive account of what one cannot but call the ineradicable, absolutely authentic, *Communist desire*, the Idea of a society which fully overcomes domination:

> Unlike the slaves, who only wished to be as free as their masters, unlike the peasants, who wanted to give the lords a tenth of their crop instead of a fifth, unlike the bourgeoisie, who only wanted

> political freedom, not economic freedom, what the workers demanded was a classless society. What the Communists promised was the abrogation of all domination. And as long as they are remembered, their promise remains.[26]

This desire is "eternal" in the simple sense that it is a shadow which accompanies all previous history which is, as Marx and Engels wrote, the history of class struggle. Jean Meslier was right: "Man will never be free until the last king is strangled with the entrails of the last priest."[27] What makes Adamczak's book unique is that she detects this desire through a very close analysis of the failures of the (European) Communist movement in the twentieth century, tracing them backwards from the Hitler–Stalin pact to the brutal suppression of the Kronstadt rebellion. The details she describes make it clear that, say, the Hitler–Stalin pact cannot be accounted for just in the terms of brutal *realpolitik* (Stalin needed time to prepare for the war that loomed on the horizon)—weird excesses disturb this image, like the fact that 1940 guards in gulags were forbidden to shout at prisoners "Fascists!" not to insult the Nazis:

> What remains incomprehensible, because irreducible to any calculation of power politics, is Beria's order forbidding the guard staff in the gulags from disparaging political prisoners—antifascists in the majority, frequently convicted of "Trotskyte-fascist deviations"—with the epithet fascist.[28]

Adamczak's focus is double, as the subtitle of her book makes clear: "On the Loneliness of Communist Specters and the Reconstruction of the Future"—the absolute loneliness of the Communists who were purged but continued to believe in the Communist Idea embodied in the Party that liquidated them, i.e., to put it in Lacan's terms, the Party remained for them the only big Other. The deadlock they faced is that the way out for them was not to insist on the purity of the Communist dream against its betrayal by the Party: this dream of the future itself had to be "reconstructed." Most of them (just recall Arthur Koestler and Ignazio Silone) failed in this task: they *gave up on their Communist desire* (in the precise Lacan's sense of *ceder sur son desir*), rejoined the liberal (or even conservative) critique of Communism, and produced writings in the style of "God that failed," rejoining the anti-Communist Cold War warriors. As Adamczak notes, the absence of the Communist desire explains why, when European Communism disintegrated around 1990,

> the jubilant cries of the Cold War victors were so unconvincing: they lacked all joy. Instead of relief at averting looming danger or shared joy at the newfound fortune of the former oppressed, it expressed something resembling embittered malevolence: the schadenfreude those who stayed at home feel for their siblings drowned at sea.[29]

Adamczak here turns around the well-known anti-Communist motto that those who do not want to talk about Stalinism should also keep quiet about Communism: "But what can be said about Stalinism by those who refuse to hear about Communism? Those who wish to write the history of this past without writing about the history of that future that was buried in it?"[30] Only Communism establishes the highest standards by which it must be judged and critically rejected, which is why "the first reproach against anticommunism must be that of downplaying the crimes of Stalinism. Not because an idea was murdered alongside the people in the gulags—how cynical—but because Communism alone brought forth into the world the historically actionable demand to accept no disenfranchisements, to tolerate no more degradation."[31] That's why the worst thing a Communist can do is to half-heartedly defend Communist states in a modest comparative way:

> Communists react defensively to the (anticommunist) critique of Communism—not everything about Communism was bad—with parries—that wasn't even Communism—or by attacking—criticism of the crimes of communism only serves to legitimate the crimes of the enemies. They are right on all counts. But what does it say about Communism to state that National Socialism was worse, that capitalism has been just as bad? What kind of verdict is it for Communism to say not everything but instead only almost everything was bad?[32]

Just recall the similar defence of Cuba: yes, revolution was a failure, but they do have good healthcare and education . . . And do we not hear a similar argumentation from those who "show understanding" for Russia although they condemn the invasion of Ukraine: "the criticism of the Russian crimes in Ukraine only serves to legitimate the crimes of the liberal West . . ."?

Adamczak also dismisses the "postmodern" Left which criticizes Communism for its focus on economy, ignoring as "secondary" feminism, the struggle against sexual oppression, and all other domains of "cultural Marxism." Such a critique comes all too close to comfortable historicism which ignores the "eternity" of the Communist Idea: the actual Communist power is not only fighting its capitalist opponents; it is betraying the emancipatory dream which brought it into existence. This is why a true critique of actually-existing socialism should not just point out that life in a Communist state was mostly worse than life in many capitalist states—its greatest "contradiction" is the antinomy in its very heart, not just the stark contrast between the Idea and reality but the less perceptible change in the Idea itself. The idealized image of future promised by the Communist power is incompatible with the Communist Idea. In the last act of *The Tempest*, Prospero says to Caliban: "This thing of darkness I acknowledge mine." Every Communist has to say something similar about Stalinism, the largest "thing of darkness" in the history of Communism: in order to really understand it, the first gesture is to "acknowledge it as mine," to fully accept that Stalinism is not a contingent deviation or misapplication of Marxism but implied as a possibility by its very core . . . But does Hegel not say something similar in his famous lines on the French Revolution?

> Never since the sun had stood in its firmament and the planets revolved around him had it been perceived that man's existence centers in his head, i.e., in thought. /. . ./ Anaxagoras had been the first to say that nous governs the world; but not until now had man advanced to the recognition of the principle that thought ought to govern spiritual reality. This was accordingly a glorious mental dawn. All thinking beings shared in the jubilation of this epoch. Emotions of a lofty character stirred men's minds at that time; a spiritual enthusiasm thrilled through the world, as if the reconciliation between the divine and the secular was now first accomplished.[33]

Note that Hegel says this a quarter of a century *after* the French Revolution, and also decades *after* he deployed how the freedom the French Revolution wanted to actualize necessarily turned into terror. And we should say exactly the same about the October Revolution *after* experiencing Stalinism as its consequence: it also was "a glorious mental dawn. All thinking beings shared in the jubilation of this epoch. Emotions of a lofty character stirred men's minds at that time; a spiritual enthusiasm thrilled through the world . . ." We have to endure fully this antinomy, avoiding both traps: the dismissal of Stalinism as an error due to contingent circumstances, as well as the quick conclusion that Stalinism is the "truth" of the Communist desire. This antinomy is brought to extreme in Lenin's *State and Revolution*, a book whose vision of the revolution is definitely grounded in the authentic Communist desire: as Lenin writes, with the revolution,

> for the first time in the history of civilized society, the mass of the population will rise to take an independent part, not only in voting and elections, but also in the everyday administration of the state. Under socialism all will govern in turn and will soon become accustomed to no one governing.[34]

This properly Communist dimension is condensed in Lenin's famous formula "Every Kitchen Maid Should Learn To Rule The State," which was endlessly repeated through the 1920s as a slogan of women's emancipation. However, it is worth taking a closer look at the precise context of Lenin's justification of this slogan which, at first sight, may appear extremely utopian, especially since he emphasizes that the slogan designates something that "can and must be made at once, overnight," not in some later Communist future. Lenin begins his line of argumentation by denying being utopian: against anarchists, he asserts his utter realism—he is not counting on "new men" but on "people as they are now, with people who cannot dispense with subordination, control, and 'foremen and accountants'":

> We are not utopians, we do not "dream" of dispensing at once with all administration, with all subordination. These anarchist dreams, based upon incomprehension of the tasks of the

> proletarian dictatorship, are totally alien to Marxism, and, as a matter of fact, serve only to postpone the socialist revolution until people are different. No, we want the socialist revolution with people as they are now, with people who cannot dispense with subordination, control, and "foremen and accountants." This subordination, however, must be to the armed vanguard of all the exploited and working people, i.e., to the proletariat. A beginning can and must be made at once, overnight, to replace the specific "bossing" of state officials by the simple functions of "foremen and accountants," functions which are already fully within the ability of the average town dweller and can well be performed for "workmen's wages."[35]

But how to do this? Here comes the key moment of Lenin's argumentation:

> the mechanism of social management is here already to hand in modern capitalism—the mechanism of the automatic functioning of a large production process where the bosses (representing the owner) just give formal orders. This mechanism runs so smoothly that, without disturbing it, the role of the boss is reduced to simple decisions and can be played by an ordinary person. So all the Socialist revolution has to do is to replace the capitalist or state-appointed boss with (randomly selected) ordinary person.[36]

To illustrate his point, Lenin uses the example of postal service:

> A witty German Social-Democrat of the seventies of the last century called the postal service an example of the socialist economic system. This is very true. At the present the postal service is a business organized on the lines of state-capitalist monopoly. Imperialism is gradually transforming all trusts into organizations of a similar type, in which, standing over the "common" people, who are overworked and starved, one has the same bourgeois bureaucracy. But the mechanism of social management is here already to hand. Once we have overthrown the capitalists, crushed the resistance of these exploiters with the iron hand of the armed workers, and smashed the bureaucratic machinery of the modern state, we shall have a splendidly-

> equipped mechanism, freed from the "parasite," a mechanism which can very well be set going by the united workers themselves, who will hire technicians, foremen and accountants, and pay them all, as indeed all "state" officials in general, workmen's wages.[37]

The first question that arises here is: but industries change, introduce new products—who will make such long-term strategic decisions? Hired technicians can make proposals—but in whose interests will these proposals be? Will the "average town dwellers" be able to do it? And how will these proposals be coordinated with the plans of other companies? Some central planning agency is needed—how will that one function? Next question: what Lenin advocates here is "the transformation of public functions from political into simple functions of administration"—so where, in this depoliticized administrative machine, is the place for popular feedback from those who are supposed to obey "iron discipline"? Lenin's solution was an almost Kantian one: freely debate at public meetings during the weekends, but obey and work while at work—the Bolsheviks must

> stand at the head of the exhausted people who are wearily seeking a way out and lead them along the true path, along the path of labour discipline, along the path of co-ordinating the task of arguing at mass meetings about the conditions of work with the task of unquestioningly obeying the will of the Soviet leader, of the dictator, during the work. . . . We must learn to combine the "public meeting" democracy of the working people – turbulent, surging, overflowing its banks like a spring flood – with iron discipline while at work, with unquestioning obedience to the will of a single person, the Soviet leader, while at work.[38]

It was often noted how Lenin gradually narrows the field here: first it is the majority, the exploited mass of people; then it is the proletariat, no longer a majority (remember that in Russia at that time more than 80 per cent of the population were peasants) but a privileged minority; then even this minority becomes a mass of confused "exhausted people" who have to be led by "the armed vanguard of all the exploited and working people"; and, as expected, we end with the unquestioning obedience to the will of a single person, the Soviet dictator. A Hegelian would immediately raise the question of *mediation* here: we have three levels, the Universal (working majority, "all"), the Particular (party, the "armed vanguard" that holds state power), and the Singular (leader). Lenin automatically identifies them, ignoring modes of mediation where the political struggle proper is taking place—this is why, as Ralph Miliband noted, there is no debate on the role of the Party when Lenin described the functioning of the socialist economic edifice.[39] This absence is all the more strange if we take into account the fact that the focus of Lenin's political work is the struggle within the Party between the true line and the different revisionists.

This brings us to another of Lenin's antinomies: in spite of his total politicization of social life (for example, for him, there is no neutral "justice" in the courts: if judges are not on our side, they are on the side of the enemy), his vision of the socialist economy is deeply technocratic: economy is a neutral machine which can run smoothly whoever is at its head. The fact that a kitchen maid can be at its head means precisely that *it doesn't matter who is at its head*: the kitchen maid strangely resembles the role attributed by Hegel to the monarch: she just gives a formal "yes" to proposals prepared by managers and specialists . . .

But why dwell on this old topic which is today obviously outdated? Because it is not outdated at all: the latest trends in corporate capitalism provide a perverted version of Lenin's dream. Let's take companies like Amazon, Facebook, or Uber. Amazon and Facebook present themselves as just mediators: they are well-functioning algorithms regulating a commons of our interaction, so why not just nationalize them, cut off the head of their owner or boss and replace him with an ordinary person who will care that the company will serve the interests of the company, i.e., that the machine will not be twisted into serving particular commercial interests which made the previous owner a multi-billionaire? In other words, can bosses like Bezos and Zuckerberg not be replaced by people's "dictators" imagined by Lenin? Plus take Uber: it also presents itself as pure mediator bringing together drivers (who own their car, their "means of production") and those who need a drive. They all allow us to keep (the appearance of) our freedom—they just control the space of our freedom. Much worse than the "iron discipline" and obedience to the Soviet dictator, we are getting now the appearance of freedom which demands from you an even more severe self-control and self-discipline. As an Uber driver, you choose when to work, but your activity is constantly monitored (how much you work, are customers satisfied with you, etc.), and all these data go into the algorithm which determines how you will be treated by the anonymous system. Do phenomena like these not justify Karl-Heinz Dellwo to talk about "domination without subject": today it is "reasonable to speak no longer about masters and servants but only about servants who command servants."[40] Servants who command servants—is this not what Lenin envisions in his slogan that "Every Kitchen Maid Should Learn To Rule The State"?

Are elements of post-party politics not already visible here and there in today's developed capitalism? Take the case of Switzerland: who knows the names of the ministers in its government? Who knows which party is in power there? Decades ago, a Communist was repeatedly elected as the mayor of Geneva, the city which stands for big capital, and nothing changed . . . (But one should also mention that Switzerland is really run by a half-secret elite board of twenty men who really decide everything.)

So yes, we have to accept the fact that it is impossible for Communism to win (in the same sense that Ukraine cannot win over Russia), i.e., that, in this sense, Communism is a lost cause—but, as G.K. Chesterton put it in his "What's Wrong With the World": "The lost causes are exactly those which might have saved the world." What can we do once we are fully aware of this antinomy? In the last pages of his book, Adamczak plays with two extreme solutions: what if Communist revolutionaries, knowing they will bring a new terror, capitulate in advance to counter-revolution to keep their morals and prevent their own counter-revolution? Her example is Salvador Allende who renounced armed struggle against the military putsch, but we should add at least the debate in the Soviet Union in the early 1920s when, after it became clear that there will be no European revolution and the Bolsheviks realized they have no chance to begin to build socialism, some among them proposed that they should simply surrender power . . . Adamczak's other extreme solution is that, after winning state power, the Communists should fight the terrorist temptation by using terror against themselves, consciously accepting the need of their own purge, of the liquidation of the first-generation revolutionaries. (But did in a way Stalin not do exactly this—liquidate the first generation of revolutionaries who won power?) What if the only imaginable solution to this antinomy is a weird short-circuit: taking power, Communists themselves organize a "counter-revolution" against their rule, organizing a state apparatus which limits their own power? How would such an immanent counter-revolution look? Let's return to Lenin who repeatedly emphasized that, in the Soviet Union, there is no "neutral" law or "justice": the state legal system is a direct tool for the implementation of the Bolshevik policy. In 1922, in his critique of the People's Commissariat for Justice, he wrote:

> The P.C.J. has "forgotten" that that is its business, that it is its duty to pull up, shake up and rouse the people's courts and teach them to be ruthless and swift in chastising—with every means, including the firing squad—for abuse of the New Economic Policy.[41]

The underlying logic is: if courts do not serve Bolsheviks, whom do they serve? It can only be the enemy . . . So we have to admit that "equality before the law was never even an aspiration of Soviet revolutionary jurisprudence. The Bolsheviks did not see the law as a means to adjudicate civil and business disputes, or to dispense justice blindly; they viewed it as a mechanism to implement their social and political agenda."[42] Plus one cannot but note how Lenin, being aware of the problematic nature of his text, explicitly prohibits any mention of it to the public:

> P.S. There must not be the slightest mention of my letter in the press. Let anyone, who so wishes, write in his own name, without any mention of mine, and provide as many concrete data as possible.[43]

To Lenin's benefit, one should note that he insists Communists (members of the Bolshevik party) should be punished three times more harshly than non-Communists for economic crimes, so his proposal does not imply simple punishment of the class enemy. However, does this insistence not prove that he ignores—but is simultaneously aware of—the fact that what generates corruption is the very identification of the state and (Bolshevik) party, i.e., the unconstrained power of the party lacking any external control?

What should be our reply to this? Here enters what I have called the counter-revolution as part of the victory of an emancipatory movement: of course, there is no neutral law, no neutral justice, but this does not automatically imply that we should abandon any notion of universality which ignores the struggle between "us" and "them." We should formulate a new universality which, while privileging those who are exploited and dominated, *does this in the form of neutral universality*, thereby guaranteeing that the new law will pose a limit also to the emancipatory movement itself. In the ongoing struggle between "us" and "them," the law should also prevent the winning emancipatory agent from exerting limitless power—the law should limit also "our side." Or, in more political terms, that's why the state law should prevail over "our" party: "we" should fight for universality, for our hegemony in its space, without directly identifying ourselves as an organ of this universality. By contrast to Lenin, Robespierre and the Jacobins were to the end aware of this distance.

Appendices II

Appendix 5

"Generalized Foreclosure"? No, Thanks!

We have to be very cautious and precise when talking about the disintegration of the big Other in today's societies: this disintegration is not a straightforward process of approaching what French psychoanalyst Jacques-Alain Miller called "generalized foreclosure," a state in which the big Other no longer serves as the symbolic space in which subjects communicate (the idea is that, today, each of us is caught in their own balloon where s/he just gets mirrored back their own message). Does a large majority of people not continue to communicate through the reliance on some figure of the big Other? Plus, is the chaotic digital space of "fake news" nonetheless not a new form of big Other, a chaotic public space in which influencers fight for numbers of clicks? When we engage in spreading (fake or not) news on Facebook, we are not directly ourselves there, we play a certain role in this new big Other. And is the space of Cancel Culture also not a very strict form of the big Other in which those "cancelled" are excluded from the public space? This is why, although I highly appreciate Duane Rousselle's analyses of our predicament, I have problems with his thoughts on the function of irony within the clinic:

> In the same way irony is suitable, according to Miller, for the psychoanalyst as well as the revolutionary (and what about the lover?) because it maintains that the social link, at its most radical, is a fraud. It is for this reason that we can claim that psychoanalysis is radical. Irony exists there within an analysis when there is no longer any subject supposed to know, when the Other does not know. Humor, on the other hand, begins with a subject supposed to know. Irony begins when that subject supposed to know has fallen. This implies that there is irony in the psychoanalytic fall of the Other, in the revolutionary fall of

> the Other, but also in the psychotic's—schizophrenic's—foreclosure of the Other.[1]

"But also in ..."—can one really posit so easily the chain of equivalences between the fall of the Other in psychoanalysis, revolution, love, and psychosis? And is irony really a good name for the subject's stance after it assumes the fall of the Other? Is revolutionary politics not based on the idea of a social link which will NOT be a fraud (a link embodied in the revolutionary subject)? And does the same not hold for psychoanalysis? Lacan proclaimed that an analyst authorizes himself only by himself—but, as he then added with a little bit of sarcasm, others have to confirm that he actually authorized himself (otherwise any idiot could proclaim himself an analyst). A new dimension of collectivity enters here: we are no longer in the intimacy of the relationship between analysand and analyst. The analysand who is a candidate for the title of the analyst has to formulate his testimony in such a way that all traces of authentic subjective truth are erased from it (or, rather, become irrelevant): his subjective position of enunciation disappears, all that matters is the enunciated content. The analysand has to formulate his testimony in such a way that the two average and neutral "passeurs" (who know nothing about the analysand's subjective struggles) will be able to get it ... to do what with it? Simply to transmit it further to the jury (composed of three analysts of the school), which will then confirm (or not) that the candidate is an analyst of the school. So why is the candidate not allowed to render his testimony directly to the jury, why is there no direct contact between him and the jury? In order to prevent any initiatic closure, to prevent the jury serving as an initiatic body with special access to the truth and deep personal contact with the candidate—everything has to happen at the level of public knowledge which can be fully transmitted by two average stupid people.

This stupidity means nothing else than to be caught in the big Other, which is why Lacan concludes his "Vers un signifiant nouveau" with: "I am only relatively stupid—that is to say, I am as stupid as all people—perhaps because I got a little bit enlightened?"[2] One should read this relativization of stupidity—"not totally stupid"—in the strict sense of non-all: the point is not that Lacan has some specific insights which make him not entirely stupid.

There is nothing in Lacan which is not stupid, no exception to stupidity, so that what makes him not totally stupid is only *the very inconsistency of his stupidity*.[3] The name of this stupidity in which all people participate is, of course, the big Other. We should turn around here the well-known phrase "You have to be stupid not to see that!"—*la verité surgit de la méprise* means that, precisely, you *have* to be stupid to see that, i.e., as Lacan put it, *les non-dupes errent*, those who are not duped are in the wrong (this is the best critical description of cynics). In order to arrive at the truth, one has to be taken into an illusion—just recall how emancipatory politics can only be sustained by a belief in the (in some sense obviously "illusory") axiom of universal justice.

The non-stupid are thus cynics, and this is where the cynic who believes only hard facts falls short: when a judge speaks, there is in a way more truth in his words (the words of the institution of law) than in the direct reality of the person of judge; if one limits oneself to what one sees, one simply misses the point. This paradox is what Lacan aims at with his *les non-dupes errent* (those in the know err): those who do not let themselves be caught in the symbolic fiction and continue to believe their eyes only are the ones who err most. What a cynic who believes only his eyes miss is the efficiency of the symbolic fiction, the way this fiction structures our (experience of) reality. And what Rousselle celebrates as irony comes dangerously close to cynicism—and one has to distinguish here between cynical irony (not being duped by the Other) and irony in its more radical Mozartean sense.

The main premise of Peter Sellars's version of *Cosi fan tutte* is that the only true passionate love is the one between the philosopher Alfonzo and Despina, who engage in their experimenting with the two young couples in order to act out the deadlock of their own desperate love. This reading hits the very heart of Mozartean IRONY, which is to be opposed to cynicism. If, to simplify it to the utmost, a cynic fakes a belief that he privately mocks (publicly you preach sacrifice for the fatherland, privately you amass profits . . .), in irony, the subject takes things more seriously than he appears to—he secretly believes in what he publicly mocks. Alfonzo and Despina, the cold philosophical experimenter and the corrupted dissolute servant-girl, are the true passionate lovers using the two pathetic couples and their ridiculous erotic *imbroglio* as instruments to confront their traumatic attachment. Now, we can formulate the uniqueness of Mozartean irony: although, in it, music is already fully autonomized with regard to words, it *does not yet lie*. Mozartean irony is the unique moment when the truth really "speaks in music," when music occupies the position of the Unconscious rendered by Lacan with his famous motto "*Moi la verité, je parle*." And it is only today, in our postmodern times, allegedly full of irony and lacking belief, that Mozartean irony reaches its full actuality, confronting us with the embarrassing fact that—not in our interior, but in our acts themselves, in our social practice—we believe much more than we are aware of.

What is foreclosed in psychosis is not the big Other as such but the Other of the Other, its master-signifier which holds the big Other together, what Lacan first called the Name-of-the-Father. This Other of the Other is, of course, a fraud, a semblance, but what we get after its fall is not a generalized foreclosure of the big Other but the space of cynical perversion filled with subjects who err because they are not duped. This is why the description of generalized foreclosure as a carnival without limitation in which every entity is an exception is misleading:

> Today the exception has become the universal. Indeed, "all X" is the multiple that occupies the place of the exception, producing an exception generalized to all speaking beings. It is thus against the background of this generalized foreclosure [of the Name of the Father] that fraternity unfolds. It finds in social networks, which have become the public square of the age, the means that are adequate to it. The "carnival," as Lacan called it in his interview with a journalist in Rome in 1974, has become a carnival without limitation of place thanks to the power of the virtual, which has modified the category of perceptual space, which until now required the displacement of the body.[4]

But is there really no limitation in this carnival? Does the limitation, in some sense much stronger than the paternal prohibition which solicits the desire to transgress it, not return with a vengeance in the Politically Correct Woke or Cancel culture? The characterization of Woke as "racism in the time of the many without the One" may appear problematic, but it hits the mark: in an almost exact opposite to the traditional racism which opposes a foreign intruder posing a threat to the unity of the One (say, immigrants and Jews to our Nation), Woke reacts to those who are suspected not to truly abandon old forms of the One ("patriots," proponents of patriarchal values, Eurocentrists . . .).

It is in these terms that we should account for the paradox of how, in Woke and Cancel Culture, non-binary fluidity coincides with its opposite. The prestigious *École Normale Supérieure* in Paris is now debating a proposal to establish in their dormitories corridors reserved exclusively for individuals who have chosen mixity/diversity (*mixité choisie*) as their sexual identity, with the exclusion of cisgender men (men whose sense of personal identity and gender corresponds with their birth sex).[5] The proposed rules are strict—for example, it is prohibited for persons who do not fit the criterion to even briefly pass through these corridors. Plus the proposal opens up the path to further restrictions: if enough individuals define their identity in narrower terms, they can reserve a corridor just for themselves. One should note three features of this proposal: (1) it excludes only cisgender men, not cisgender women; (2) it is not based on any objective criteria of classification but only on subjective self-designation; (3) it calls for further classificatory subdivisions, demonstrating how all the emphasis on plasticity, choice and diversity ends up in what one cannot but call a new apartheid, a network of fixed identities. This is why the Woke stance provides the supreme case of how permissiveness turns into universal prohibition: in a Politically Correct regime, we never know if and when some of us will be cancelled for his/her acts or words, the criteria are murky.

This murkiness brings us to a key aspect of every actual state power edifice: no matter how democratic and responsive to its subjects it is, one can easily detect an implicit but unmistakable signal in it: "Forget about our limitations—ultimately, we can do whatever we want with you!" This excess is not a contingent supplement spoiling the purity of power but its necessary constituent—without it, without the threat of arbitrary omnipotence, state power is not a true power, it loses its authority. And we have to stop playing games of limiting power to a rational-democratic extent: we have to accept this excess fully. It is the Trumpian populists who undermine it.

Appendix 6

Shamelessly Ashamed

To understand what is false in today's Cancel Culture, we have to take a closer look at the notion of shame, and at how this notion changed recently. In his *Two Revelations on Shame*, Robert Pfaller[1] convincingly refutes two common notions of shame as opposed to guilt (shame comes from outside in contrast to guilt; shame comes from our failure, from a not-good-enough). Guilt comes in different grades, it involves rational (counter)argumentation and the possibility of pardon, while shame overwhelms us all of a sudden—we just wish to disappear, no rational way out is offered to us. Pfaller demonstrates how the role of shame changed in today's culture: shame is no longer the shame of failure or weakness, but the shame of an obscene too-muchness which can be success itself. I am not ashamed of my lack or insufficiency—I myself appear to myself as an obscene excess, an element out of place, "I just want to disappear, sink into the ground (because I am too fat, I emit flatulence in public. . .)." "The Ego perceives itself as an obscene excess,"[2] as an element that lacks its own proper place in the symbolic order which defines the coordinates of our reality: "Shame is not triggered by a not-enough, but by a too-much. It comes from below, not from above."[3] I experience shame not when something in me doesn't fit my super-ego but when my ego is disturbed by something from my sub-ego (*Es* which precedes symbolic castration). Here, perhaps, Pfaller proceeds too quickly: symbolic castration does not run between *Es* and *Ich*, it is at work already in the very heart of *Es*, and the so-called "normal" functioning of the Ego is based on the disavowal of the trauma of castration. This is also why the weird agency of the "innocent observer" (on which Pfaller focuses) is not located in the Id: it is a figure of the big Other, an agent of pure appearance, and the duty of the Ego is to maintain appearances, to prevent the "innocent observer" from noticing them. Pfaller deploys this functioning perfectly:

> Shame doesn't arise when all know about a painful matter. Shame bursts out only when an "as-if" breaks down. /. . ./ When the attempt to maintain a public secret fails, shame arises in everybody who is present.[4]

This means that shame is not simply external: I can feel ashamed also when I am alone. What we call "manners" or "tact" means that we learned to pretend that the big Other didn't notice the disturbing element. This role of the innocent observer (the guardian of appearances) also accounts for the strange fact that I can feel shame for others who should be ashamed of themselves: when the "innocent observer" (a figure of big Other) registers the excess, we all who admit this agency of innocent observer feel equally ashamed since it became obvious that we all knew the reality and just discreetly ignored it.

Let's say that somebody in a closed social circle (like behind a large table) does something socially inappropriate, like emit a loud flatulence; the proper thing to do is not to smile at him kindly with the message "Ok, you did it, but no problem . . ."; the proper thing is to ignore it totally, to go on as if nothing happened. A different version of such a way to react happened to Queen Elizabeth I: when, at a court reception, she emitted a loud flatulence, one of her courtiers turned to her and said "Sorry, your majesty, I couldn't stop it!" taking the inappropriate act upon himself. (According to the legend, he was amply rewarded by the Queen for saving her face.)

Stalinism is perhaps the clearest political case of such an innocent observer—we all know how absolutely crucial appearances were in Stalinism: the Stalinist regime reacted with total panic whenever there was a threat that appearances would be disturbed (say, that some accident which rendered clear the failure of the regime would be reported in the public media: there were, in the Soviet media, no black chronicles, no reports on crimes and prostitution, not to mention workers or public protests). Let us just recall why it never rained during the first of May parades in Moscow: the authorities feared that the rain disturbing the parade would be perceived as an indication that the party is not all-powerful, so they sprayed the sky above Moscow with gases that prevented the formation of clouds. What characterizes Stalinism is precisely this conjunction of raw brutal terror and the need to protect appearances—even if we all know something is not true, the big Other (of appearances) should not notice it . . . With today's new breed of obscene leaders, relations are turned around. Donald Trump is famous not in spite of his obscenities but on account of them. In the old royal courts, a king often had a clown whose function was to destroy the noble appearance with sarcastic jokes and dirty remarks (thereby confirming, by contrast, the king's dignity). Trump doesn't need a clown, he already is his own clown, and no wonder that his acts are the inversion of the standard situation: Trump is not a dignified person about whom obscene rumours circulate; he is an (openly) obscene person who wants his obscenity to appear as a mask of his dignity. Alenka Zupančič elaborated the contrast between this logic and the classic logic of domination in which

> the smear of the king's image is simultaneously the smear of the king himself and as such inadmissible. The new logic is: let the image be castrated in all possible ways while I can do more or less everything I want. Even more, I can do what I want precisely because of and with the help of this new image.[5]

This, again, is how Trump functions: his public image is smeared in all possible ways; people are surprised at how he, again and again, manages to shock them by reaching a new depth of obscenity, but at the same time he governs in the full sense of the term, imposing unheard-of presidential decrees, etc.—castration is here turned around in an unheard-of way. The basic fact of what Lacan calls "symbolic castration" is the gap that separates me, my (ultimately miserable) psychic and social reality, from my symbolic mandate (identity): I am a king not because of my immanent features but because I occupy a certain place in the socio-symbolic edifice, i.e., because others treat me like a king. With today's obscene master, "castration" is displaced onto his public image—Trump makes fun of himself and deprives himself of almost the last vestiges of dignity, he mocks his opponents with shocking vulgarity, but this self-depreciation not only in no way affects the efficiency of his administrative acts, it even allows him to perform these acts with the utmost brutality as if the open assuming of the "castration" of the public image (renouncing the insignia of dignity) enables the full "non-castrated" display of actual political power. It is crucial to see how the "castration" of the public image is not just a signal that this image doesn't matter, that it is only actual administrative power that counts—the full deployment of administrative power, of enforcing measures, is possible only when the public image is "castrated."

And what about shame here? Lacan was known for shamelessly emitting flatulences and burping in public without restraint, not caring not only for the innocent observer but also for the embarrassment of the others around him. One should nonetheless raise the question: did Lacan really just ignore public manners or was his behaviour part of a strategy to embarrass others? And maybe something similar holds for Trump: in a kind of interpassive shaming, he counts on us, his subjects, to be ashamed for him. And the "Left" gladly participates in this game:

> Instead of a rebellious, enlightening Left ready to debate every question with its enemy since it feels assured about its better arguments, now a fussing pseudo-Left appears which fears argumentative confrontation and wants to close the mouth especially to its own people.[6]

Why? Because of the clear link between shame and enjoyment: a subject can secretly enjoy feeling shame (especially when he is feeling shame for what another did or is). What is missing today is the reflexivity of shame: in our new culture of shame, we experience what Pfaller calls a "shame which became shameless."[7] The all-pervasiveness of shame thus at the same time signals its lack: we are not embarrassed by our shame, we *shamelessly enjoy it*. The PC stance is "permeated by a common disappearing of desire"[8] which, one might add, culminates in the desire to disappear, and the exemplary case of this desire to just disappear is a strong feeling of shame.

The excess which causes shame is profoundly linked to some kind of surplus-enjoyment: I feel shame (if I see myself observed by the big Other) when doing something that I secretly enjoy (like emitting flatulence), plus—and this reflexive turn is crucial—I enjoy this shame itself. In some of his acts (but not all of them), Trump acts without shame; the liberal Leftists feel shame for him, and this shame attributed to the Other is in itself a source of pleasure (I enjoy others feeling shame for what I am doing). However, Trump's shamelessness is not unlimited—say, he would never shamelessly claim he is bisexual or gay; in his eyes, those whom he dismisses as non-patriotic should be ashamed of themselves. But, in contrast to the liberal Left, Trump would not feel himself ashamed on behalf of what the Left is doing.

Shame is thus simply not a reliable indicator that something is wrong. Recall how, in Mark Twain's *Huck Finn*, Huck does the right thing (helping the black slave Jim to escape), but he feels ashamed of it . . . We should begin with shame that something outrageous is possible, but the next step is to submit to critical analysis the entire situation, our shame included. How, then, can we do things which, according to the predominant figure of the big Other, should make us ashamed without actually feeling shame? There is a form of perversion at work today which allows us to avoid shame: to exclude oneself from a reality regulated by a big Other and intervene in it from a safe distance. An exemplary case of such a perversion is provided by *Sarajevo Safari* (Miran Zupanič, Slovenia, 2022), a documentary about the arguably most bizarre pathological event that took place during the siege of Sarajevo from 1992 to 1996. It is well known that snipers on the hills surrounding Sarajevo occupied by Serb forces were shooting arbitrary residents on the streets below them. It was also well known that selected Serb allies (mostly Russians) were invited to shoot a couple of shots on Sarajevo, but this was considered an honour, a sign of special appreciation, not business. Now we learn about the real business. Dozens of rich foreigners (mostly from the US, UK, and Italy, although some also from Russia) paid high fees for the chance to shoot at the residents of besieged Sarajevo. The trip was organized by the Bosnian Serb Army: the customers were transported from Belgrade to Pale (the capital of the Serb Bosnia in mountains near Sarajevo) and then brought to a safe place with a view of Sarajevo down the valley.[9]

We learn from the documentary that not only the top command of the Serb Bosnian Army but NATO peacekeeping forces in Bosnia were also aware of this safari—so why didn't they render it public or simply bomb the sniper place? But what is of special interest here is the form of the subjectivity of a safari "hunter": victims were not personalized, they remained anonymous; a symbolic wall separated the hunter from the target; it was nonetheless not a video game, victims were part of reality, and the awareness of this fact accounts for the perverse thrill of such "hunting." To be more precise, it is not the victim who was here de-realized, it was the "hunter" himself who excluded himself from ordinary reality and perceived himself as located in some safe place above reality. This is how reality itself became part of a spectacle in which the hunter can pretend that he is not personally involved.

For this reason, *Sarajevo Safari* arguably goes even a step further than another documentary, *The Act of Killing* (directed by Joshua Oppenheimer and Christine Cynn, Final Cut Film Production, Copenhagen, 2012) The film—shot in Medan, Indonesia, in 2007—reconstructs the story of Anwar Congo and his friends, who are now respected politicians, but were gangsters and death squad leaders playing a key role in the 1966 killing of circa 2.5 million alleged Communist sympathizers, mostly ethnic Chinese. After their victory, their terrible acts were not relegated to the status of the "dirty secret," the founding crime whose traces are to be obliterated—on the contrary, they boast openly about the details of their massacres (the way to strangle a victim with a wire, the way to cut a throat, how to rape a woman in a most pleasurable way . . .). In October 2007, the Indonesian state TV produced a talk show celebrating Anwar and his friends; in the middle of the show, after Anwar says their killings were inspired by gangster movies, the beaming moderator turns to the cameras and says: "Amazing! Let's give Anwar Congo a round of applause!" When she asks Anwar if he fears the revenge of the victim's relatives, Anwar answers: "They can't. When they raise their heads, we wipe them out!" His henchman adds: "We'll exterminate them all!", and the audience explodes into exuberant cheers . . . One has to see this to believe it's possible.

However, with all the horror it discloses, *The Act of Killing* reports on (and re-enacts for the camera) something that already happened, while in *Sarajevo Safari* the killing itself is organized as a spectacle. There is something perversely honest in this: are top corporate managers not engaged in a similar safari? Their decisions may ruin many lives, thousands may lose jobs—and we can imagine some of them observing the ruined families of a guy they fired or in another way destroyed. And—our final example of the same madness—did Dmitry Medvedev, a former Russian president who now serves as deputy chairman of Russia's Security Council, not rely on a similar logic when he recently said that

> the U.S.-led NATO military alliance would be too scared of a "nuclear apocalypse" to directly enter the conflict in response to Russia using tactical nuclear weapons . . . I believe that NATO will not directly intervene in the conflict even in this situation. After all, the security of Washington, London, Brussels is much more important for the North Atlantic Alliance than the fate of a dying Ukraine that no one needs. . . . The supply of modern weapons is just a business for Western countries. Overseas and European demagogues are not going to perish in a nuclear apocalypse. Therefore, they will swallow the use of any weapon in the current conflict.[10]

Are we aware of what these sentences imply? Medvedev is ready to risk the lives of billions for a small piece of land—billions in Latin America, Africa and Asia who are NOT involved in the Ukrainian conflict. Back in August 2022, Medvedev already said that a proposal to punish Russia for war crimes in Ukraine threatened the existence of mankind, given Moscow's nuclear arsenal.[11] Again, where does Medvedev speak from when he talks like that, what is his subjective position? He does not include himself amongst those who will perish, as if he will somehow survive the global nuclear catastrophe—as if humanity is like Sarajevo in a valley and he is at a safe distance on a hill above it. Of course, he knows that he will be affected by the end of mankind, but he speaks as if he doesn't know it.

It is clear to everybody that Medvedev's words have to be read against the background of Russia's formal annexation of the Russian-occupied parts of Ukraine: in this way, any Ukrainian intrusion into those parts could be declared a threat to the survival of Russia as a state, and thus justify the use of tactical nuclear weapons . . . Not being a specialist, I ignore here the wider context of this move (Russian military setbacks, etc.); I just want to follow Medvedev's logic to the end. He also said Russia will "do everything" to prevent nuclear weapons from appearing in "our hostile neighbors" like "Nazi Ukraine"—but since it is Russia which threatens the very existence of another state (Ukraine), does this other state not also the right to defend its existence by tactical nuclear weapons? We should thus take seriously the idea that it is Ukraine which should be given nuclear weapons to establish a basic parity with Russia. Recall Putin's words:

> In order to claim some kind of leadership—I am not even talking about global leadership, I mean leadership in any area—any country, any people, any ethnic group should ensure their sovereignty. Because there is no in-between, no intermediate state: either a country is sovereign, or it is a colony, no matter what the colonies are called.[12]

From these lines it is clear that, in Putin's view, Ukraine falls into the latter category: it is a colony, no matter what it is called. Our strategy should be precisely NOT to treat Ukraine as anyone's colony. This is also why we should resolutely reject Harlan Ullman's argument that, in the same way peace in Korea was achieved by direct negotiations between the US and the opposite side, bypassing South Korea, the powerful Western states should also intervene directly, bypassing Ukraine:

> How does this war end if Putin is determined to win? Should we not be at least considering acceptable terms for all parties to end the war? Clemenceau observed that 'war is too important to be left to the generals.' In this case, is Ukraine too important to be left to Zelensky? The United States needs a strategy with an off-ramp to seek an end to the violence and the war.[13]

But is this not precisely what Russia wants? I have no doubt that some Leftist peaceniks will reject with horror my suggestion, interpreting Medvedev's statements as a warning to Ukraine and the West to show constraint—we shouldn't push Russia too much into a corner . . . This, however, is precisely the stance we should avoid at any price. The peaceniks who are against NATO and sending arms to Ukraine ignore the key fact that *it was Western help that allowed Ukraine to resist*—without it, Ukraine would be all long occupied. This help led to today's stalemate which created the conditions for a possible peace compromise. So, in Germany, I fully support the stance of the Green Party which not only advocates full support for Ukraine but also proposes to use the ongoing oil and gas crisis as a unique opportunity to make our industries greener. The Greens thus go in the exactly opposite direction with regard to the predominant Western politics which struggles with the problem of how to help Ukraine while limiting the impact of this help on our established way of life: the German Green party's plan is to use the Ukrainian war in a positive way, not just as an obstacle but as an incentive for a general reorientation of our economy and social life. Two of their ministers in Olaf Scholz's government occupy posts where they can act in this direction: Annalena Baerbock advocates a "post-pacifist" foreign policy, and Robert Habeck serves as Federal Minister for Economic Affairs and Climate Action.

The most despicable figures in our public space are the peaceniks from Chomsky through Varoufakis to Peterson: they first insisted that Ukraine simply CANNOT win a war against Russia, but now when it IS winning they repeat that it SHOULDN'T (be allowed to) win (or even gain too much) because this may provoke Putin's ire and he may push the button—the idea is now that Putin is not a ruthless conqueror but a dangerous madman, so peace (preventing nuclear war) should have priority over all other considerations . . . For months the West is obsessed by what is going on in Putin's mind (although to me his goals are pretty clear)—I think it is much more enigmatic and ambiguous what goes on in the Western liberal mind. Recall how, in the first days of the war, Western powers offered Zelensky to take him out of Kyiv with a special plane, implying that the situation is already lost, so let's get over it fast . . . This hysterical precipitous offer made palpable the true desire of the West (to get over the crisis fast), a desire which was spoiled by the unexpected Ukrainian resistance. We hear again and again that Russia should be allowed to save face—but statements like Medvedev's make it impossible for Ukraine and the West to save *their* faces, declaring in advance a compromise, proof of Western cowardice! One of the arguments against Ullman is the true enigma of Medvedev's words: why is he publicly saying what he is saying? Why does he add insult to injury and in advance interpret the Western refusal to respond with a nuclear counter-attack as a sign of timidity?

Here we unexpectedly enter the domain of philosophy: Putin's and Medvedev's words clearly echo the most famous passage in Hegel's *Phenomenology*, the dialectic of master and servant. If, in the confrontation of the two self-consciousnesses engaged in the struggle for life and death, each side is ready to go to the end in risking its life, then there is no winner—one dies, the other survives but without another to recognize it. The whole history of freedom and recognition—in short, the whole of history, the whole of human culture—can take place only with an original compromise: in the eye-to-eye confrontation, one side (the future servant) "averts its eyes," it is not ready to go to the end. Medvedev presumes that the decadent hedonist West will avert its eyes—however, what complicates the situation is that, as we know from the Cold War, in a nuclear confrontation there is no winner, both sides disappear.

But the true madness resides in the fact that we are talking about the threat of nuclear annihilation while we are ALL committing collective suicide by way of ignoring environmental changes—as if the self-annihilation towards which we already are slowly drifting can be made less terrifying if we focus on the potential future of nuclear war . . . This threat of nuclear destruction makes us (not all of us but those who can push the buttons) a version of *homo deus*, but in a negative sense: the only divine act we are now able to commit is the one of self-destruction—something that, as we learned recently, a stupid virus is also able to do.

This brings us back to the fact that *Sarajevo Safari* is becoming more and more the basic situation of the privileged elite not just in the West but in all parts of the world. We don't live IN the real world; reality is in the valley that we observe from a safe distance, and we intervene in it for a thrilling experience that does not endanger us. Unfortunately, reality catches up with us from time to time, and we mostly react to it like the peace-loving West, trying not to provoke too much the beast in the valley.

Appendix 7

A Muddle Instead of a Movie

To prevent the excessive use of exploding firecrackers in the holiday period, the Slovene Ministry of Defence posted on December 23, 2021, a tweet entitled "Become a soldier!" which says: "DON'T THROW FIRECRACKERS!!! Become a volunteer soldier, ignite an explosive, throw a bomb!" The pragmatic reason is clear: Slovenia doesn't have mandatory military service and lacks soldiers, plus throwing firecrackers can occasionally cause some damage. However, the brutal irony of this tweet cannot but strike the eye. The common wisdom is that, in order to avoid actual violence, we should channel our need for it into its more sublimated forms like competitive sport events (boxing). We read a lot about the potentially harmful consequences of children playing violent video games of killing opponents—the debate is: do such games incite real violence or do they allow players to act out their destructive impulses in a harmless way and thus prevent real violence? But the case of the Slovene ministry tweet is almost the opposite: in order to avoid throwing firecrackers (which is, in spite of the dangers, a minimally sublimated form of violence), become a soldier and train for the real violence of wounding and killing people! This perverted logic is the hidden truth of many of today's complaints that we live in a fake virtual world and that we should return to real life, whatever the risks. Far from being opposed to the fascination with fictions, the escape into the Real is its immanent other side—both extremes characterize what was once called postmodernism, and the problem with *The Matrix Resurrections*[1] is that it proposes a postmodern solution in an era which left postmodernism behind.

What is postmodernism reduced to its minimum? In the opening scene of the TV version of Agatha Christie's *Hickory*

Dickory Dock, a mouse scurries through the walls of a boarding house in London searching for morsels of food. Having made his way to a bedroom upstairs, he pauses and twitches his whiskers: the crumbs from a bedtime cookie are lying on a saucer, but something strange is happening and he dare not advance to the plate of crumbs—one of the humans is killing the nice young girl who always eats cookies at bedtime.[2] The mouse knows the murderer's identity, but the police are confused until Poirot enters the scene. From time to time, the mouse is shown in a close-up crawling in the background; it is noticed by humans only at the very end, after Poirot explains the case—at that very moment, the mouse appears on the bookshelf behind Poirot, Poirot's secretary Ms Lemon notices it and emits a terrified scream. So Poirot finally puts in words what the mouse knew all the time . . . But already this reading of the presence of the mouse in contrast to the narrative line is too much, it ignores the stupid meaningless presence of the mouse as a little bit of the real totally indifferent to human concerns—this is how postmodernism works. And my first reaction to *The Matrix Resurrections* was that it has too many persons who, although officially part of the narrative, are effectively nothing but mice running around. There was much praise for the "complexity" of the story, as if the blurring of clear choices somehow makes the movie psychologically more "realist." In a properly postmodern way, this complexity is inscribed into the narrative form itself as a wealth of self-reflexive moments: "quotes" from the preceding *Matrix* trilogy, bits of dialogue which evoke theories about the *Matrix* series or theories which served as its foundation (Baudrillard, especially)—as Rightist rednecks like to say about intellectuals, Lana Wachovsky is often too bright for her own good.

The first thing that strikes the eye in the multitude of reviews of *The Matrix Resurrections* is how easily the movie's plot (especially its ending) was interpreted as a metaphor for our socio-economic situation. Radical Leftist pessimists read it as an insight into how, to put it bluntly, there is no hope for humanity: we cannot survive outside the Matrix (the network of corporate capital that controls us), freedom is impossible. Then there are social-democratic pragmatic "realists" who see in the movie a vision of some kind of progressive alliance between humans and machines: sixty years after the destructive Machine Wars, "the human survivors have allied with some of the machines to fight an anomaly that jeopardizes the whole Matrix. Scarcity among the Machines led to a civil war that saw a faction of Machines and programs defect and join human society."[3] Humans also change: Io (a human city in reality outside the Matrix led by General Niobe) is a much better place to live than Zion, their previous city in reality (there are clear hints of destructive revolutionary fanaticism in Zion in previous Matrix movies).

At this point, we have to introduce a key factor and a new person. The scarcity among the Machines refers not just to the devastating effects of the war but above all to the lack of energy produced by humans for the matrix. Remember the basic premise of the *Matrix* series: what we experience as the reality we live in is an artificial virtual reality generated by the "Matrix," the mega-computer directly attached to all our minds; it is in place so that we can be effectively reduced to a passive state of living batteries providing the Matrix with the energy. So when (some of the) people "awaken" from their immersion in the Matrix-controlled virtual reality, this awakening is not the opening into the wide space of external reality, but first the horrible realization of this enclosure, where each of us is effectively just a foetus-like organism, immersed in pre-natal fluid . . . This utter passivity is the foreclosed fantasy that sustains our conscious experience as active, self-positing subjects—it is the ultimate *perverse* fantasy, the notion that we are ultimately *instruments* of the Other's (Matrix's) *jouissance*, sucked out of our life-substance like batteries.[4] Therein resides the true libidinal enigma of this dispositif: *why* does the Matrix need human energy? The purely energetic solution is, of course, meaningless: the Matrix could have easily found another, more reliable, source of energy which would have not demanded the extremely complex arrangement of the virtual reality coordinated for millions of human units. The only consistent answer is: the Matrix feeds on human's *jouissance*—so we are here back at the fundamental Lacanian thesis that the big Other itself, far from being an anonymous machine, needs the constant influx of *jouissance*. This is how we should turn around the state of things presented by the film: what the film renders as the scene of our awakening into our true situation is effectively its exact opposite, the very fundamental fantasy that sustains our being.—But how does the Matrix react to the fact that humans produce less energy? Here a new figure called "Analyst" enters: he discovers that if the Matrix manipulates the fears and desires of humans, they produce more energy that can be sucked by the machines:

> The Analyst is the new Architect, the manager of this new version of the Matrix. But where the Architect sought to control human minds through cold, hard math and facts, the Analyst likes to take a more personal approach, manipulating feelings to create fictions that keep the blue-pills in line. (He observes that humans will "believe the craziest shit," which really isn't very far off from the truth if you've ever spent any time on Facebook.) The Analyst says that his approach has made humans produce more energy to feed the Machines than ever before, all while keeping them from wanting to escape the simulation.[5]

With a little bit of irony we could say that the Analyst corrects the falling profit rate of using humans as energy batteries: he realizes that just stealing enjoyment from humans is not productive enough, we (the Matrix) should also manipulate the experience of humans that serve as batteries so that they will experience more enjoyment. The problem is just that, although the new regulator of the Matrix is called "Analyst" (with an obvious reference to the psychoanalyst), he doesn't act as a Freudian analyst but as a rather primitive utilitarian following the maxim of avoiding pain and fear and getting pleasure. There is no pleasure-in-pain, no "beyond the pleasure principle," no death drive, in contrast to the first film in which Smith, the agent of the Matrix, gives a different, much more Freudian explanation:

> Did you know that the first Matrix was designed to be a perfect human world? Where none suffered, where everyone would be happy? It was a disaster. NO one would accept the program. Entire crops [of the humans serving as batteries] were lost. Some believed we lacked the programming language to describe your perfect world. But I believe that, as a species, human beings define their reality through suffering and misery. The perfect

> world was a dream that your primitive cerebrum kept trying to wake up from. Which is why the Matrix was re-designed to this: the peak of your civilization.[6]

One could effectively claim that Smith (let us not forget: not a human being like others but a virtual embodiment of the Matrix—the big Other—itself) is the stand-in for the figure of the analyst within the universe of the film much more than the Analyst. This regression of the last film is confirmed by another archaic feature: the affirmation of the productive force of sexual relationships:

> Analyst explains that after Neo and Trinity died, he resurrected them to study them, and found they overpowered the system when they worked together, but if they are kept close to each other without making contact, the other humans within the Matrix would produce more energy for the machines.[7]

In many media *The Matrix Resurrections* was hailed as less "binary," as more open towards the "rainbow" of transgender experiences—but, as we can see, the old Hollywood formula of the production of a couple matrix is here again: "Neo himself has no interest in anything except rekindling his relationship with Trinity."[8]

This brings us back to the basic point: what does the Matrix Machine stand for if we read it not as a direct description of our reality but as a metaphor for our actual situation? It stands for two big Others, two alienated substances that control us: *capital* and *the symbolic order*, the order of symbolic fiction that structures our reality. In both cases, the danger to resist is that of a paranoiac reading—as if capital is impersonated by corporate bosses or bank managers who control the game, or as if the symbolic universe is programmed by a Matrix-like machine.

The best-known scene in the first *Matrix*[9] movie occurs when Morpheus offers Neo the choice between Blue Pill and Red Pill. But this choice is a strange non-choice: when we live immersed in virtual reality we didn't take any pill, so the only choice is "Take the red pill or do nothing." The blue pill is a placebo, it changes nothing. Plus we don't have only virtual reality regulated by the Matrix (accessible if we choose the blue pill) and external "real reality" (the devastated real world full of ruins accessible if we choose the red pill); we have the Machine itself which constructs and regulates our experience (this, the flow of digital formulas and not the ruins, is what Morpheus refers to when he says to Neo "Welcome to the desert of the real.") This Machine is (in the film's universe) an object present in "real reality": gigantic computers constructed by humans which hold us prisoners and regulate our self-experiences.

The choice between the blue pill and the red pill in the first *Matrix* movie is false, but this does not mean that all reality is just in our brain: we interact in the real world but through the fantasies imposed on us by the symbolic universe in which we live. This brings us back to the beginning of the movie where Neo visits a therapist (Analyst) in recovery from a suicide attempt. The source of his suffering is that he has no way of verifying the reality of his confused thoughts, so he is afraid of losing his mind. In the course of the film, we learn that "the therapist is the least trustworthy source that Neo could have turned to. The therapist is not just part of a fantasy that might be a reality, and vice versa [. . .] He is just one more layer of fantasy-as-reality, and reality-as-fantasy, a mess of whims, and desires, and dreams that exist in two states at once." Is, then, Neo's suspicion which drove him to suicide not just confirmed?

The film's ending brings hope by merely giving the opposite spin to this insight: yes, our world is composed just of layers of "fantasy-as-reality, and reality-as-fantasy, a mess of whims, and desires," there is no Archimedean point which eludes the deceitful layers of fake realities. However, this very fact opens up a new space of freedom—the freedom to intervene and rewrite fictions that dominate us. Since our world is composed just of layers of "fantasy-as-reality, and reality-as-fantasy, a mess of whims, and desires," this means that the Matrix is also a mess: the paranoiac version is wrong, there is no hidden agent (Architect or Analyst) who controls it all and secretly pulls the strings. The lesson is that "we should learn to fully embrace the power of the stories that we spin for ourselves, whether they be video games or complex narratives about our own pasts [. . .] – we might rewrite *everything*. We can make of fear and desire as we wish; we can alter and shape the people who we love, and we dream of." The movie thus ends with a rather boring version of the postmodern notion that there is no ultimate "real reality," just an interplay of the multitude of digital fictions:

> Neo and Trinity have given up on the search of epistemic foundations. They do not kill the therapist who has kept them in the bondage of The Matrix. Instead, they thank him. After all, through his work, they have discovered the great power of re-description, the freedom that comes when we stop our search for truth, whatever that nebulous concept might mean, and strive forever for new ways of understanding ourselves. And then, arm in arm, they take off, flying through a world that is theirs to make of.[10]

The film thus ends at the lowest point of ideology, celebrating "the great power of re-description" which enables us to obliterate every Real as a temporary obstacle that can be undone through re-description. It obliterates the horror of our utter submission to the Matrix, of our reduction to its source of energy, which is the Real sustaining our false freedom to circulate in different realities regulated by the Matrix.

Every reader has for sure noticed that, in my description of the movie, I heavily rely on a multitude of reviews which I extensively quote. The reason is now clear: in spite of its occasional brilliance, the film is ultimately not worth seeing—which is why I also wrote this account without seeing it. The editorial that appeared in *Pravda* on January 28, 1936, brutally dismissed Shostakovich's opera *Lady Macbeth of the Mtsensk District* as "Muddle Instead of Music" (the text's title). Although *The Matrix Resurrections* is very intelligently made and full of admirable effects, it ultimately remains a muddle instead of a movie. *Resurrections* is the fourth film in the *Matrix* series, so let's just hope that Lana's next movie will be what the fifth symphony was for Shostakovich, an American artist's creative response to justified criticism.

Appendix 8

How to Love a Homeland in Our Global Era

Perhaps the ultimate form of the self-annihilating negation of negation is a certain mode of melancholy, a melancholy which arises when, say, I am leaving my home permanently: what makes the situation melancholic is not just seeing how my beloved home is disappearing from my life but the sadness of knowing that *this disappearance itself will disappear*: there will be a moment when I will no longer miss my home but simply stop caring about it, a moment when homesickness itself, not just home, will disappear . . . However, what if a home appears "as such," is experienced as a home, only through (the threat of) its disappearance? In her *How to love a homeland*,[1] Oxana Timofeeva deals with this topic, combining in a very productive way autobiography and theory: apropos her childhood memories of living in small Siberian towns, she provides the outlines of "loving your homeland" which is starkly opposed to nationalist-patriotic "territorialization." Her theoretical references reach from Platonov through Deleuze and Guattari to Michael Marder, and her vision of a "homeland" consists of a unique combination of humans, animals, plants, landscapes and wind—a texture of what Saroj Giri calls "objects as comrades."[2] The far-reaching importance of her small book is that it recaptures for the Left a topic usually monopolized by the Rightist blood-and-soil populists. When she talks about "homeland," her starting point is not a big ethnic group organized as a nation-state but displaced nomadic groups.

In his great masterpieces, Platonov focuses on a post-revolutionary situation when the new Communist power tries to mobilize these groups for the Communist struggle: each of his works "departs from the same political problem of how to build communism: of what communism means and how the communist idea meets the concrete conditions and reality of the post-revolutionary society."[3] Platonov's answer to this problem is paradoxical, far from the usual dissident rejection of Communism. His result is a negative one, all his stories are stories of a failure, the "synthesis" between the Communist project and the displaced nomadic groups ends in a void; there is no unity between proletarians and less-than-proletarians. The wandering organic intellectuals are a supplement to the wandering masses, classes and communities, and they are all accompanied in their migration by animals, plants and the natural landscape. The protagonist of *Dzhan* (*Soul* in English translation),[4] Nazar Chagataev, returns to his native town in Turkestan on a party errand to find the lost nomadic nation Dzhan, from which he had come, in order to establish a socialist order. Although the typically Platonovian utopian group is still here—the "nation," a desert community of marginals who lost the will to live—the hero is now a Stalinist educator schooled in Moscow; he returns to the desert to introduce the "nation" to scientific and cultural progress and thus restore their will to live. Platonov, of course, remains faithful to his ambiguity: at the novel's end, the hero has to accept that he cannot teach others anything. So the radical cut Platonov depicts is not between the "spontaneous" proletarian crowd and the organized Communist forces but between the two aspects of the proletarian crowd itself, between the two social "nothings": the strictly proletarian "nothing" of the modern workers generated by capitalism, and the "less-than-nothing" of those not integrated into the system, not even as its immanent negativity, as it is made clear in this short exchange from *Chevengur*:

> "Who did you bring us?" Chepurny asked Prokofy [...] "That's proletarians and others", Prokofy said. Chepurny was disturbed, "What others? Again the layer of residual swine?" [...] "The others are the others. Nobody. They're even worse than the proletariat."[5]

Incidentally, these "others" who are "even worse than the proletariat" (i.e., who are not exploited in the classic Marxist sense of producing surplus-value) abound today, from women's unpaid labour to aborigines whose environment is ruined by exploitation, from refugees wandering around to precarious workers whose only land is "nomadland." (Crucial distinctions are to be introduced here. Işık Barış Fidaner (in a personal communication) characterized the proletariat's subjective stance as masculine versus the precariat's as feminine: proletarians act like obsessionals who do not really hurry (even/especially when they put it on as a show) since they wait for their Master to die (for capitalism to disintegrate), while precarians act like hysterics compelled to really hurry (even/especially when they display absolute patience) as their Master is obviously already dead. This opposition perfectly captures the contrast between the two groups of the exploited today: assured of its relatively stable situation (in Western developed countries, at least), with safe employment and the prospect of retirement, the proletarians wait, while the precarians live under permanent pressure and cannot afford to relax.

Plus, back to Hegel, are these "others" again not a case of the negation of negation? The proletariat is the embodied negation of the existing order, those who are within this order negated, reduced to substance-less subjectivity, deprived of substantial content (property), while "others" as "even worse" are in this sense *less than nothing*, "the layer of residual swine," a nothing besmirched by a fragmentary residual content which they don't want to abandon, a nothing that remains rooted in an "indivisible remainder" of the lost homeland. In literature, exemplary are the cases of Joyce and Beckett, who both moved abroad in order to create an image of their Irish homeland. There are thus different modes of belonging and territorialization, not only along the axis of the centralized state and migrants but also along the opposition between plants and animals. (Most of) the plants are rooted in a certain place, while (most of) the animals move around and sometimes choose, construct or mark their territory (den, nest . . .). Along these lines, Michael Marder analyses plant behaviour and the vegetal heritage of human thought so as to affirm the potential of vegetation to resist the logic of totalization and to exceed the narrow confines of instrumentality. For him, "plant-thinking" is "the non-cognitive, non-ideational, and non-imagistic mode of thinking proper to plants, as much as the process of bringing human thought itself back to its roots and rendering it plantlike."[6] This "plant-thinking" reaches far beyond giving flowers as a symbolic act—Marder evokes the well-known clip from the Ukrainian war that shows an older woman confronting a heavily armed Russian soldier on a city street. She gives the soldier some sunflower seeds and tells him: "Take these seeds and put them raw in your pockets. At least, sunflowers will grow there where you fall on our soil." Flowers as symbols of resistance to military operations are quite familiar—just think about carnation revolutions, etc. However, the anonymous Ukrainian woman did something else:

> She did not cull flowers in a symbolic gesture of peaceful resistance to military onslaught. She did not offer the life of these flowers as a secular sacrifice on the high altar of human coexistence. Instead, her gesture was oriented toward the postwar future /.../ The seeds will outlive those who put them in the pockets of their military fatigues. They will live on and flourish as flowers, fed by the death of the occupiers, who will enrich with their decomposing corpses the soil of the country they invaded. There is a moment of posthumous redemption for the Russian soldiers themselves in the woman's offer. Their vegetal afterlife will partly atone or compensate for violence and destruction wrought in their human incarnation [...] she is willing to admit them into the more-than-human community of a local ecosystem in the guise of the flowers they would metamorphose into.[7]

In order to describe such a horizontal intermingling of different levels of reality, Saroj Giri borrows from the early years of the Soviet Union the term "comrade as object."[8] This term does not imply that we should observe and manipulate ourselves from a cold "objective" distance, which is why it is to be supplemented by its inversion, "object as comrade": "Instead of going over to the fetishistic powers of the commodity, one had to go towards the 'hidden' engineering/ artistic powers of things, objects and materials: this would, as it were, allow the object to commune and speak, providing us the first contours of the 'object as comrade.'"[9] This "object as comrade" displays what Giri calls idealism in the (material) thing itself, of what we may call spiritual corporeality as opposed to the fetishist idealism which imposes on a thing from the outside a social dimension as its reified property: to treat an object as "comrade" means to open oneself up to the virtual potentials of an object in an intense interaction with it. Maybe a surprising link can help us understand what is meant by "object as comrade" which supplements "comrade as object": today's object-oriented-ontology—here is Graham Harman's concise description of the object-oriented-ontology's basic stance:

> The arena of the world is packed with diverse objects, their forces unleashed and mostly unloved. Red billiard ball smacks green billiard ball. Snowflakes glitter in the light that cruelly annihilates them, while damaged submarines rust along the ocean floor. As flour emerges from mills and blocks of limestone are compressed by earthquakes, gigantic mushrooms spread in the Michigan forest. While human philosophers bludgeon each other over the very possibility of "accede" to the world, sharks bludgeon tuna fish and icebergs smash into coastlines.[10]

Such a way of treating objects as a "comrade" also opens up a new way of being ecological: to accept our environment in all its complex mixture that includes what we perceive as trash or pollution, as well as what we cannot directly perceive since it is too large or too minuscule (Timothy Morton's "hyperobjects"). Along these lines, for Morton, being ecological

> is not about spending time in a pristine nature preserve but about appreciating the weed working its way through a crack in the concrete, and then appreciating the concrete. It's also part of the world, and part of us. Reality is populated with "strange strangers"—things that are "knowable yet uncanny." This strange strangeness, Morton writes, is an irreducible part of every rock, tree, terrarium, plastic Statue of Liberty, quasar, black hole, or marmoset one might encounter; by acknowledging it, we shift away from trying to master objects and toward learning to respect them in their elusiveness. Whereas the Romantic poets rhapsodized about nature's beauty and sublimity, Morton responds to its all-pervading weirdness; they include in the category of the natural everything that is scary, ugly, artificial, harmful, and disturbing.[11]

There is thus, in resistance to abstract global "citizenship" with no territorial base (split into immigrants and wealthy travellers with no home), a "home" retroactively constructed from dispersed fragments of memory, material details ... Such a notion of homeland opens up also a new approach to national anthems: we can imagine a different anthem, not the usual anthem which celebrates a nation-state's strength and pride, its resoluteness to destroy all its enemies. Let's compare this with "Djelem, djelem," the Roma official national anthem:[12] here is no defence of a territory here, the basic notion is that of travelling, of taking long roads which have now opened, the only place of (temporary) stability are "tents on happy roads." It would be a wonderful miracle if, in a unique short circuit between tradition and our time, today's migrant groups (precarious workers, etc.) were to celebrate this same mobility. One should also mention here that there is an alternate version of the second part of the Roma anthem, a shift to passionate sexual love.[13]

The fact that the celebration of passionate love is part of an anthem is in itself breathtaking—although the unhappy ending of this love is included ... So what about making "Strosse to Stroma sou" ("Prepare the mattress for the two of us," a Mikis Theodorakis song which is already a national treasure in Greece—when it is performed publicly, people join clapping and singing) a Greek national anthem? It describes a passionate sexual encounter, and, again, there is no "happy forever after" here: what comes after the ecstatic love-event is the more miserable existence of a beggar desperately searching for the crumbs that remain ... and one should definitely include this song itself among these crumbs. But there is also no regret hidden in this sad aftermath: there is not the slightest doubt that the love encounter was worth the price, which is why "I go around collecting what I tossed away with you."[14]

But is this enough? Frederic Lordon endeavours to provide a philosophical grounding of the Leftist rehabilitation of "belonging" (to a particular community, way of life, etc.) in Spinoza's thought: he attacks the Cartesian individualist tradition of an abstract subject of free choice, with no substantial roots, which survives in existentialism and today's postmodern celebration of hybridity, from the position of Spinoza as "the thinker who can emancipate us from the delusions of free will or untrammelled individual choice, allowing us to grasp human struggles for existence in a disabused materialist fashion."[15] Against post-national individualism and direct universalism, Lordon advocates

> a Spinozian conception of the community constituted by convergence around a shared emotion—a common view of good and evil, for example—which the vertical of sovereignty then establishes as a condition of membership. The community's feeling for itself exceeds the individual emotions of its members, creating something that is part of them yet goes beyond them. For Spinoza, this excess is the potential of the multitude, which will duly bring forth a potestas.[16]

The mechanism which accounts for the constitution and closure of social totalities, the mechanism that regulates how individuals are "captured" into a social space, is that of the "imitation of affects," and its status is universal, it is an "anthropological necessity of closure and exclusion,"[17] the elementary mechanism of how groups as self-enclosed bodies which exclude others emerge. The imitation of affects works at a more basic level than the liberal-individualist notion of singular subjects who establish links that fit their interests. Spinoza's starting point is not individual but multitude, a pluriverse field of chaotic interconnections which resists centralization (subordination to a One).

Lordon thus proposes a kind of "structuralism of passions." Social and economic structures determine individuals directly, at a sub-individual level of collectivized passions: "human beings are in the first instance moved by their passions, which in turn, in the final analysis, are determined by social structures." Unless we get rid of political and social philosophies of the subject, we cannot supplement objective structures with a regime of desires and affects grounded in these structures. Even Communism as the most radical idea of universal emancipation should not be deprived of "belonging" as the fundamental feature of every social link:

> Governed by divergent passions, humans will never be combined and pacified in spontaneous harmony [. . .] To simply assert a communism of reason is to wish away the weight of common affect. To avert implosion, all numerous collectives require a vertical right or power—which, having the multitude as its only basis [. . .] nevertheless rises up over it.[18]

Consequently, any post-nationalism is "the denial of this fragmentary condition of human social life, its separation in different groupings of belonging"[19]—vertical forms of emancipation can only emerge on the basis of a shared affective belonging. Lordon thus attacks the anti-nationalist left, dismissing their demands as "'the grotesque claims of the well-off' for a 'liberation from belonging', without acknowledging how much they benefit from their own belonging." Once again, Lordon contrasts this hidden belonging of self-proclaimed rootless universalists with "the reality of statelessness, the nightmare of absolute non-inclusion, surviving like the sans-papiers without rights—and indeed fighting for citizenship, for belonging":[20]

> To disavow national affects in the metropole while allowing them, romantically or condescendingly, for the subaltern, is mere hypocrisy. One is never totally free of national belonging: we are seized by a nation from our very first day.[21]

Lordon attacks here Habermas and Ulrich Beck for their lifeless universalism: in Europe today, the nationalist popular call for sovereignty against its financial confiscation "signals the urgency of rethinking the national state in its relation to collective emancipation."[22] We should get rid of the dangerous idea that every "territorialization"—delimitation, drawing a line of separation—is in itself almost proto-Fascist, a possessive act of separating "ours" from "theirs," and only the limitless open flow is truly "progressive," as if there is not also a properly Leftist way of drawing a border. The irony of such a passion for "de-territorialization" is that it occurs at a time when, from Palestine to many other places, desperate activities to protect a territory against capitalist global free flow are abounding. In "Liberalism Needs the Nation,"[23] his reaction to the Ukrainian war, Francis Fukuyama points out how the patriotic defence of one's nation can also function as a defence of liberal notions—it all depends on which values does one's "nation" contain. Does not the last century offer numerous examples of radically-Left patriotic struggle against foreign domination?

Today's predominant ideology rejects any particular "belonging" and celebrates the "fluidification" of any identity: Lordon demonstrated the inconsistency of "cosmopolitan" anti-nationalist intellectuals who advocate a "liberation from belonging" and *in extremis* tend to dismiss every search for roots and every attachment to a particular ethnic or cultural identity as an almost proto-Fascist stance. Lordon contrasts this hidden belonging of self-proclaimed rootless universalists with the nightmarish reality of refugees and illegal immigrants who, deprived of basic rights, desperately search for some kind of belonging (like a new citizenship). Lordon is quite right here: it is easy to note how the "cosmopolitan" intellectual elites despising local people who cling to their roots belong to their own quite exclusive circles of rootless elites, how their cosmopolitan rootlessness is the marker of a deep and strong belonging. (This is why it is an utter obscenity to put together elite "nomads" flying around the world and refugees desperately searching for a safe place where they would belong—the same obscenity as that of putting together a dieting upper-class Western woman and a starving refugee woman.) This paradox is properly Hegelian: within each particular community (nation), today's universal class of managers and university elite appears as a particular group isolated from the majority by their entire lifestyle—a humanities professor in New York has much more in common with a humanities professor in Paris or even Seoul than with a worker who lives on Staten Island. The form of appearance of a universal class which reaches across particular nations is extreme particularity within its nation—universality divides a particular identity from within.

So Lordon is right in emphasizing the link between multicultural hybridity and today's global capitalism—however, in our global era, belonging can be easily appropriated by the Rightist nationalists to exclude enemies who are "not really one of us," who don't really belong to our community, like the denouncing of the Jews who are critical of Zionism as "self-hating" Jews. The same goes for Lordon's denunciation of the state as a universal apparatus elevated above social networks of belonging and, as such, a correlate of the Cartesian subject: both ignore particular "passionate" links that make a specific way of life. But is there not also a liberating aspect of the state as an apparatus elevated above specific ways of life? Is every belonging not immanently inconsistent, not only with regard to other belongings but also with regard to itself? Is in this sense the state apparatus not the figure of a big Other, a neutral terrain within which different belongings can coexist without exploding into animosity? We can observe the disintegration of the social big Other at its purest in today's Sweden. When I was a child, Sweden had a mythic status of a country which is so safe that when you left your house you didn't even lock the doors. A last echo of this stance was felt even at the beginning of the pandemic when Sweden avoided lockdown and other obligatory measures with the justification that Swedes are people with a highly developed sense of community so legal regulations are not necessary. As we have learned from crime writers like Henning Mankel, this image was largely an illusion, but it was an illusion which worked. Now we find in the media headlines like "Ultraviolent gangs are threatening to subvert the rule of law in Sweden" and we read: "Once one of the most peaceful countries in Europe, Sweden is plagued by the worst rates of deadly gun violence in Europe, 10 times higher than Germany. Its problems offer a warning of what can happen when integration fails."[24] Integration is mentioned here because violence is condensed, even de facto normalized, in ghettos like Hjällbo, a suburb of Gothenburg where

> social exclusion and lack of cultural integration for immigrants provide fertile ground for gangs. [Hjällbo police inspector] Olsson says identity is also a driving issue. The most violent offenders, he says, are seen as occupying "no-man's land." He adds: "They don't obey the rules of their parents' generation and they haven't really integrated into Swedish society. So they make up their own level of social capital." Hjällbo's segregation is complete, cut off from Gothenburg by forest and hills. Hjällbo is also dominated by the city's most brutal criminal network, an organization that openly challenges the state and whose

gangland lifestyle not only threatens to reshape Swedish politics but also to undermine its democracy.[25]

To blame immigrants for their refusal to integrate, as well as to blame the Swedish indigenous white majority for its non-readiness to integrate immigrants, is both wrong and misleading. The basic fact is that immigrant gangs are not just simply criminal—in all its brutality, their community relies on their own ethics, on a set of very stringent norms and prohibitions which are incompatible with the norms and prohibitions of the majority. The problem is that there is no all-encompassing big Other that would regulate the interaction between the two: although we can still talk about the big Other in the sense of a "normal" Swedish society into which gangs got integrated, the danger is that this big Other is disintegrating, so that if the process of ghettoization goes on, what is awaiting us is a multitude of "tribal" communities of belonging less and less held together by a common rule of Law. When critics of the Soviet Union drew attention to the fact that, contrary to the Marxist predictions about the state gradually withering away in Socialism, the Soviet state apparatus grew stronger and stronger, the defenders of the Soviet Union replied with the "paradox" that the Soviet state withers away through the strengthening of its organs. And is, at a different level, this not happening today? The state as a public space safeguarding the common good is weakening while its—financial, police, control—organs strengthen.

However, this does not mean that the universal common space is simply elevated above particular identities: there is a particular sub-group in which it comes to exist as such, and it is this sub-group whose key role is ignored by Lordon. In Orwell's *1984*, there is a famous exchange between Winston and O'Brien, his interrogator. Winston asks him: "'Does Big Brother exist?' 'Of course he exists. The Party exists. Big Brother is the embodiment of the Party.' 'Does he exist in the same way as I exist?' 'You do not exist,' said O'Brien." Should we not say something similar about the existence of universality? To the nominalist claim that there is no pure neutral universality, that every universality is caught in the conflict of particular ways of life, one should reply: no, today it's the particular ways of life that do not exist as autonomous modes of historical existence, the only actual reality is that of the universal capitalist system. This is why, in contrast to identity politics which focuses on how each (ethnic, religious, sexual) group should be able to fully assert its particular identity, the much more difficult and radical task is to enable each group full access to universality. This access to universality does not mean a recognition that one is also part of the universal human genus or the assertion of some ideological values which are considered universal. It means recognizing one's own universality the way it is at work in the fractures of one's particular identity, as the "work of the negative" which undermines every particular identity, or, as Buck-Morss put it, "universal humanity is visible at the edges":[26]

> rather than giving multiple, distinct cultures equal due, whereby people are recognized as part of humanity indirectly through the mediation of collective cultural identities, human universality emerges in the historical event at the point of rupture. It is in the discontinuities of history that people whose culture has been strained to the breaking point give expression to a humanity that goes beyond cultural limits. And it is in our emphatic identification with this raw, free, and vulnerable state, that we have a chance of understanding what they say. Common humanity exists in spite of culture and its differences. A person's nonidentity with the collective allows for subterranean solidarities that have a chance of appealing to universal, moral sentiment, the source today of enthusiasm and hope.[27]

Buck-Morss provides here a precise argument against the postmodern poetry of diversity: it masks the underlying *sameness* of the brutal violence enacted by the culturally diverse cultures and regimes:

> Can we rest satisfied with the call for acknowledging "multiple modernities," with a politics of "diversity," or "multiversality," when in fact the inhumanities of these multiplicities are often strikingly the same?[28]

This, however, is not the whole story. The Slovene art group NSK (its best-known element is the band Laibach) actualized the ingenious idea of a virtual state, "NSK State," a state without territory which exists in time only—but it functions, providing citizenship with a proper passport that could be bought (cheaply)—the paper material was given to NSK by their supporter Zoran Thaler who was at that time (in the 1990s) Slovenia's foreign minister. I remember that at a "serious" press conference he first reported on some diplomatic troubles with Italy, and then went on with "great good news": the Republic of Slovenia and NSK State recognized each other and established full diplomatic relations ... Also at the 57th Venice Biennale NSK had its own pavilion along with other actual states.[29] It is important to bear in mind the possibility of such a virtual state without territory, to add it to the series of actual territorial states. Although the NSK state was founded on extremely "dogmatic" authoritarian principles, its virtual status immediately cancelled the social reality of these principles.

Finale: The Four Riders of the Apocalypse

In politics, *larvatus prodeo* (I progress masked) is often quite appropriate: a revolutionary force, when it takes over, at first does not show its true colours and just claims it wants to make better the existing system. But is it not even more appropriate to turn the saying around: *larvatus redeo*? When I am forced to retreat, I assume a deceiving mask to cover up the depth of my defeat ... However, what if—the lesson of psychoanalysis—the naked face itself is already a mask (which is why in the analytic session the analyst does not see the face of his patient), and I am authentic only by adopting a mask I fully identify with? So when I retreat, I pretend to drop my mask and offer my true face—which is the ultimate deception. Is this not what politicians—who (often late in their age) betray their radical roots and claim that they are now no longer possessed by false visions do? ("I renounce my ideological illusions, now I am just who I truly am").This is where we stand today.

The crises we are all caught in evoke more and more ominously the four riders of the apocalypse from the Book of Revelations: plague, war, hunger, death.[1] These four riders cannot be simply dismissed as figures of evil—Trevor Hancock pointed out that they are "remarkably close to what we might call the four horsemen of ecology that regulate population size in nature."[2] Referring to Charles Elton, he suggests that the "four riders" play a positive role in preventing over-population: "increases in numbers are held in check by predators, pathogens, parasites and food supply." The problem is that, in the long term, this regulatory function didn't seem to work for us, humans:

> The human population has more than tripled in the past 70 years, from 2.5 billion in 1950 to 7.8 billion today. So what

> happened to Elton's four ecological horsemen? Why we are not controlled? Is there a fifth horseman that will cause our populations to crash at some point, as lemmings do?[3]

Until recently, humanity was able to hold in check the four riders through medicine, science and technology; however, now we are threatened by the "massive and rapid global ecological changes we have triggered. So although of course an asteroid strike or super-volcano eruption could wipe us out, the greatest threat to the human population, the 'fifth horseman' if you like, is us."[4]

What this means is that we (humanity) are now facing a key decision: we are the "fifth horseman" who can cause our destruction or save us. Although global awareness of the threat is growing, it is not followed by adequate activity, so the four riders are galloping faster and faster:

- Plague: at the end of 2019, Covid exploded and changed our lives forever—it is still here and we can expect new waves as well as other viral pandemics.
- War: with the Russian attack on Ukraine, we got a true hot war in Europe—a sobering reminder that nobody can afford to observe war from a safe distance. Even if some kind of truce will be enforced, war forcefully asserted itself as a general condition of our lives and peace as a temporary exception—whichever way we turn, World War Three is on the horizon, and what is needed is not just or even primarily the strength to counter the aggressors but a radical change of the entire global system.
- Hunger: it is also on the horizon—here are some of the recent big media titles: "The War in Ukraine Is Creating the Greatest Global Food Crisis Since WWII"[5]; "War in Ukraine could lead to food riots in poor countries."[6] Because of global warming, "The India and Pakistan heatwave is 'testing the limits of human survivability,' an expert says," with massive crop failures there.[7] Are we getting ready for the mass migrations and riots that global hunger will trigger?
- Death is in itself (until the full biogenetic control over our lives, at least) part of life—suffice it to recall a deeply true

> Polish graffiti definition of life: a disease transmitted by sex which always ends with death. But what I mean with death as the fourth rider is something more radical, not just the excessive deaths caused by the other three riders. It is our "second death" through the latest modes of the digital control of our daily lives, especially the prospect of the "wired brain" (the direct link of our thinking with digital machines)—will we still be human, and in what sense, if this happens? More closely, there are three levels of this threat to being-human today: digital control and manipulation; biogenetic changes in our DNA; wired brain (the direct link between our thought process and a digital machine).[8] With each new level, the threat gets more internalized: the digital control just closely observes our external behaviour, our acts and reactions, so we still can claim to enjoy the freedom of our flow of inner thoughts; with changes in our DNA, others can directly influence our physical and psychic properties well beyond the trivialities of the colour of my eyes—my "natural" itself becomes a human product. However, what remains out of reach of direct manipulation is our flow of thoughts, the unique outcome of the interaction between nature and nurture which (according to some interpreters) cannot be reduced to its causes—and the wired brain closes even this last loophole, making accessible to a machine the very core of our Self.

What is becoming more and more obvious is the inability of the parliamentary liberal democracy to cope with these multiple crises and apocalyptic prospects. But why do I mention Communism here? What we need is not twentieth-century Communism with all its horrors but, as we have already seen, more global cooperation, the limitation of the market and the social regulation of the economy . . . in short, a new kind of Communism. (Today debates are going on in many countries about how to cope with global warming—should we limit the use of coal, oil or/and of nuclear energy, how reliable are solar or wind collectors . . . It is important to note that these debates concern basic social decisions without regard for the market profitability, so they introduce an element of

Communism—no wonder titles like "green politics has ruined Europe" abound recently, desperately trying to sabotage this process.) What we need is simply to take literally, to really do, what even our big media declare that we should do. One can easily imagine a new variation of the well-known line from Monty Python's *The Life of Brian*: "All right, but apart from the sanitation, the medicine, education, wine, public order, irrigation, roads, a fresh water system, and public health, what have the Romans ever done for us? Nothing!"—"All right, but apart from universal healthcare, social regulation of economy, free education ... what will such new Communism do for us? Nothing!"

De-Nazifying Ukraine, Kosovo ... Europe

And all the ongoing conflicts should be located within this global context. After new tensions erupted in northern Kosovo, Vladimir Djukanovic from the ruling Serbian Progressive Party wrote on Twitter that "he believes Serbia might be forced to engage in the 'de-Nazification' of the Balkans." Note two details in this statement: the expression "forced to engage" (aggressors today never simply attack, they are always *forced* to do it—in their view, the true aggressor is the one they attack); and the mention of "Balkans," not just of Kosovo—a hint that Bosnia is also included in this "de-Nazification" project ... What awaits us at the end of this line is clear: ultimately, all of Europe will have to be "de-Nazified" since it is caught in the vortex of self-destructive degeneration (LGBT+, gay marriages, no clear distinction of sexes ...)—a crazy case of how, in the view of Russian new conservativism, Nazism, Communism, and Woke hedonism ultimately amount to the same. Recall that, in late March 2022, Aleksandr Dugin said in an interview: "We are fighting the absolute evil embodied in Western civilization, its liberal-totalitarian hegemony, in Ukrainian Nazism ..." The truth of this identity of opposites that is too much even for the most hardline of Hegelians is that it reflects the obvious immanent inconsistency of the neoconservatives, from the pro-Russian ones to the American alt-Right: while they pretend to deplore the multicultural hedonism and present themselves as the embodiment of traditional Christian values, their words and acts display extraordinary vulgarity, sexism and racism.

I am referring here to an obscene event that occurred back in 2012: in an effort to explain his stance on abortion, Representative Todd Akin, the Republican Senate nominee from Missouri, provoked ire across the political spectrum by saying that in instances of what he called "legitimate rape," women's bodies somehow blocked an unwanted pregnancy.[9] Responding to this ire, Akin claimed that he has "misspoken": he really wanted to say that there are "legitimate cases of rape" where penetration is really enforced, but that, if the victim shows signs of consent (say, getting wet and excited), this, then, is no longer a legitimate case of rape . . . I think this confusion reveals the truth—what Akin really wanted to say precisely what his "misspoken" formulation says: in some cases rape is legitimate since the victim showed signs of participation, which means it really wasn't a rape . . . (We encounter here a clear case of surplus-enjoyment: far from being a mere neutral mistake, Akin's "misspoken" formulation brings out the obscene enjoyment (of humiliating raped women) which sustains his entire line of argumentation.)

A closer look at the clitoris makes clear the mistake of Akin's reasoning. The clitoris is the pleasure centre of the feminine reproductive anatomy. It is not just the tiny nub of flesh located at the top of the genitals (vulva): it consists of a complex network of erectile tissue and nerves, with parts located inside and outside your body. The Greek word "kleitoris" means "little hill," but this little hill (protected by a cloak of skin, or the "clitoral hood," which is found over the urethral opening) is just the tip of a much larger octopus-like organ.[10]

We should not be afraid to go a little bit further here and take this metaphor of octopus a little bit more literally: the true counterpart of male castration is not just cliterodectomy (in the narrow sense of cutting out the tiny nut that is visible) but the excision of the entire organ seen on the image. What remains is a "castrated vulva": a flat surface with the vaginal hole that doesn't react to his caressing and penetration—no rhythmic squeezing that bears witness to pleasure. We should therefore conceive the entire octopus-like clitoris as a kind of parasite, a foreign body attaching itself to the space around the vaginal opening: it is only this parasite which sexualizes the vaginal area. The distinction between vaginal and clitoral orgasm, as well as the distinction between who is active and who is passive in sexual intercourse, is thus rendered problematic: the bodily reactions associated with feminine orgasm (rhythmic squeezing of the muscles around the vaginal hole) are products of the clitoral muscles. The form of sex that renders this fact clear is the so-called "Singapore grip," the sexual act in which during intercourse both the man and the woman are stationary: the man lies on his back while the woman sitting on him brings both to orgasm not by her movements but just by clenching her vaginal muscles. (There is, of course, a colonial reading of this grip: a white man in Singapore was too lazy to even properly make love to a local woman, she had to do the work ... But there is also a feminist reading which undermines the predominant opposition of man as active and woman as passive.)

My Octopus Teacher (2020, Pippa Ehrlich and Craig Foster, South Africa), the Oscar-winning documentary about a man establishing a kind of relationship with an octopus which circles around him and plays with him, massively changed our eating habits, making thousands all around the world abandon eating octopuses. However, the film avoids the key question: do octopuses establish the same intense links also among themselves, or was the octopus in the movie just "hystericized" by the weird behaviour of the diver? Whichever is the right answer, can we not imagine the movie as the metaphor of a man erotically interacting with a clitoris which playfully circulates around him and even comes to rest on his chest?

Back to Akin, all this renders problematic the idea that how the body reacts to penetration determines if rape was endorsed or not by the woman: the fact that the vaginal hole gets humid has nothing to do with clitoral muscles which generate pleasure. However, leaving behind the obvious falsity and vulgarity of Akin's reasoning (his "misspeaking" reveals his anti-feminist "surplus-enjoyment"), I want to draw a parallel with the Russian attack on Ukraine since the metaphor of rape was also evoked from the Russian side. At a press conference on February 7, 2022, Putin noted that the Ukraine government does not like the Minsk agreement and then added:

"Like it or not, it's your duty, my beauty."[11] The saying has well-known sexual connotations: Putin appeared to be quoting from "Sleeping Beauty in a Coffin" by the Soviet-era punk rock group Red Mold. The song talks about a sleeping beauty in a coffin who, if she likes it or not, will be fucked by the narrator.[12] There is a clear reference to rape here: there are cases when the rape of a country is "legitimate," i.e., justified. Such male-chauvinist obscenities are the (not even so hidden) truth of the proponents of traditional Christian values.

Two conclusions are to be drawn from this. First, the notion of "de-Nazification" used by Russia and Serbia is that of the "legitimate rape" of a country—this notion serves as the legitimization of such a rape. Second, the link between Akin and Putin is not external and contingent but immanent: they both need to mobilize obscenities in order to sustain their project . . . Should we then simply support Ukraine and the liberal West? Everybody knows that Volodymyr Zelensky first played the Ukrainian president in a popular TV series *The Servant of the People*,[13] and then became one—a fact that gave birth to many ironic comments and led many commentators to not take him seriously (as if having a president who was before a KGB agent is better or at least more normal . . .). Many people know the basic plot of the series:

> Filmed by a student when launching a profane rant about corruption in Ukraine, who uploads the footage to YouTube, Vasily Petrovych Goloborodko, an absent-minded high-school history teacher who lives with his parents, turns into an Internet sensation overnight. Goloborodko's students launch a crowdfunding campaign for registering his candidacy in Ukraine's presidential race unbeknownst to him, eventually propelling their flabbergasted teacher to political victory as the new President of Ukraine. While in office, Vasily is confused at his newfound responsibilities, but gradually eases into his presidential duties and decides to weed out corruption by the oligarchy in his government.

Those who are close to Zelensky claim that, upon becoming a president, he effectively tried to live up to his role in the TV series—but did he succeed? One thing is sure: the image of Ukraine in

Zelensky's TV series fully fits reality. Of all the post-Communist countries in Eastern Europe, Ukraine has been hardest hit by the "shock therapy" of capitalist restoration: during the thirty years after independence, incomes and quality of life have remained below 1990 levels; poverty is rampant (worse than much-decried Belarus), law enforcement totally failed in curbing corruption, courts were a farce … in short, the "conversion" to capitalism has followed the usual pattern: a class of oligarchs and a narrow elite have enriched themselves disproportionately by despoiling the public sector with the complicity of the political class. If we add to this the strings attached to the financial help from the West ("the cash was strongly tied to reforms that Ukraine was required to implement, all under the banner of fiscal restraint and austerity"), a very sad picture emerges. This, not a thriving democracy, is the land Russia invaded.

From my links in Russia (which, for obvious reasons, have to remain anonymous), I learned that, on top of a group of conservative Orthodox advisers, Putin also organized a group of Marxists to counsel him on how to present Russia's position in the Third World. One can find traces of such a "Marxist" approach in Putin's speech on August 16, 2022:

> The situation in the world is changing dynamically and the outlines of a multipolar world order are taking shape. An increasing number of countries and peoples are choosing a path of free and sovereign development based on their own distinct identity, traditions and values. These objective processes are being opposed by the Western globalist elites, who provoke chaos, fanning long-standing and new conflicts and pursuing the so-called containment policy, which in fact amounts to the subversion of any alternative, sovereign development options.[14]

Two details, of course, spoil this "Marxist" image. Sovereignty "based on their own distinct identity, traditions and values"—which means let's tolerate what the state is doing in North Korea or in Afghanistan. True Leftist solidarity is based on antagonisms in each "distinct identity," on building a network of links between the struggles for emancipation in each country—in Afghanistan, we should focus on the plight of women who suffer the consequences of its "distinct identity." "The subversion of any alternative, sovereign development options"—is Russia not doing exactly this in Ukraine, or does Ukraine not deserve this option? This "Marxist" image should thus not deceive us: it is a key component of all alt-Right movements all around the way. In France, lawyer, politician and National Rally member Marine le Pen presents herself as the protector of ordinary working people against the big international corporations which promote multiculturalism and sexual depravity to undermine national identities. The US alt-Right not only often sounds like the old radical Left, attacking the "deep state" and even advocating its violent overthrow; they sometimes openly declare themselves the successors of the radical Left from the 1960s and 1970s. Steve Bannon, former White House chief strategist, is a self-proclaimed "Leninist" and advocates the coalition of the alt-Right with the radical Left as the only way to beat the reign of financial and digital elites. And, to reach back to go to the original model, let's not forget that Hitler headed the National-*Socialist* German *Workers* Party!

When today's Leftists criticize the Western support of Ukraine, they as a rule repeat the cliché about how the ongoing war drags on because it serves as a boost for the Western military-industrial complex—a rather stupid cliché which could well be applied to World War Two: didn't it give a big boost to the US military industry since it was only after World War Two that the US effectively left behind the Great Depression? There is another aspect of what goes on in Ukraine that deserves much greater attention. In the conditions of global warming and other ecological disturbances, the possession of fertile land is viewed as a very important asset—that's why Bill Gates and other billionaires invest a good part of their wealth into owning large agricultural estates or forests.

And fertile land is the greatest asset of Ukraine—its fields are full of chernozem ("black ground"), a black-coloured soil containing a high percentage of humus and high percentages of phosphoric acids, phosphorus, and ammonia. Chernozem is very fertile soil and can produce high agricultural yields with its high moisture storage capacity. No wonder, then, that, for decades, big corporations have shown great interest in acquiring land in Ukraine—at least one-third of it is already owned by American and West European big companies. Aware of this threat, twenty years ago Ukraine imposed a moratorium on sales of land to foreigners which the US State Department, IMF and World Bank had repeatedly called to be removed—under this immense pressure, it was finally repealed by the Zelensky government in 2020.

The small good news brought by the horrors of war is that the ongoing war seems to have disrupted the current grand neoliberal project in the short term: since war demands social mobilization and the coordination of production, it offers a unique chance to put a brake on this process, as well as a chance to get rid of the excesses of corruption and oligarchy which were abundant in Ukraine after it gained sovereignty. But will Ukraine be able to exploit this chance? The cruel irony is that, while Russia is now colonizing Ukraine with the brutal force of arms, there is a moment of truth in Russia's claim that, after 1990, Ukraine was a Western economic colony.

Even if Ukraine will—hopefully—protect its independence, its victorious defence will be its moment of truth. They will have to learn the lesson that it is not enough for them to catch up with the West and join the EU for two reasons. First, Western democracy is itself in a deep crisis, there is a deep discontent broiling—the US is getting close to ideological civil war, Europe is falling apart with post-Communist countries getting close to a new illiberal authoritarianism incompatible with the basic values of the EU. Second, will the victorious Ukraine deeply indebted to the US and EU be able to resist an even stronger pressure to become economically colonized by the Western big powers, so that its freedom will be largely limited to cultural matters?

Beneath our fascination with the war and Ukraine's heroic resistance, this struggle is already going on. We can only hope that, as it often happened with the Western help to countries struggling for freedom and democracy, the final result will not be neoliberal colonization. To achieve this, Ukraine will have to reinvent itself, not just try to catch up with the West. To be an economic colony of the West may be better than to disappear as a nation in the new Russian empire, but it is not good enough. It doesn't limit in any way the four riders of the apocalypse, only a new Communism will do this job.

Some observers in the West mockingly dismiss the Ukrainian admiration of Europe, its resolute desire to become part of

European civilization, as a naive misrecognition of the much more brutal reality of Europe. Simultaneously, the predominant Western European stance towards Ukraine is patronizing: this poor and badly abused country should be helped and allowed to join us, to catch up with us who offer the best model of how a good society should look ... Both stances miss something crucial. What Ukrainians see in Europe (and for what they are fighting) is not European reality: they see in Europe something we don't see or don't take seriously. In some sense, then, Ukrainians are more European than we, "real" Europeans—they are ready to suffer and fight for Europe, while most of us are caught in passive apathy, worrying about small changes in our standard of living. So it is not only that Ukraine needs Europe, our help, we Western Europeans also need Ukraine to remind us of the emancipatory vision that sustains a united Europe. Ultimately it is not the Ukraine which needs to catch up with Western Europe, we need to catch up with Ukraine. Let's hope the Ukrainian struggle will awaken us, Western Europeans, from the dogmatic torpor and make us aware of the urgency to mobilize—not only militarily, but also and above all against all other threats that challenge our very survival. (Helping Ukraine is not enough—in this case also, the words of an Australian Aboriginal activist hold: "If you have come here to help me, then don't waste your time. But if you have come here because your liberation is bound up with mine, then come, let us join in the struggle together."[15])

The End of Nature

There is no necessity in this possible rise of new Communism: the existing order will (and already is) forcefully acting against it—this predicament was best described by Álvaro García Linera:

> The contingency of history, which always existed but was hidden behind a triumphalist mantle of free market, privatization, and globalization as the naturalized destiny of humanity, is today shown in all its unpredictability. And as the inevitable collective suffering caused by the pandemic and economic hecatomb

> increases in the coming months, an exceptional moment of collective willingness to revoke old beliefs, to replace aged certainties, to listen, to process new understandings, and new procedural and moral reasons for the organization of personal life and the world is becoming possible. It is a moment of propensity to some kind of cognitive epiphany capable of giving the imagined world a stable sense of destiny to engage the meaning of personal decisions; a period of collective desire towards new signifiers to stabilize each individual's world order.[16]

However, Linera is far from elevating such moments of "epiphany" into a mystical radical rupture. Long hard work is ahead which prohibits any return to a "closed economy" as a cure against capitalist limitless self-expansion. The main candidate for this "closed economy" is today ecology which tends to perceive Nature itself as the limit to our expansion, and enjoins us, humans, to renounce our hubris, our ruthless exploitation of nature. Now that God or Tradition can no longer play the role of the highest Limit, Nature takes over this role. But what kind of nature will this be? Even when we imagine global warming, we are aware that we are approaching a new world in which "England" will designate a barren dry country, while "Death Valley" will designate a big lake in California. However, we still picture it as a new stability, with "regular and repeatable weather patterns": "once humanity reaches the limit of carbon output, Earth's climate stabilizes at a new, higher average temperature. This higher temperature is overall bad for humans, because it still leads to higher sea levels and more extreme weather events. But at least it's stable: The Anthropocene looks like previous climate ages, only warmer, and it will still have regular and repeatable weather patterns."[17] However, recent researches find it more probable that

> Earth's climate leads to chaos. True, mathematical chaos. In a chaotic system, there is no equilibrium and no repeatable patterns. A chaotic climate would have seasons that change wildly from decade to decade (or even year to year). Some years would experience sudden flashes of extreme weather, while others would be completely quiet. Even the average Earth temperature may fluctuate wildly, swinging from cooler to

> hotter periods in relatively short periods of time. It would become utterly impossible to determine in what direction Earth's climate is headed.[18]

Such an outcome is not only catastrophic for our survival it also runs against our (human) most basic notion of nature, that of a repeatable pattern of seasons. As such, it reminds us of what Georg Lukács pointed out in his *History and Class Consciousness*:[19] "nature" is a social category, i.e., what we perceive as "nature" is always overdetermined by a social context. So while everything that there is is nature (we are part of nature), the obverse also holds at the level of our understanding: nature is a cultural category, what strikes us as "unnatural" is always socially determined. In "Are we entering a post-anthropocentric era?," a BBC report on the 2022 Venice bienniale, we read that its curator, Cecilia Alemani, "imagines a world where humans are 'not at the top of the pyramid', and live in a more horizontal relationship not only with each other but also with nature and animals, with organic and non-organic beings."[20] The least one can say is that such a "post-anthropocentric" vision of a horizontal relationship between humans, living beings and non-organic entities *is only accessible to us, humans*: non-organic entities are simply part of their environment, while animals and plants relate to it from their narrow perspective and definitely cannot imagine a global natural order of which they are only a small part. A horizontal texture of beings is no less "anthropocentric" than a pyramidal one.

The temptation to be resisted here is to continue to rely on our basic notion of nature and, consequently, proclaim chaos as somehow "unnatural." It is as if our Earth is gradually turning into Trisolaris, the strange planet from *The Three-Body Problem*, Liu Cixin's sci-fi masterpiece.[21] Trisolaris has three suns which rise and set at strange and unpredictable intervals: sometimes far too far away and horribly cold, sometimes far too close and destructively hot, and sometimes not seen for long periods of time. Devastating hurricanes, droughts and floods, not to mention global warming—do they all not indicate that we are witnessing something for which the only appropriate term is "the end of nature"? ("Nature" is to be understood here in the traditional sense of a regular rhythm of seasons, the reliable background of human history, something on which we can count always to be there.)

Our survival depends on certain natural parameters which we automatically take for granted. The lesson of global warming is that the freedom of humankind was possible only against the background of the stable natural parameters of life on earth (temperature, the composition of the air, sufficient water and energy supply, etc.): humans can "do what they want" only insofar as they remain marginal enough so that they don't seriously perturb the parameters of life on earth. The limitation of our freedom that becomes palpable with global warming is the paradoxical outcome of the very exponential growth of our freedom and power, i.e., of our growing ability to transform nature around us up to destabilizing the very basic geological parameters of life on earth. We are thus entering a new phase in which it is simply nature itself which melts into the air: the main consequence of the scientific breakthroughs in biogenetics is the end of nature. Once we know the rules of its construction, natural organisms are transformed into objects amenable to manipulation. Nature, human and inhuman, is "desubstantialized," deprived of its impenetrable density, of what Heidegger called "earth."

Let me confess one of my guilty pleasures for which the contempt of almost all of my friends befell me: I quite like Roland Emmerich's 2022 film *Moonfall* whose premise is that our Moon is an artificial megastructure constructed by the ancestors of humanity (who were more technologically advanced than their present-day descendants) as an ark to repopulate humanity; these ancestors were hunted by a rogue artificial intelligence that grew too strong . . . Two features I find interesting in the film are: (1) the conflict that structures the entire human history is the one between two strands of Artificial Intelligence, not between humanity and AI; (2) the denaturalization of what we spontaneously perceive as a gigantic natural object—the Moon's ragged surface is just a mask aimed at deceiving humans and concealing a complex machine inside. So what if we universalize this premise and conceive nature itself, what if we perceive its most "natural" features (spontaneity, chaos . . .) as a deceiving appearance concealing a machinic inside? It is crucial to bear in mind that the rise of the post-human era and the end of nature are the two sides of the same process. So if development will render *homo sapiens* obsolete, what will follow it? A post-human *homo deus* (with abilities that are traditionally identified as divine) or a quasi-omnipotent digital machine?[22]

With regard to the possibility of new forms of awareness emerging, one should bear in mind Metzinger's warning. While he considers artificial subjectivity possible, especially in the direction of hybrid bio-robotics, and, consequently, an "empirical, not philosophical"[23] issue, he emphasizes its ethically problematic character: "it is not at all clear if the biological form of consciousness, as so far brought about by evolution on our planet, is a *desirable* form of experience, an actual *good in itself*."[24] This problematic feature concerns conscious pain and suffering: evolution "has created an expanding ocean of suffering and confusion where there previously was none. As not only the simple number of individual conscious subjects but also the dimensionality of their phenomenal state spaces is continuously increasing, this ocean is also deepening."[25] And it is reasonable to expect that new artificially generated forms of awareness will create new "deeper" forms of suffering.

As Yuval Harari points out, the most realist option of the biotechnology and computer algorithms joining their powers in producing "bodies, brains and minds" will be a radical division, much stronger than the class division, within human society itself. With the gap exploding "between those who know how to engineer bodies and brains and those who do not": "those who ride the train of progress will acquire divine abilities of creation and destruction, while those left behind will face extinction."[26] The main threat is therefore that of the rise of a

> small and privileged elite of upgraded humans. These superhumans will enjoy unheard-of abilities and unprecedented creativity, which will allow them to go on making many of the most important decisions in the world. [...] However, most humans will not be upgraded, and they will consequently become an inferior caste, dominated by both computer algorithms and the new superhumans. Splitting humankind into biological castes will destroy the foundations of liberal ideology.[27]

Is this option not a new version of the old joke from Stalin's era about a debate in the Politburo about money in Communism: the Rightists claim there will be money in Communism because money is needed to regulate exchanges in a complex society, while the Leftists claim that, since money belongs to a society of commodities, there will be no money in Communism. Stalin replies that they are both wrong, a Rightist and a Leftist deviation—the truth is a dialectical synthesis of the opposites: there will be money in Communism and there will be no money in Communism. The members of the Politburo praise Stalin for the creative solution but nonetheless ask him to explain how this will work. Stalin calmly answers: "It's very simple. Some people will have money and others will not have it . . ."

Crucial here is the interdependence of man and nature: by reducing man to just another natural object whose properties can be manipulated, what we lose is not (only) humanity but *nature itself*. In this sense, Francis Fukuyama is right: humanity itself relies on some notion of "human nature" as what we inherited as simply given to us, the impenetrable dimension in/of ourselves into which we are born/thrown. The paradox is thus that there is man only insofar as there is impenetrable inhuman nature (Heidegger's "earth"): with the prospect of biogenetic interventions opened up by the access to the genome, the species freely changes/redefines *itself*, its own coordinates; this prospect effectively emancipates humankind from the constraints of a finite species, from its enslavement to the "selfish gene." However, this ultimate freedom (of genetic self-reconstruction) coincides with the ultimate non-freedom: I am myself reduced to an object which can be endlessly refashioned.

DON'T Be True to Yourself!

The ultimate lesson is here that we should accept the meaningless stupidity of nature. Humanity owes its existence to the immense destruction and suffering that befell life on earth. Without the extinction of dinosaurs, there would not be human life on earth. Our main sources of energy (coal, oil) are the leftovers of unimaginable destructions that occurred in the past. Our daily habits rely on global suffering—just think about what happens in industrial farms with chickens and pigs. We are not only a catastrophe for our environment, we emerged out of this catastrophe and even today live off it.[28] And all these sacrifices will never be redeemed in some kind of new Nuremberg court condemning us for our crimes against natural life. The most difficult thing is not to find some deeper meaning of suffering but to really accept its meaninglessness.

In their short book *Memo sur la nouvelle classe ecologique*, Latour and Schultz[29] confront the big problem: although the media bombard us with news about the pandemic and the threat of ecological catastrophe, why does all this not trigger a mass political mobilization at the level of previous big mobilizations (the Third Estate movement against feudalism, the Socialist movement against capitalist exploitation, even the Fascist mobilization)? While Latour and Schultz try to locate ecological struggle as the last (and most universal) in the series of emancipatory class struggles, they point out the difference: the "ecological class" is universal, it includes not only all of us, humans, but even our natural environs, and it breaks with the progressive paradigm that sustained previous class struggles (more material development). So its basic promise is just survival, better life, not a higher standard of life, and to achieve this, it is aware that great material and social sacrifices will be needed, especially in the "developed" countries. Is this the reason that it fails to trigger mass mobilization? I think the situation is more complex since, with the exception of new populists, political mobilization is failing in the entire domain of politics characterized by growing apathy.

Do we not find a similar passivity already in the work of Adorno and Max Horkheimer? In Horkheimer's stance towards the developed West, we can discern a strange echo of ontological difference: at the ontological level, the developed Western consumerist society is the worst possible, the culmination of the "dialectic of Enlightenment," the society of total technological manipulation, but at the ontic level, as one of the social orders compared with others, it is still the best and we should defend it. (That's why in the late 1960s Horkheimer refused to condemn the US intervention in Vietnam, claiming that the US Army always brings freedom ...) Thus Horkheimer's stance cannot but recall Churchill's famous definition of democracy: the worst possible political system, but all others are worse.

As Latour and Schultz point out, although the ecological class should strive towards unity with democratic and socialist forces, their unity is not guaranteed. The obstacles are not just "reactionary" forces interested in further capitalist expansion but also "progressive" forces unable to abandon the paradigm of infinite growth—decades back, many trade unions were opposed to the first ecological warnings, dismissing them as an attempt by the capital to limit workers' demands, and even in today's conspiracy theories, there is a tendency to dismiss ecological limitations as a plot by the establishment to control population. The ecological class thus often cuts across other struggles, and we should not reduce this tension to a passing moment that should be gradually overcome through building a global solidarity. Maybe, if we want to re-actualize the notion of Communism, we should accept the basic inadequacy of the idea of working-class power. In his very last text, Christopher Hitchens wrote that "at the very end of his life, cut off in Mexico and aware of his own declining health, [Trotsky] admitted, after the outbreak of the Second World War, that the conflict might just end without a socialist revolution. In that event the whole Marxist-Leninist project would have to be abandoned"[30]—here is a passage from Trotsky's last text:

> We would be compelled to acknowledge that [Stalinism] was rooted not in the backwardness of the country and not in the imperialist environment, but in the congenital incapacity of the proletariat to become a ruling class. Then it would be necessary to establish in retrospect that ... the present USSR was the precursor of a new and universal system of exploitation.[31]

Trotsky is clear here: one has to leave behind the very basic idea of the "proletarian power," of the wretched of the earth able to organize alternate power. "In retrospect" means that this idea was from the very beginning doomed. Today, we are in a position to draw the full consequences of this fact, the most important of them being the already quoted line from Karl-Heinz Dellwo that today it is "reasonable to speak no longer about masters and servants but only about servants who command servants." (And, as Gandhi put it, the fate of the serf is worse than that of the slave, for the slave has lost only his liberty, but the serf has become unworthy of it.) What this means is that we should leave behind the characterization of the global capitalist reproduction as an expression of the "will to power": capital reproduces itself without a will, will is on the contrary something that would only characterize a "voluntarist" revolutionary attempt to interrupt this mad dance: "Today the one who doesn't want revolution doesn't want anything." This is also why we should resist the nostalgic search for a (new) revolutionary subject: there is no predestined agent of a revolution, the only solution is that we ourselves, each of us who experiences the need for global change, assert ourselves as such: "I will not raise the question about the revolutionary subject. If we are not this, then others are also not this."[32] In short, no one is allowed to take the easy path of expecting from another group (especially so-called "nomadic proletarians") to appear as a privileged agent which will show us the path—there is an absolute egalitarianism at work here, the "objective social situation" is strictly secondary.[33] This should be our version of the statement (wrongly) attributed to Gandhi: "Be yourself the change you want to see in the world." The message is the exact opposite of "be true to yourself": there is no inner truth deep in you (as psychoanalysis amply shows), so obliterate yourself, don't be free but become an object-instrument of Freedom.

Whose Servant Is a Master?

It's time to conclude and bring together the dispersed threads of this book. There is a general narrative gradually emerging of what is going on in the last decades—to cut a long story short, it is the return of what was repressed in the age of modernity and Enlightenment. More precisely, the antagonism we encounter today is not just the one between the Enlightenment and its repressed, it is at its most basic an antagonism which runs through the Enlightenment edifice itself, back to Ancient Greece: the antagonism between Plato and Aristotle, Sparta and Athens, French Revolution and English reform, rationalism and empiricism, egalitarian freedom and liberty rooted in customs. It is the antagonism between radical universalism and a particular experimental approach, and the truth is by far not on the side of a cautious empirical approach.

The dissatisfaction with the ideological coordinates of modernity expresses itself in the guise of its opposite, as a redoubled surplus-enjoyment: not the surplus-enjoyment and/or surplus-value which sets in motion the capitalist edifice but a surplus over this surplus itself, the surplus palpable in the obscenity of the populist discourse permeated by racist and sexist enjoyment.[34] We are learning the hard way that the attempt of modernity to dispense with traditional forms of domination (the father of the family, Master . . .) and install secular democracy failed: the dimension of the Master is returning with a vengeance in all its forms (patriarchal values, political authoritarianism, religious fundamentalism . . .). It was clear already to Freud that the decline of paternal authority is an ambiguous process: the father as a figure of moral authority enables the child to adopt a stance of moral autonomy resisting the pressure of his/her peers and of the corrupted social environment. Following Freud, in his study on authority and family written back in the 1930s, Max Horkheimer made the same point, while, in the same spirit, Adorno pointed out that Hitler is not a paternal figure. And in his classic *Auf dem Weg zur vaterlosen Gesellschaft*,[35] Alexander Mitcherlich analyses in detail the process of the loss of paternal authority and how it gives birth to new forms of domination.

The obvious answer to this crisis is: no authorities should rule the people, people themselves should reign. But in today's populism, the dark obscene side of the reference to the people also made itself palpable. The People to which populism refers does not exist: populism is by definition a mask of power, it is a fantasized entity evoked by new masters to justify their role as the servants of the people, enabling them to dismiss their opponents as the enemies of the people. The first step towards populism was made centuries ago when, to counter the loss of traditional authority, the leader (king) proclaimed himself a servant. Friedrich the Great defined himself as "the first servant of State," and this is how, from the early Enlightenment onwards, a master justifies his rule: he is in reality the greatest servant, the servant of all his subjects/servants.[36] But there are different modalities of this position of "serving the servants," from technocracy and religious fundamentalism to obscene master-clown, or even, as Mao Zedong can be characterized, to a "Lord of Misrule," a master who periodically organizes rebellion against the order installed by himself. The obscene Master is not a direct reaction to the failure of the traditional Master, it is a reaction to the fact that knowledge (S_2, the agent of the University discourse) cannot properly function at the place of the agent of a discourse (social link) so that it has to be supplemented by a new obscene figure.[37] Insofar as the obscene Master operates as a superego figure, we should recall here Jacques-Alain Miller's old claim that the superego is on the side of S_2, not on the side of S_1. The point of this disintegration is not that the empirical bearer of a symbolic function (father, leader) cannot live up to his symbolic mandate (say, that a father doesn't properly function as a father) but that this mandate itself is losing its power.[38]

The reaction to this critical predicament is double. We can reluctantly accept the need to return to some form of social authority since, if the symbolic Law (Name-of-the-Father) loses its authority, desire itself (sustained by the prospect of transgressing it) vanishes. Along these lines, some Lacanians claim that the problem today is the decline of the Name-of-the-Father, of the paternal symbolic authority: in its absence, pathological Narcissism explodes, evoking the spectre of the primordial Real Father. Consequently, we should try to restore some kind of Law as the agent of prohibition. Although this idea is to be rejected, it correctly points out how the decline of the Master in no way automatically guarantees emancipation but can well engender much more oppressive figures of domination. Is, however, the return to Prohibition sustained by Law the only way out? It seems that the very last Lacan, aware of this problem, proposed another solution which Miller, in his reading of Lacan, calls "cynical"—we cannot return to the authority of the Law, but what we can do is act as if we sustain the Law... in short, Miller's solution is: we are psychotics who try to play normal hysterics. Miller has fearlessly spelt out the political implications of this stance: a psychoanalyst "acts so that semblances remain at their places while making sure that the subjects under his care do not take them as *real* ... one should somehow bring oneself to remain *taken in by them* (fooled by them)."[39] The axiom of this cynical wisdom is that "one should protect the semblances of power for the good reason that one should be able to continue to *enjoy*. The point is not to attach oneself to the semblances of the existing power, but to consider them necessary."[40] (Miller repeats here the famous line from Kafka's *The Trial*: the law is not true, it is just necessary.) Is this cynical stance the only way out?

Another perhaps more refined form of the return of the repressed is that the repressed returns as a fiction, and, well aware that it is only a fiction, we emotionally fully commit ourselves to it. The TV spectacle we were able to watch on September 9, 2022—the ceremony of Queen Elizabeth's burial—reminds us of how the British monarchy embodies a similar paradox: the more not only the British monarch but also the United Kingdom as a state lost its superpower status and became a local power, the more the status of the British royal family become the stuff of ideological fantasies all around the world—according to the official estimates, the ceremony was watched by four billion people around the world. We should not dismiss this as ideology masking actual power relations: the British royal fantasy is one of the key components which enable actual power relations to reproduce themselves. This fantasy doesn't concern only the present royal family: remember how, in 2012, an archaeological excavation was commissioned by the Richard III Society on the site previously occupied by Grey Friars Priory. The University of Leicester identified the skeleton found in the excavation as that of Richard III as a result of radiocarbon dating, comparison with contemporary reports of his appearance, identification of trauma sustained at the Battle of Bosworth and comparison of his mitochondrial DNA with that of two matrilineal descendants of his sister Anne. He was reburied in Leicester Cathedral on March 26, 2015, and, again, the ceremony of burial (where only a hundred or so people were expected) was witnessed by over one hundred thousand people. Facts like these cannot be dismissed as reactionary fantasies: the correct insight they bear is the distinction between the symbolic top of power and the actual executive power. Kings and queens reign, they don't rule; their reign is ceremonial and as such crucial.

The paradox of a monarch (or of any other form of the symbolic peak of power) is that, precisely as a unique figure, the One, the traditional dignified Master is already in him/herself interchangeable. Since it is a contingent body attached to a name (and as such a purely performative agency), nothing really changes if s/he is replaced by a double. No wonder that leaders, and precisely those who were perceived as unique, are as a rule suspected to have doubles who appear publicly on their behalf (from Tito to Saddam). But is it true that nothing changes? The ideological fantasy is that everything may change. In Ivan Reitman's 1993 film *Dave*, Dave Kovic, a good-natured and caring Temp Agency operator, by a staggering coincidence looks exactly like the actual president, the philandering and distant Bill Mitchell, president of the United States. As such, when Mitchell wants to escape an official luncheon, the Secret Service hires Dave to stand in for him. Unfortunately, Mitchell suffers a severe stroke whilst having sex with one of his aides, and Dave finds himself stuck in the role indefinitely. The corrupt and manipulative Chief of Staff Bob Alexander plans to use Dave to elevate himself to the White House—but unfortunately, he doesn't count on Dave enjoying himself in office, using his luck to make the country a better place . . . A prior version of this fantasy is provided in Alexandre Dumas's *The Man in the Iron Mask*:[41] Philippe, Louis XIVs twin brother, is locked in a prison with an iron mask on his face so that nobody can recognize him; the three musketeers and d'Artagnan liberate Philippe and replace Louis (who is put in a prison with iron mask) with him—Philippe becomes the Louis XIV we all know, leading France to glory.

Is then the solution to take care that the One on the top nonetheless meets certain criteria (moral integrity, politeness and kindness, pragmatic sense of reckoning)? The moment we think this way, what awaits us at the end is the figure of a Stalinist Leader who is the very opposite of a monarch: he is definitely not a traditional Master, also not an obscene Master, and also not an agent of liberal-democratic stance or of contemporary scientific knowledge based on rational reasoning and experimentation. He is rather a pathological distortion of the University discourse, the return of its repressed: in Stalinism, the Master-signifier directly overlaps with the space of knowledge. There is no post-truth here, no obscene multiplicity and self-irony: knowledge is acting as Truth itself.

But why a master at all? The other way to deal with the decline of traditional authority is the anarchist way, and anarchism is having a revival today, from Noam Chomsky to David Graeber. Anarchism is not against public power—Catherine Malabou, another neo-anarchist, refers to Jacques Rancière who asserts "radical equality between citizens who are considered able to both command and obey."[42] There is an essential relationship between drawing lots and democratic expression: there is public power, but "true democracy would rely on the contingency of who governs and who is governed because governing does not require any particular skill."[43] In his reply to Malabou, Etienne Balibar goes to the crux of the problem:

> The anarchist will say that we are able to imagine and realize in practice now an alternative social fabric because the whole society could, one way or another, emerge from forms of self-government and self-organization that can be experienced and experimented with at the level of cooperatives, towns and so on. Today, this idea is becoming increasingly influential and people give us examples of what the Kurdish fighters tried in Rojava, what the Zapatistas are trying in Chiapas, and so forth. From there they extrapolate and say what works at the local level could work at the global level, provided you find the right forms of federation.[44]

Malabou herself points out two other problems; first, anarchism is becoming today a key feature of global capitalism:

> Our current epoch is characterized by a coexistence between a de facto anarchism and a dawning or awakening anarchism. De facto anarchism is the reign of anarcho-capitalism, which is contemporaneous with the end of the welfare state, creating in citizens a feeling of abandonment—just think of the state of hospitals and healthcare today. My contention is that current capitalism is undertaking its anarchist or libertarian turn: a generalized 'Uberization' of life.[45]

Second, this anarcho-capitalism is the other side of new authoritarianism:

> Authoritarianism does not contradict the disappearance of the state; it is its messenger—the mask of this so-called "collaborative" economy which, by bringing professionals and users into direct contact through technological platforms, pulverizes all fixity.[46]

One should only add here that this mask is not only a mask, it is also the hidden truth of the anarchic collaborative economy.

What this means is that the rising authoritarianism is the other side of the disappearance of the state—more precisely, of the most precious function of the state, that of providing public services. We thereby touch on the vast domain of public services (healthcare, education ...) which cannot be provided through expanding cooperatives and other forms of local self-organizations. Balibar makes this point clear:

> If you look at the poor in American suburbs, mainly African Americans and other migrant groups, what they suffer from is the fact that America never really had a welfare state or a social state in the British, French or German sense. The catastrophe for them is not that there is too much state, it's that there is not enough of the state.[47]

So yes, popular mobilization outside party politics and state apparatuses is needed—but communities evoked by anarchists rely on a thick texture of "alienated" institutional mechanisms: where do electricity and water come from? Who guarantees the rule of law? To whom do we turn for healthcare? The more a community is self-ruling, the more this network has to function smoothly and invisibly.

Consequently, the usual oppositions (alienation versus disalienation, unconditional state power versus a state power limited to providing public services) have to be left behind: we do not overcome alienation by desalienation, we do not overcome master by eliminating him, we do not overcome public power by limiting it to useful public services. The non-alienated autonomous liberal individual is itself a product of alienation in capitalist society; a master effectively serving the people, taking care of them, is a fetish created to prevent the possibility that individuals will themselves take care of themselves; the idea of power serving society justifies power and thus obfuscates its constitutive excess. Since today permissiveness and free choice are elevated into a supreme value, social control and domination can no longer appear as infringing on the subject's freedom: it has to appear as (and be sustained by) the very self-experience of individuals as free. Unable to break out of this vicious cycle alone, as isolated individuals, since the more we act freely the more we get enslaved into the system, we need to be "awakened" from this "dogmatic slumber" of fake freedom from outside, by the push of a Master figure. This is why Isolde Charim is fully justified in characterizing today's post-patriarchal narcissistic subject as a subject practicing voluntary servitude:[48] When I focus on my Ego, its potentials, interests and needs, I am far from being free, I remain enslaved to the socio-symbolic space within which my Ego was shaped.

There was a trace of the authentic Master's call even in Obama's motto from his first presidential campaign: "Yes, we can!" A new possibility was thereby opened—but, one might say, did Hitler also not do something formally similar? Was his message to the German people not "Yes, we can . . ."—kill the Jews, squash democracy, act in a racist way, attack other nations? A closer analysis immediately brings out the difference: far from being an authentic Master, Hitler was a populist demagogue who carefully played upon people's obscure desires. A true Master doesn't try to guess what people want; he simply obeys his own desire so that it is up to the people to decide if they will follow him. In other words, his power stems from his fidelity to his desire, from not compromising it. Therein resides the difference between a true Master and, say, a Fascist or Stalinist leader who pretends to know (better than the people themselves) what people really want (what is really good for them), and is then ready to enforce this on them even against their will.

In short, in order for the individuals to "reach beyond themselves," to break out of their passivity and engage themselves as direct political agents, the reference to a Leader is necessary, a Leader who allows them to pull themselves out of the swamp like Baron Munchhausen. Badiou's thesis is that a subject needs a Master to elevate itself above the "human animal" and to practice fidelity to a Truth-Event:

> The master is the one who helps the individual to become subject. That is to say, if one admits that the subject emerges in the tension between the individual and the universality, then it is obvious that the individual needs a mediation, and thereby an authority, in order to progress on this path. The crisis of the master is a logical consequence of the crisis of the subject, and psychoanalysis did not escape it. One has to renew the position of the master, it is not true that one can do without it, even and especially in the perspective of emancipation.[49]

And Badiou is not afraid to oppose the necessary role of the Master to our "democratic" sensitivity: "This capital function of leaders is not compatible with the predominant 'democratic' ambience, which is why I am engaged in a bitter struggle against this ambience (after all, one has to begin with ideology)."[50] But does this not involve a contradiction with Lacan's claim that there is no big Other? How to read together the fact that the big Other doesn't exist and the utter self-sacrificial reliance on the figure of an Other? The obvious reading of the fact that there is no big Other would have been for the bearer of authority to admit openly to those subjected to him that he is not qualified to exert authority and to simply step down, leaving his subjects to confront reality as they can—Hannah Arendt outlines this gesture apropos parental authority:

> Modern man could find no clearer expression for his dissatisfaction with the world, for his disgust with things as they are, than by his refusal to assume, in respect to his children, responsibility for all this. It is as though parents daily said: "In this world even we are not very securely at home; how to move about in it, what to know, what skills to master, are mysteries to us too. You must try to make out as best you can; in any case you are not entitled to call us to account. We are innocent, we wash our hands of you."[51]

Although this imagined answer of the parents is factually more or less true, it is nonetheless existentially false: a parent cannot wash his/her hands in this way. (The same goes for saying: "I have no free will, my decisions are the product of my brain signals, so I wash my hands, I have no responsibility for crimes that I committed!" Even if this is factually true, it is false as my subjective stance.) This means that "the ethical lesson is that parents should pretend (to know what to do and how the world works), for there is no way out of the problem of authority other than to assume it, in its very fictionality, with all the difficulties and discontents this entails."[52]

But, again, how does this differ from Miller's cynical solution? Paradoxically, it is that the subject, although fully aware of his/her incompetence to exert authority, assumes it not with a cynical distance but with full sincerity, ready even to sacrifice his/her life for it if needed. The opposite of fundamentalism is the awareness that the authority we refer to has no real fundament but is self-referentially grounded in an abyss. Let's take a perhaps surprising example: the finale of Wagner's *Rhinegold*[53] which ends with the contrast between Rhinemaidens bemoaning their lost innocence and the majestic entrance of the Gods into Valhalla, a powerful assertion of the rule of Law. It is customary to claim that the sincere and authentic complaint of the Rhinemaidens makes it clear how the triumphant entrance of the Gods into Valhalla is a fake, a hollow spectacle; however, what if it is precisely the saddening background of the Rhinemaidens' song which gives to the entry into Valhalla its authentic greatness? The Gods know they are doomed, but nonetheless they heroically perform their ceremonial act. This is why we are not dealing here with the usual fetishist disavowal but with a courageous act of taking a risk and ignoring my limitations, along the lines of Kant's *Du kannst, denn du sollst!*—I know I am too weak to do it, but I'll nonetheless do it—a gesture which is the very opposite of cynicism. In Wagner's opera, the cynic is Loge (Loki), the embodiment of knowledge (S_2), the demi-god of fire, Wotan's clever, manipulative executive servant who does not follow the gods to Valhalla; he says in an aside that he is tempted to destroy the complacent gods by fire, but he will think it over . . . Far below, the Rhinemaidens mourn the loss of their gold and condemn the gods as false and cowardly—Roger Scruton writes of this lament: "And yet, ever sounding in the depths, is the lament of the Rhine-daughters, singing of a natural order that preceded the conscious will that has usurped it. This lament sounds in the unconsciousness of us all, as we pursue our paths to personality, sovereignty and freedom . . ." These are the last voices that are heard in the opera, "piercing our hearts with sudden longing, melting our bones with nostalgic desire," before the gods, "marching in empty triumph to their doom," enter Valhalla to a thunderous orchestral conclusion . . . Is this triumph really empty? Is there not in it a heroic dignity, an indication that Wotan takes risk, well aware that his authority is not properly grounded?[54]

But, again, are we here not back at the cynical position—authority is not true, just necessary? No, because, to quote Miller himself, the cynical position "resides in saying that enjoyment is *the only thing that is true*," while in the case evoked by Arendt, the fiction is more true than reality, we are ready to risk our life for it precisely because it is a fiction—we are here back at Lacan's "the truth has the structure of a fiction." "There is no big Other" doesn't mean that if there is no God then everything is permitted—as Lacan knew, it means the exact opposite, that everything is prohibited, and to break out of this prohibition I have to act counterfactually. "There is no big Other" is not a cold description of the state of things—such a description implies that I occupy the place of a big Other, a neutral view on reality, in the same sense that universal historicism exempts me from historical relativism. "There is no big Other" means that, in a maximum of subjective engagement, I have to identify myself as the hole in the big Other, as the crack in its edifice.

So, to go to the end, one has to correct Lacan here: the last, most radical, subjective position is not that of the analyst. After achieving this, after traversing the fantasy and assuming that there is no big Other, the only way to avoid cynicism is to heroically pass to the position of a new Master.

Notes

Introduction

1. What follows is taken from a personal communication to me by Peng Tai'ming.
2. Martin Heidegger, *Logic as the Question Concerning the Essence of Language*, Albany: SUNY Press 2009, p. 73.
3. See Grant Farred, *Martin Heidegger Saved My Life*, Minneapolis: University of Minnesota Press 2015.
4. Living with the ghost of Martin Heidegger—University of Minnesota Press Blog (uminnpressblog.com), proper details.
5. Alain Badiou, *The True Life*, Cambridge: Polity Press 2017, p. 7
6. "Niemand ist mehr Sklave, als der sich für frei hält, ohne es zu sein." (Johann Wolfgang Goethe, Die Wahlverwandtschaften, Hamburger Ausgabe, Bd. 6, dtv Verlag, München: dtv Verlag 1982, p. 397)
7. "Mao Zedong," Wikipedia, The Free Encyclopedia, https://en.wikipedia.org/w/index.php?title—ao_Zedong&oldid=1156088558
8. See Mladen Dolar, *Od kod prihaja oblast?* (in Slovene), Ljubljana: Analecta 2021, pp. 84–85.
9. Immanuel Kant, "Lectures on pedagogy," in *Lectures on Ethics*, Cambridge: Cambridge University Press 1997, p. 437.
10. Ibid., p. 438.
11. Ibid., p. 369.
12. "Grass Mud Horse," Wikipedia, The Free Encyclopedia, https://en.wikipedia.org/w/index.php?title=Grass_Mud_Horse&oldid=1151326242
13. Gilles Deleuze, *Cinema 2: The Time-Image*, London and New York: The Athlone Press 2005 [1985], pp. 178–179.

14. https://minimalistquotes.com/agnes-sligh-turnbull-quote-243926/. The quote is often attributed to Agnes Sligh Turnbull, but may be originally that of the French diplomat Charles-Maurice de Talleyrand-Périgord.
15. See "Torn Curtain," Wikipedia, The Free Encyclopedia, https://en.wikipedia.org/w/index.php?title=Torn_Curtain&oldid=1151212392

1 Freedom and Its Discontents

1. Étienne Balibar, *Spinoza and Politics*, New York: Verso 1998, p. 88.
2. "Liberty," Wikipedia, The Free Encyclopedia, https://en.wikipedia.org/w/index.php?title=Liberty&oldid=1154099098
3. "Lust, Caution," Wikipedia, The Free Encyclopedia, https://en.wikipedia.org/w/index.php?title=Lust,_Caution&oldid=1153441169
4. "Today's version of 'I command you to freely sign this document!'," Žižek (reddit.com), https://www.reddit.com/r/zizek/comments/x2pjlb/todays_version_of_i_command_you_to_freely_sign/
5. See "Even what's secret is a secret in China," *The Japan Times*, June 16, 2007, p. 17.
6. Franz Kafka, "The Problem of Our Laws," in *The Complete Stories*, New York: Schocken Books 1995, p. 437.
7. Jacques Derrida, *Acts of Literature*, New York: Routledge 1992, p. 201.
8. See (in Slovene) Ingrid Meger, "Milena Miklavčič, 'Avtorica knjige Ogenj, rit in kače niso za igrače: Kako so seksali in rojevali pred sto leti'," *Dnevnik*, April 12, 2014, https://www.dnevnik.si/1042659827
9. Noah Gordon, "Paris Alive: Jean-Paul Sartre on World War II," *The Atlantic*, September 2014, https://www.theatlantic.com/
10. See the interview with Mansur Tayfuri, a Kurdish researcher (available on "Interview with Mansour Tayfuri on Kurdish exodus of 1979 in Mariwan – Rawej", Sunday, November 20, 2016 on Vimeo, https://vimeo.com/193933442), on his master's thesis on the resistance of people of Mariwan, "La dernière barricade de la revolution. Forme de résistance en Kurdistan après la révolution iranienne de 1979," presented to the Université Paris VIII-Saint Denis in September 2014.

11. Friedrich Engels,"Anti-Duhring," ch. 9, available online at https://www.marxists.org/archive/marx/works/1877/anti-duhring/ch09.htm. G.W.F. Hegel, *The Science of Logic*, Cambridge: Cambridge University Press 2010, p. 509.
12. Quoted from Somerset Maugham, *Sheppey* (a play, 1933), last publication in *W. Somerset Maugham, Plays*, Vol. I, London: Bloomsbury 1997. Agatha Christie also refers to this story in her *Appointment with Death* (1938).
13. Quoted from Daniel Gilbert,"Buried by bad decisions," available online at https://www.nature.com/articles/474275a
14. See Peter Sloterdijk, *Critique of Cynical Reason*, Minneapolis: Minnesota University Press 1988, p. 11.
15. Quoted from Alenka Zupančič,"Perverzniu obrat utajitve," (manuscript in Slovene) – translation mine.
16. See Alenka Zupančič,"The End" (manuscript).
17. I resume here a line of thought from the Introduction to my *The Courage of Hopelessness*, London: Penguin Books 2017.
18. Monir Ghaedi,"Viral protests: Russians continue to denounce war, risking imprisonment", *DW*, March 3, 2022, https://www.dw.com/
19. From the 1939 American comedy *Ninotchka*, directed by Ernst Lubitsch.
20. See Benjamin Libet,"Unconscious Cerebral Initiative and the Role of Conscious Will in Voluntary Action," in *The Behavioral and Brain Sciences*, 1985, Vol. 8, pp. 529–539; and Benjamin Libet,"Do We Have Free Will?," in *Journal of Consciousness Studies*, 1999, Vol. 1, pp. 47–57.
21. Surprisingly (or not), the work of Edith Wharton, usually perceived as a chronicle of snobbish high society, provides an exemplary portrait of the intersection between "economic base" and "ideological superstructure": her refined psychological portraits focus on the desperate reaction to class struggle and financial inequality. Just recall *The House of Mirth*, whose heroine Lily fails in her love life since she persists in marrying for money. Incidentally, the same holds for the TV series *The Guilded Age* (created by Julian Fellowes, HBO, first season 2022), which deals with the conflict between "old money" (bent on maintaining high society traditions) and "new money" (train and other barons who brutally amass money and struggle to enter "society," to be accepted by it) in New York in the 1880s: all the refined psychological and ideological conflicts have sense only against the background of this economic struggle.

2 Is There Such a Thing as "Free Will"?

1. See Benjamin Libet, "Unconscious Cerebral Initiative and the Role of Conscious Will in Voluntary Action," in *The Behavioral and Brain Sciences*, 1985, Vol. 8, pp. 529–539; and Benjamin Libet, "Do We Have Free Will?," in *Journal of Consciousness Studies*, 1999, Vol. 1, pp. 47–57.
2. Quoted from Thorsten Jantschek, "Ein ausgezehrter Hase," *Die Zeit*, July 5, 2001, Feuilleton, p. 26.
3. Bill McKibben, *Enough: Staying Human in an Engineered Age*, New York: Henry Holt and Company 2004, p. 127.
4. See Georg Lukács, *The Ontology of Social Being*, Vols. 1–3, London: Merlin Press 1978–1980.
5. Daniel Dennett, "Back from the Drawing Board," in *Dennett and His Critics*, ed. Bo Dahlbom, Oxford: Blackwell 1993, pp. 204–205.
6. Ibid., p. 40.
7. Ibid., p. 43.
8. Antonio Damasio, *Descartes' Error: Emotion, Reason, and the Human Brain*, New York: Quill 1995, p. 30.
9. Ibid., p. 51.
10. Jean-Paul Sartre, *Nausea*, London: Penguin 2000.
11. T.S. Eliot, "Tradition and the Individual Talent," originally published in *The Sacred Wood: Essays on Poetry and Criticism* (1922).
12. "Correspondance: Lettres de Louis Althusser à Fernanda Navarro à propos de l'édition de Philosophie et marxisme, précédées d'une lettre à Mauricio Malamud (1984-1987)," *Sur la philosophie* [ed. Olivier Corpet], Paris: Gallimard, 1994, p. 121.
13. Ibid., pp. 127–128.
14. Louis Althusser, "Ideology and Ideological State Apparatuses," in *Essays in Ideology*, London: Verso 1984, p. 163.
15. I resume here a more detailed critical reading of Althusser's notion of ideology from Chapter 3 of Slavoj Žižek, *The Metastases of Enjoyment*, London: Verso Books 2006.
16. Here I follow the perspicacious observations of Henry Krips—see his excellent unpublished manuscript "The Subject of Althusser and Lacan."
17. Michael Egnor, "Does Superdeterminism Resolve Dilemmas Around Free Will," *Mind Matters*, December 26, 2021, https://mindmatters.ai/

2021/12/does-superdeterminism-resolve-dilemmas-around-free-will/

18. I have written about this extensively in my previous books, so I do not want to lose space here for explaining it.
19. See David Chalmers, *Reality*+, New York: Norton 2022.
20. Martin Heidegger, *Zollikoner Seminare*, Frankfurt: Vittorio Klostermann 2017, p. 260.
21. See Britannica, T. Editors of Encyclopaedia, "Pascal's wager." Encyclopedia Britannica, December 13, 2022. https://www.britannica.com/topic/Pascals-wager.
22. I rely here on Dominiek Hoens, "Is Life but a Pascalean Dream?," *Psychoanalytische Perspectivien*, Vol. 36/2, pp. 169–185, available online at https://www.psychoanalytischeperspectieven.be/vol-36-2-2018/is-life-but-a-pascalian-dream-a-commentary-on-lacans-louvain-lecture
23. "Reponse de Jacques Lacan a une question de Marcel Ritter," *Lettres de l'Ecole freudienne* 18 (1975), 7–1, p. 2.
24. https://www.marxists.org/archive/lenin/works/cw/pdf/lenin-cw-vol-38.pdf
25. "Bulletproof Monk," Wikipedia, The Free Encyclopedia, https://en.wikipedia.org/w/index.php?title=Bulletproof_Monk&oldid=1152759310
26. G.K. Chesterton, *Orthodoxy*, San Francisco: Ignatius Press 1995, p. 145.
27. Sigmund Freud, "The Ego and the Id," quoted from https://www.sigmundfreud.net/the-ego-and-the-id-pdf-ebook.jsp.
28. I rely here extensively on Alenka Zupančič, *Ethics of the Real: Kant and Lacan*, London: Verso Books 1995.
29. Rachel Metz, "AI won an art contest, and artists are furious", *CNN Business*, September 3, 2022, https://edition.cnn.com/2022/09/03/tech/ai-art-fair-winner-controversy/index.html

3 Indivisible Remainder and the Death of Death

1. Robert Pippin, "The Return of Metaphysics: Hegel vs Kant," IAI TV, January 21, 2022, https://iai.tv/articles/the-return-of-metaphysics-hegel-vs-kant-auid-2032?_auid=2020

2. I owe this joke to Todd MacGowan.
3. Terry Pinkard, "Should Hegelian Political Philosophy Jettison the Absolute? Hegel's Political Philosophy Two-hundred Years Later," *Crisis and Critique* 8, no. 2 (2021), https://www.crisiscritique.org/storage/app/media/2021-12-13/cc-82-terry-pinkard.pdf
4. Terry Pinkard, *Hegel: A Biography*, Cambridge: Cambridge University Press 2000, pp. VIII–IX.
5. There are theological readings of my work which elaborate this point—see, for example, https://www.youtube.com/watch?v=4oK2kZS2gNQ.
6. F.W.J. von Schelling, *Ages of the World*, Ann Arbor: The University of Michigan Press 1997, pp. 181–182. See also Chapter 1 of Slavoj Zizek, *The Indivisible Remainder*, London: Verso Books 1997.
7. Jacques Derrida, *Adieu à Emmanuel Levinas*, Paris: Galilee 1997, p. 87.
8. See Frank Ruda, *Abolishing Freedom*, Winnipeg: Bison Books 2016.
9. Etienne Balibar, "'Tod des Todes'. From the Philosophy of Religion to the Phenomenology," in *Zweite Natur. Stuttgarter Hegel-Kongress 2017*. Herausgegeben von Julia Christ und Axel Honneth, Frankfurt: Vittorio Klostermann 2022, p. 326.
10. Ibid., pp. 323–324.
11. Ibid., pp. 637–638
12. Ibid., p. 331.
13. John 4:12, The Holy Bible, New International Version.
14. Balibar, op. cit., p. 636.
15. G.W.F. Hegel, *Lectures on the Philosophy of Religion, Volume III: The Consummate Religion*, Oxford: Clarendon Press 2007, p. 206.
16. Ibid., p. 337.
17. Adrian Johnston, "Conclusion: The Modest Absolute: or, Why I am not an agnostic (or even an agnostic atheist)" (manuscript).
18. I owe this reference to Delport, Hook and Moss to Stephen Frosh (Birkbeck College, University of London).
19. Quoted from Derek Hook, "White anxiety in (post)apartheid South Africa," *Psychoanalysis, Culture & Society* 25 (2020): 612–631, doi:10.1057/s41282-020-00178-1. Hook2020_Article_WhiteAnxietyInPostApartheidSou.pdf.

20. Donald Moss, "On Having Whiteness," *Journal of the American Psychoanalytic Association* 69, no. 2 (2021): 355–371. https://journals.sagepub.com/doi/abs/10.1177/00030651211
21. Ibid.
22. "Who Really Killed Malcolm X?" *The New York Times* (2020). https://www.nytimes.com/2020/02/06/nyregion/malcolm-x-assassination-case-reopened.html
23. "Assassination of Malcolm X," Wikipedia, The Free Encyclopedia, https://en.wikipedia.org/w/index.php?title=Assassination_of_Malcolm_X&oldid=1154232503
24. See "Still Alice," Wikipedia, The Free Encyclopedia, https://en.wikipedia.org/w/index.php?title=Still_Alice&oldid=1151043822
25. Sigmund Freud, *The Interpretation of Dreams*, Harmondsworth: Penguin Books 1976, p. 446.
26. There is a nice case of a short-circuit between the frame and its content in *Midsomer Murders*. The series is introduced (plus some passages and scenes are accompanied) by a simple melodic motif which we (spectators) take as part of the frame, not of the reality depicted in the series. However, in one of the episodes, there is a scene that takes place in a village fair, with a wind orchestra playing the very motif that introduces each episode of the series—as if those who act in the series somehow were aware that they are in the series and knew the accompanying music . . .

    There is another version of the short-circuit between frame and its content in today's cinema. The Russian-Kazakh director and producer Timur Bekmambetov (now living in LA) is the main proponent of Screenlife or computer screen film where all the movie events occur on a computer, tablet or smartphone screen. According to "Timur Bekmambetov," Wikipedia, The Free Encyclopedia, https://en.wikipedia.org/w/index.php?title=Timur_Bekmambetov&oldid=1152326419, a computer screen film should take place on one specific screen, never move outside of the screen, the camerawork should resemble the behaviour of the device's camera, all the action should take place in real time, without any visible transitions and all the sounds should originate from the computer. (See "Screenlife," Wikipedia, The Free Encyclopedia, https://en.wikipedia.org/w/index.php?title=Screenlife&oldid=1145738133)
27. Herbert Marcuse, *Eros and Civilization*, Boston: Beacon Press 1974, p. 37.

28. Ibid., pp. 37–38.
29. I resume here the line of thought from the chapter "Parataxis" of my *Less Than Nothing*, London: Verso Books 2013.
30. I rely here on the line of thought deployed by Aaron Schuster and Alenka Zupančič.
31. See "Frome," Wikipedia, The Free Encyclopedia, https://en.wikipedia.org/w/index.php?title=Ethan_Frome&oldid=1151110419
32. Quoted from *Ethan Frome. A Norton Critical Edition*, New York: Norton 1995, pp. 120–121.
33. Lionel Trilling, "The Morality of Inertia," in *Ethan Frome. A Norton Critical Edition*, op. cit., p. 126.
34. See John Rodden, *Lionel Trilling and the Critics: Opposing Selves*, Lincoln: University of Nebraska Press 1999.
35. Frederic and Mary Ann Brussat, "Ethan Frome: Film Review," *Spirituality & Practice* (n.d.). https://www.spiritualityandpractice.com/films/reviews/view/6220
36. Edith Wharton, "Ethan Frome Epilogue Summary & Analysis," LitCharts. https://www.litcharts.com/lit/ethan-frome/epilogue
37. I follow here the reading by Jean Frantz Blackall in his "Edith Wharton's Art of Elipsis," in *Ethan Frome. A Norton Critical Edition*, op. cit., p. 174.
38. Cynthia Griffin Wolff, "The Narrator's Vision," in *Ethan Frome. A Norton Critical Edition*, op. cit., p. 145.
39. The movie version (John Madden, 1993) misses it all: the narrator is a new priest in the town (so the parallel between the narrator and Ethan—both are/were in their youth ambitious and interested in technical education—is lost), there is full sex between Ethan and Mattie, but the trauma—indicated by Mrs Hale's final words—is censured.
40. Tana French, *Broken Harbour*, London: Penguin Books 2013. In my observations on *Broken Harbour*, I rely heavily on Amy Adams's blog – see The Book Blog of Evil: Broken Harbor, by Tana French, http://maebookblog.blogspot.com/2012/08/broken-harbor-by-tana-french.html
41. I rely here on the line of thought deployed by Mladen Dolar.
42. I resume here my line of thought from "Corollary 2: Circular Time" in *Sex and the Failed Absolute*, London: Bloomsbury 2019.

43. An exemplary case of the tension between the universal and the particular is the case of a symptom. Let us imagine that somebody has to report on his/her/it's very traumatic experience. If its reporting gets stuck or if there are inconsistencies in it, this should of course be treated as a symptom and to be interpreted. But if the report is perfect, if it runs smoothly, without deadlocks and interruptions (i.e., if the fact that the report deals with a traumatic content is not somehow inscribed into the way the story is narrated), this is an even greater symptom, an indication that the report as such is a fake—how come the subject who experienced the trauma was not affected by it, how come that they are able to report about it coolly, as if they are an external observer?

Appendix 1

1. Quotes are from Adrian Johnston's monumental *Infinite Greed: Money, Marxism, Psychoanalysis* (Columbia University Press, 2024).
2. Ricardo Sanín Restrepo, "Many Worlds Interpretation, Critical Theory and the (Immanent) Paradox of Power", *Critical Legal Thinking* (online, 2021). https://criticallegalthinking.com/2021/11/22/many-worlds-interpretation-critical-theory-and-the-immanent-paradox-of-power/
3. Quoted in Marcelo Gleiser, "Can quantum mechanics explain consciousness?," *Big Think* (November 4, 2021). https://bigthink.com/13-8/quantum-consciousness-2/
4. Sabine Hossenfelder and Tim Palmer, "How to Make Sense of Quantum Physics," *Nautilus* (online 2020). https://nautil.us/how-to-make-sense-of-quantum-physics-237736/
5. Donna Lu, "What is a Quantum computer?," *New Scientist* (online, n.d.). https://www.newscientist.com/question/what-is-a-quantum-computer/

Appendix 2

1. Jean Casimir, *The Haitians: A Decolonial History*, Chapel Hill: The University of North Carolina Press 2020. I rely here on Rocio Zambrana's "Hegelian History Interrupted" (Columbia University Press, 2024).

2. "Guarani language," Wikipedia, The Free Encyclopedia, https://en.wikipedia.org/w/index.php?title=Guarani_language&oldid=1153210540.
3. The actual role of colonizers in language was, of course, more complex and ambiguous. In Canada, Inuits were called by other indigenous people who lived to the south of them *Askamiciw*, "those who eat raw food"; Christian missionaries then transcribed this as *Excominqui*, "excommunicated," and the general public condensed it into "Eskimos." Our task should be not just to restore the original term but to reconstruct the interaction of cultures so that we will not just use the term "Inuits" as an exotic intruder into our mode of speaking and thinking.

Appendix 3

1. Wendy Powers and Robin McLeod, *The Testament of Judith Barton*, San Francisco: PM Press 2011.
2. Review of *The Testament of Judith Barton*, Kirkus Reviews. https://www.kirkusreviews.com/book-reviews/wendy-powers/the-testament-of-judith-barton/
3. Powers and McLeod, *The Testament of Judith Barton*, p. 278.
4. For a more detailed analysis of this scene, see chapter II.2 of my *Organs Without Bodies* (New York: Routledge 2012).

Appendix 4

1. Quoted from Georg Wilhelm Friedrich Hegel, *The Philosophy of History*, trans. J. Sibree, Batoche Books, 2001. Available online at https://socialsciences.mcmaster.ca/econ/ugcm/3ll3/hegel/history.pdf
2. Boris Groys, quoted from "The Cold War between the Medium and the Message: Western Modernism vs. Socialist Realism," *e-flux Journal* no. 104 (2019). https://www.e-flux.com/journal/104/297103/the-cold-war-between-the-medium-and-the-message-western-modernism-vs-socialist-realism/. In my description, I rely heavily on Groys's text.
3. "Jail cells 'made from modern art,'" BBC News Online: Entertainment: Arts (March 28, 2003). http://news.bbc.co.uk/1/hi/entertainment/2698177.stm

4. Quoted from Groys, op. cit.
5. Ibid.
6. Ibid.
7. One should mention here another surprising exception: Irving Reis's *Crack-Up*, a *noir* from 1946 in which the elite proponents of modern non-realist art are presented as corrupted Fascist villains who aim at confusing masses of ordinary people; the film's hero is an art critic who attacks modern art and defends the taste of ordinary people.
8. Steven Pinker, *The Blank Slate: The Modern Denial of Human Nature*, London: Penguin 2002.
9. Robert B. Pippin, *After the Beautiful: Hegel and the Philosophy of Pictorial Modernism*, Chicago: University of Chicago Press, 2014, p. 69.
10. I resume here my argumentation from chapter 4 of *Disparities*, London: Bloomsbury Press, 2016.

4 Marx Invented Not Only Symptom But Also Drive

1. Quoted from Karl Marx, *Capital A Critique of Political Economy. Volume I, Book One: The Process of Production of Capital*. Available online at http://www.marxists.org/archive/marx/works/1867-c1/ch04.htm.
2. Karl Marx, *A Contribution to the Critique of Political Economy*, New York: International Publishers 1970, p. 134.
3. Karl Marx, *Theories of Surplus-Value*, Moscow: Progress Publishers 1963, pp. 282–283.
4. Quoted from Karl Marx, *Economic & Philosophic Manuscripts of 1844* available online at https://www.marxists.org/archive/marx/works/download/pdf/Poverty-Philosophy.pdf
5. Robert Pippin, "The Return of Metaphysics: Hegel vs Kant," *IAInews* blog (January 21, 2022). https://iai.tv/articles/the-return-of-metaphysics-hegel-vs-kant-auid-2032?_auid=2020
6. Quoted from Adrian Johnston's monumental *Infinite Greed* (to appear in 2024 at Northwestern University Press, Evanston.). All non-accredited quotes in this chapter are from *Infinite Greed*.
7. See Adrian Johnston, "Capitalism's Implants," *Crisis and Critique*, op.cit.

8. Peter Coffin, *Cancel Culture. Mob Justice or a Society of Subscriptions?*, Las Vegas: Independently published 2022, pp. 31 and 36.
9. See James Godley, "In the Shadow of Fire" (intervention at the conference *In the Wake of the Plague: Eros and Mourning* in Dartmouth College, April 21–24, 2022).
10. I rely here on Robert Pfaller, *Illusionen der Anderen*, Frankfurt: Suhrkamp 2003.
11. I owe this point to Sabina Livadariu.
12. See Adrian Johnston's "Capitalism's Implants," *Crisis and Critique* 8, no. 2 (2021). https://www.crisiscritique.org/storage/app/media/2021-12-13/cc-82-adrian-johnston.pdf
13. John Vidal, "Floods, storms and heatwaves are a direct product of the climate crisis—that's a fact, so where is the action?," *The Guardian* (2022). https://www.theguardian.com/commentisfree/2022/aug/04/floods-storms-heatwaves-direct-product-climate-crisis
14. See Peter Sloterdijk, *Critique of Cynical Reason*, Minneapolis: Minnesota University Press 1988.
15. Ibid.
16. See Alenka Zupančič, "Teorija zarote brez zarote," *Mladina*, Ljubljana, January 28, 2022, pp. 54–56.
17. See Zupančič, "Teorija," op. cit.
18. We should furthermore complicate the relationship between act and ignorance: to act, one should not just "know it all," i.e., base one's act on knowledge as comprehensive as possible, but also simplify the complexity and ambiguity of the situation, reduce it to a simple choice: yes or no, attack or not . . . The paradox is that such a choice also changes the "objective" situation, making it visible in a different way.
19. Ben Adler, "The case for climate reparations through carbon removal: An interview with David Wallace-Wells," *Yahoo!news* (January 7, 2022). https://news.yahoo.com/the-case-for-climate-reparations-through-carbon-removal-an-interview-with-david-wallace-wells-151155418.html
20. See Johnston, "Capitalism's Implants," op. cit.
21. Shlomo Avineri, *The Social and Political Thought of Karl Marx*, Cambridge: Cambridge University Press 1968, p. 148.
22. One should note that, throughout the book, Johnston unquestionably relies on the so-called "labor theory of value," which not only

postulates labour as the only source of value (a postulate that can be defended since value is a social relationship) but, in Marx, also involves the reduction of complex to simple labour in a way that is problematized even by a Marxist like David Harvey. What about non-valorized victims of capital's expansion like house-wives or indigenous people whose conditions of existence are ruined although they are not formally exploited since they do not produce any value at all and, consequently, also no surplus-value? Johnston also ignores the big debate that ravages today interpreters of the critique of political economy: is value something generated in the production process, prior to the entry of a commodity into exchange, or does a commodity effectively assume value only through social acts of exchange? Traditional Marxists regress here to something that vicious critics call the medieval realism of value: as if a commodity has a value in itself, independently of being an object of exchange. I accept the opposite claim (made, among others, by Michael Heinrich): there is no value outside market exchange.

23. Sigmund Freud, *The Interpretation of Dreams*, Harmondsworth: Penguin Books 1976, p. 561.
24. *The Seminar of Jacques Lacan, Book XVII: The Other Side of Psychoanalysis*, New York: W.W. Norton and Company 2007, p. 98.
25. Quoted from Johnston, *Infinite Greed*, op. cit.
26. The Mayakovsky quotes are taken from https://www.scribd.com/document/317353225/Vladimir-Vladimirovic-Mayakovski-Poems#
27. Quoted from Johnston, op. cit.
28. Ibid.

5 The Path to Anarcho-feudalism

1. Bill Gertz, "China 'brain control' warfare work revealed," *Washington Times* (December 29, 2021). https://www.washingtontimes.com/news/2021/dec/29/pla-brain-control-warfare-work-revealed/
2. Jim Waterson and Dan Milmo, "Facebook whistleblower Frances Haugen calls for urgent external regulation," *The Guardian* (October 25, 2021). https://www.theguardian.com/technology/2021/oct/25/facebook-whistleblower-frances-haugen-calls-for-urgent-external-regulation

3. See Douglas Rushkoff, "What Zuckerberg's metaverse means to our humanity," *CNN* blog (October 29, 2021). https://edition.cnn.com/2021/10/28/opinions/zuckerberg-facebook-meta-rushkoff/index.html
4. See Yanis Varoufakis, "Why the rise of a new cloud-based ruling class is crushing democracy," YouTube. https://www.youtube.com/watch?v=wNf3dN0VXqE
5. In what follows, I condense my line of argumentation from Slavoj Žižek, *The Parallax View*, Part II, Chapter 2, Cambridge (MA): MIT Press 2009.
6. Daniel Dennett, "Back from the Drawing Board," in *Dennett and His Critics*, ed. Bo Dahlbom, Oxford: Blackwell 1993, pp. 204–205.
7. See Lucijan Zalokar, "Moraš uživati—čeprav se ne strinjaš," *Delo*. (February 2, 2022). https://www.delo.si/nedelo/moras-uzivati-ceprav-se-ne-strinjas/
8. "50 Difficult Songs To Get Out Of Your Head," Novelodge.com advertisement (2021). https://tinyurl.com/ctcdf49t
9. Jacques Lacan, *The Other Side of Psychoanalysis. The Seminar of Jacques Lacan, Book XVII*, New York: Norton 2007, p. 78.
10. Lorenzo Chiesa, "*Anthropie*: Beside the Pleasure Principle," in *Continental Thought & Theory* 3, no. 2 (2021), available online at https://ir.canterbury.ac.nz/handle/10092/101634
11. Jacques Lacan, *The Other Side of Psychoanalysis.*
12. See Jeremy Rifkin's *The Age of Access*, New York: JP Tarcher 2001. Along similar lines, Gerhard Schulze proposed the concept of *Erlebnisgesellschaft*, the "society of [lived] experience," in which the dominant norms are those of pleasure and quality of life-experiences—see Gerhard Schulze, *Die Erlebnisgesellschaft. Kultursoziologie der Gegenwart*, Frankfurt and New York: Campus Verlag 1992.
13. Fuat Firat and Alladi Venkatesh, quoted from Rifkin, *The Age of Access*, p. 173.
14. See Benedict Anderson, *Imagined Communities*, London: Verso Books 1991.
15. Rifkin, op. cit. pp. 35.
16. Ibid., p. 173.
17. Quoted from Rifkin, op. cit., p. 171.

18. For an attempt to assert the potentially liberating aspects of the rise of the "Protean subject," see Robert Lifton, *The Protean Self: Human Resilience in an Age of Fragmentation*, Chicago: University of Chicago Press 1999.
19. Joshua Zitser, "A reality star who says she made $200K from selling her farts in Mason jars is pivoting to selling them as NFTs," *Yahoo!news*, (January 8, 2022). https://www.yahoo.com/news/reality-star-says-she-made-115059034.html
20. Quoted from Hegel, *Philosophy of Right*, Third Part: Ethical Life, ii Civil Society, available online at https://www.marxists.org/reference/archive/hegel/works/pr/prcivils.htm#PR245
21. Private exchange.
22. Jack Simpson, "The NFT: A Wealth and Poverty Of Imagination," *Aesthetics for Birds* (March 18, 2021). https://aestheticsforbirds.com/2021/03/18/nfts-a-wealth-and-poverty-of-imagination/
23. Nelson Wan, "NFTs and SPACs: the insanity of casino capitalism," *Socialist Appeal* (March 31, 2021). https://socialist.net/nfts-and-spacs-the-insanity-of-casino-capitalism/
24. Jack Simpson, op. cit.
25. Thom Dunn, "Peter Thiel claims AI is 'Leninist' and 'literally communist' in a sprawling speech for a think tank," *boingboing* (December 3, 2019). https://boingboing.net/2019/12/03/peter-thiel-claims-ai-is-len.html
26. Ibid.
27. Quoted from Cihan Tuğal, "The Rise of the Leninist Right," Verso blog (January 20, 2018). https://www.versobooks.com/blogs/3577-the-rise-of-the-leninist-right
28. See Carole Cadwalladr, "'I made Steve Bannon's psychological warfare tool': meet the data war whistleblower," *The Guardian* (March 17, 2018). https://www.theguardian.com/news/2018/mar/17/data-war-whistleblower-christopher-wylie-faceook-nix-bannon-trump
29. Amanda Marcotte, "NFTs aren't art — they're just the Cult of Crypto's latest scam," *Salon* (February 16, 2022). https://www.salon.com/2022/02/16/nfts-arent-art--theyre-just-the-of-cryptos-latest-scam/
30. Catherine Malabou (trans. Robert Boncardo), "Cryptocurrencies: Anarchist Turn or Strengthening of Surveillance Capitalism? From Bitcoin to Libra," *Australian Humanities Review* (March 31, 2020).

https://australianhumanitiesreview.org/2020/05/31/cryptocurrencies-anarchist-turn-or-strengthening-of-surveillance-capitalism-from-bitcoin-to-libra/

31. Quotes within this quoted passage are from Simon Brunfaut, "Quand Facebook deviant un Etat," L'Echo 24, June 2019, available online at https://www.lecho.be/entreprises/technologie/quand-facebook-devient-un-etat/10139091.html
32. Quotes within this quoted passage are from Jeremy Rifkin, *The Zero Marginal Cost Society*, London: St. Martin's Press, 2014.

6 The State and Counter-Revolution

1. Quoted from Patrick Frater, "'Fight Club' Censored in China, Gets New Ending in Censorship Wars," *Variety* (January 25, 2022). https://variety.com/2022/film/asia/fight-club-china-ending-censored-1235162643/
2. In all fairness, one should add that two weeks later, after a public outcry, the original ending was restored.
3. Quoted from Ben Westcott, "West is paying the price for supporting Hong Kong riots, Chinese state media says," *CNN* online (October 21, 2019). https://edition.cnn.com/2019/10/21/asia/china-hong-kong-chile-spain-protests-intl-hnk/index.html
4. Rory Sullivan, "Western nations more concerned about their economies than civilian deaths in Ukraine, says Zelensky," *Independent* (April 7, 2022). https://www.independent.co.uk/news/world/europe/zelensky-western-sanctions-nato-weapons-b2052877.html
5. Quoted from freely available online version "Full text of Graeber & Wengrow – *The Dawn of Everything*." https://archive.org/stream/graeber-wengrow-dawn/The%20Dawn%20of%20Everything%20-%20David%20Graeber%20%26%20David%20Wengrow_djvu.txt
6. "Full text of Graeber and Wengrow," op. cit.
7. Ibid.
8. Simon Griffiths, "What can the Left learn from Friedrich Hayek?," *British Politics and Policy at LSE* blog (February 16, 2015). https://blogs.lse.ac.uk/politicsandpolicy/what-can-the-left-learn-from-friedrich-hayek/

9. Ibid.
10. Ibid.
11. Karl Marx, *Capital*, Volume One, New York: Penguin 1976, p. 173.
12. Álvaro García Linera, "The State in Times of Coronavirus: The pendulum of the 'Illusory Community'," *Crisis Critique* 7, no. 3 (2020). https://www.crisiscritique.org/storage/app/media/2020-11-24/alvaro-garci-a-linera.pdf
13. See Eric L. Santner, "Remarks on Agamben" (unpublished manuscript). Available online at https://www.artforum.com/print/201203/giorgio-agamben-s-the-kingdom-and-the-glory-30322
14. Ibid.
15. Linera, op. cit.
16. Ibid.
17. Ibid.
18. I owe this line of thought to Matt Christman (Chapo Trap house).
19. Sewell Chan and Eric Neugeboren, "Texas Republican Convention calls Biden illegitimate and rebukes Cornyn," *The Texas Tribune* (June 18, 2022). https://www.texastribune.org/2022/06/18/republican-party-texas-convention-cornyn/
20. Christopher J. Bickerton and Carlo Invernizzi Accetti, *Technopopulism: The New Logic of Democratic Politics*, Oxford: Oxford University Press 2021. See also the excellent review of the book in *London Review of Books* 44, no. 2 at https://www.lrb.co.uk/the-paper/v44/n02/wolfgang-streeck/in-the-superstate?referrer=https%3A%2F%2Fwww.google.si%2F
21. The problem is that the stance advocated here—fidelity to the need for radical change while pragmatically engaging in politics, from elections to strategically supporting reformist measures (strengthening the welfare state, advocating feminist and anti-racist rights)—is among the great losers of the last decade: from *Podemos* in Spain to *Die Linke* in Germany, they are all losing substantial support. The exemplary case here is, of course, the fate of Syriza in Greece.
22. See Jodi Dean's "Neofeudalism: The End of Capitalism?," *Los Angeles Review of Books* (May 12, 2020). https://lareviewofbooks.org/article/neofeudalism-the-end-of-capitalism/
23. I owe this joke to Kamran Baradaran, Tehran.

24. See Claudia Chwalisz, "Citizens' Assemblies Can Help Repair Dysfunctional Democracies," *Noēma* (May 12, 2022). https://www.noemamag.com/a-movement-thats-quietly-reshaping-democracy-for-the-better/
25. See Bini Adamczak, *Yesterday's Tomorrow*, Cambridge, MA: MIT Press 2021. After reading this book and trying to select quotes from it, I was overwhelmed by a weird feeling that the entire book should be quoted.
26. Ibid., p. 80.
27. This quotation has been attributed to Voltaire and Denis Diderot, but its origin was with Jean Meslier (1664–1729), French Catholic priest and closet atheist.
28. Adamczak, op. cit., p. 34.
29. Ibid., p. 79.
30. Ibid., p. 80.
31. Ibid., p. 82.
32. Ibid., p. 140.
33. G. W. F. Hegel, *The Philosophy of History*, New York: Dover 1956, p. 447.
34. Quotes from V. I. Lenin, *The State and Revolution* (1918), available online at https://www.marxists.org/ebooks/lenin/state-and-revolution.pdf
35. Ibid.
36. Ibid.
37. Ibid.
38. "The Immediate Tasks of the Soviet Government," in *Collected Works*, Moscow: Progress Publishers 1972, Volume 27, p. 261. Non-accredited quotes that follow are from this book.
39. See Ralph Miliband, "Lenin's The State and Revolution," *Jacobin* (August 14, 2018). https://jacobin.com/2018/08/lenin-state-and-revolution-miliband
40. Karl-Heinz Dellwo, "Subjektlose Herrschaft und revolutionaeres Subjekt. Friday for Future?," a talk in Leipzig on January 12, 2021. Quoted from the manuscript available online at https://www.bellastoria.de/veranstaltung/wer-herrscht-ueber-uns
41. V. I. Lenin, "On the tasks of the People's Commissariat for Justice under the new economic policy," available online at https://www.marxists.org/archive/lenin/works/1922/feb/20c.htm

42. Dmitry Dubrovsky, "The Bolsheviks and the Law: The Legacy of Arbitrary Justice," *Eurasianet* (November 7, 2017). https://eurasianet.org/the-bolsheviks-and-the-law-the-legacy-of-arbitrary-justice
43. Lenin, "On the tasks of the People's Commissariat for Justice under the new economic policy."

Appendix 5

1. Duane Rouselle, "The Ironic Clinic. Jacques-Alain Miller's lecture on the. . ." *Medium* blog (December 24, 2020). https://duanerousselle.medium.com/the-ironic-clinic-551964a854cb
2. Jacques Lacan, "Vers un signifiant nouveau," *Ornicar?* 17–18, Paris 1979, p. 23.
3. A nice example of Lacan's "stupidity": once, at a clinical presentation of a patient, the latter spoke about "Formula One"—totally ignorant of the universe of car racing (the patient was, of course, talking about this), Lacan thought the patient was referring to his own attempts at the formalization of the signifying structures . . .
4. Marie-Hélène Brousse, "WOKE or Racism in the Time of the Many Without the One" (Part 2), *The Lacanian Review* (May 29, 2021, LRO 299) (thelacanianreviews.com).
5. I owe this information to Elias Cohen, ENS, Paris.

Appendix 6

1. Robert Pfaller, *Zwei Enthuellungen ueber die Scham*, Frankfurt: Fischer 2022.
2. Ibid., p. 56.
3. Ibid., p. 89.
4. Ibid., pp. 76, 82.
5. Alenka Zupančič (private communication).
6. Pfaller, op. cit., p. 48.
7. Ibid., p. 137.
8. Ibid., p. 59.

9. See "SARAJEVO SAFARI", Arsmedia video. https://arsmedia.si/en/feature-films/sarajevo-safari
10. Guy Faulconbridge and Caleb Davis, "Medvedev raises spectre of Russian nuclear strike on Ukraine," Reuters (September 27, 2022). https://www.reuters.com/world/europe/russias-medvedev-warns-west-that-nuclear-threat-is-not-bluff-2022-09-27/
11. Brendan Cole, "NATO Would Be Too Scared to React if Russia Drops Nuke First—Putin Ally," *Newsweek* (27 September, 2022). https://www.newsweek.com/dmitry-medvedev-russia-nuclear-weapons-nato-ukraine-1746638
12. Nathan Hodge, "Vladimir Putin: Restoration of empire is the endgame for Russia's president," CNN (June 10, 2022). https://edition.cnn.com/2022/06/10/europe/russia-putin-empire-restoration-endgame-intl-cmd/index.html
13. Harlan Ullman, "U.S. needs strategic off-ramp to end Russian war in Ukraine," *UPI News* (September 28, 2022). https://www.msn.com/en-gb/news/world/u-s-needs-strategic-off-ramp-to-end-russian-war-in-ukraine/ar-AA12kMOB?ocid=msedgntp&cvid=905166c2af0146a8bae52a8401544010

Appendix 7

1. *The Matrix*, American film franchise, Warner Bros. 2021. https://en.wikipedia.org/w/index.php?title=The_Matrix_(franchise)&oldid=1155083839
2. Description taken from Amazon.com: Customer reviews: Poirot – Hickory Dickory Dock. https://www.amazon.com/Poirot-Hickory-Dickory-David-Suchet/product-reviews/B00005RIWY?pageNumber=2
3. John Saavedra, "The Matrix Resurrections Ending Explained and Spoiler Questions Answered", *Den of Geek* (December 22, 2021). https://www.denofgeek.com/movies/the-matrix-resurrections-ending-spoilers/
4. I refer here to my reading of the first *Matrix* movie available online at https://www.lacan.com/zizek-matrix.htm
5. Saavedra, op. cit.
6. Ibid.

7. Ibid.
8. Adi Robertson, "The Matrix Resurrections is more interested in being self-aware than being good", *The Verge* (December 21, 2021). https://www.theverge.com/2021/12/21/22841582/matrix-resurrections-lana-wachowski-keanu-reeves-carrie-anne-moss-review
9. *The Wachowskis*, Warner Bros. 1999.
10. Joseph Earp, "Nothing But A Brain: The Philosophy Of The Matrix: Resurrections", The Ethics Centre (December 26, 2021). https://ethics.org.au/nothing-but-a-brain-the-philosophy-of-the-matrix-resurrections/

Appendix 8

1. Oxana Timofeeva, *How to love a homeland*, Beirut: Kajfa ta 2021.
2. Quoted from Saroj Giri, "Introduction," in K. Murali, *Of Concepts and Methods*, Keralam: Kanal Publishing Center 2021. The book is now unavailable, I quote from the digital version I got from the author.
3. Maria Chehonadskih, "Soviet Epistemologies and the Materialist Ontology of Poor Life: Andrei Platonov, Alexander Bogdanov and Lev Vygotsky" (unpublished manuscript).
4. See Andrey Platonov, *Soul*, London: Vintage Classics 2013. ("Dzhan" is usually translated into English as "Soul.")
5. I rely here on Maria Chehonadskih, op. cit.
6. See Michael Marder, *Plant-Thinking: A Philosophy of Vegetal Life*, New York: Columbia University Press 2013.
7. Michael Marder, "Vegetal Redemption: A Ukrainian Woman and Russian Soldiers", *The Philosophical Salon* (February 26, 2022). https://thephilosophicalsalon.com/vegetal-redemption-a-ukrainian-woman-and-russian-soldiers/
8. I deal more in detail with this topic in "Finale" of my *Surplus-Enjoyment* (London: Bloomsbury 2022).
9. Giri, op. cit., p. 6.
10. Graham Harman, *Towards Speculative Realism*, Winchester: Zero Books 2010, p. 93, quoted from Morgan Meis, "Timothy Morton's Hyper-Pandemic," *The New Yorker* (June 8, 2021). https://www.newyorker.com

11. Quoted from Morgan Meis, "Timothy Morton's Hyper-Pandemic."
12. Djelem, djelem lyrics + English translation (lyricstranslate.com).
13. Ibid.
14. Strose to stroma sou—English Lyrics (greeksongs-greekmusic.com). One should add here that even Theodorakis's famous "Song of Songs" from his Mauthausen cycle enframes the horror of the Nazi concentration camp within a lover's remembrance of his beautiful love.
15. Quoted in Alberto Toscano, "A Structuralism of Feeling?," *New Left Review* 97 (January–February 2016), p. 78.
16. Ibid., p. 86
17. Ibid., p. 91.
18. Ibid., pp. 84–85.
19. Ibid., p. 85.
20. Ibid., p. 85.
21. Ibid., p. 18.
22. Ibid., p. 89.
23. See Francis Fukuyama, "Liberalism Needs the Nation," *Foreign Affairs* (April 1, 2022). https://www.foreignaffairs.com/articles/ukraine/2022-04-01/francis-fukuyama-liberalism-country
24. Jon Henley, "Sweden's gun violence rate has soared due to gangs, report says," *The Guardian* (May 26, 2021). https://www.theguardian.com/world/2021/may/26/fatal-shootings-have-risen-in-sweden-despite-fall-across-europe-report-finds
25. Mark Townsend, "How the murder of a Swedish rapper shocked a nation and put police on the back foot," *The Guardian* (December 4, 2021). https://www.theguardian.com/world/2021/dec/04/how-the-of-a-swedish-rapper-shocked-a-nation-and-put-police-on-the-back-foot
26. Susan Buck-Morss, *Hegel, Haiti, and Universal History*, Pittsburgh: University of Pittsburgh Press 2009, p. 151.
27. Ibid., p. 133.
28. Ibid., pp. 138–139.
29. An interesting detail is that in Nigeria, of all places, thousands applied for the citizenship.

Finale: The Four Riders of the Apocalypse

1. I owe this application of the "four riders of the apocalypse" to today's condition to Mladen Dolar.
2. Trevor Hancock, "There is a fifth horseman of the Apocalypse—and it is us", *Healthy Debate* (November 5, 2020). https://healthydebate.ca/2020/11/topic/there-is-a-fifth-horseman-humans/
3. Ibid.
4. Ibid.
5. See Rhea Mogul, Esha Mitra, Manveena Suri and Sophia Saifi, "Ukraine War Creating Biggest Global Food Crisis Since WWII," CNN (May 2, 2022). https://edition.cnn.com/2022/05/02/asia/india-pakistan-heatwave-climate-intl-hnk/index.html
6. See Larry Elliott, "War in Ukraine could lead to food riots in poor countries, warns WTO boss," World Trade Organization, reported in *The Guardian* (March 24, 2022). https://www.theguardian.com/world/2022/mar/24/war-ukraine-food-riots-poor-countries-wto-ngozi-okonjo-iweala-food-prices-hunger
7. Rhea Mogul, Esha Mitra, Manveena Suri and Sophia Saifi, "India and Pakistan heatwave is 'testing the limits of human survivability,'" CNN (May 2, 2022). https://edition.cnn.com/2022/05/02/asia/india-pakistan-heatwave-climate-intl-hnk/index.html
8. I owe this triad to Yuval Noah Harari.
9. https://www.nytimes.com/2012/08/20/us/politics/todd-akin-provokes-ire-with-legitimate-rape-comment.html
10. Maria Cohut, "Five things you should know about the clitoris," *Medical News Today* (June 22, 2018). https://www.medicalnewstoday.com/articles/322235
11. Bill Bostock, "Putin quoted song lyrics about rape and necrophilia to explain Russia's demands from Ukraine," *Insider* (February 8, 2022). https://www.businessinsider.com/putin-macron-meeting-quote-obscene-lyrics-show-russia-ukraine-demands-2022-2
12. https://www.youtube.com/watch?v=DvPVfgjfhRg
13. *The Servant of the People*, created and produced by Volodymyr Zelenskyy, Kvartal 95, 2015–2019.
14. https://www.reuters.com/world/putin-western-countries-want-extend-nato-like-system-asia-pacific-region-2022-08-16/

15. Lilla Watson, https://www.goodreads.com/quotes/844825-if-you-have-come-here-to-help-me-you-are
16. Álvaro García Linera, "The State in Times of Coronavirus: The pendulum of the 'Illusory Community'," *Crisis Critique* 7, no. 3 (2020). https://www.crisiscritique.org/storage/app/media/2020-11-24/alvaro-garci-a-linera.pdf
17. Paul Sutter, "Physicists predict Earth will become a chaotic world, with dire consequences," *Space* (blog) (May 29, 2022), msn.com
18. Ibid.
19. Quoted from Georg Lukacs, *History and Class Consciousness*, available at https://www.marxists.org/archive/lukacs/works/history/hcc07_1.htm
20. "Are we entering a post anthropocentric era? Video by Anna Bressanin, filmed by Ilya Shnitser," BBC Reel (May 19, 2022). https://www.bbc.com/reel/
21. Liu Cixin, *The Three-Body Problem*, Tor Books 2014.
22. See Yuval Noah Harari, *Homo Deus. A Brief History of Tomorrow*, London: Harvill Secker 2016.
23. Thomas Metzinger, *Being No One*, Cambridge, MA: MIT Press 2004, p. 620.
24. Ibid., p. 620.
25. Ibid., p. 621.
26. Harari, op. cit., p. 273.
27. Ibid., p. 346.
28. The gigantic volcanic eruption on the Tonga islands in January 2022 was a welcome reminder that it is not only humanity which brings havoc to our environment—nature in itself is in a fragile state of balance that can at any moment explode.
29. See Bruno Latour and Nikolaj Schultz, *Memo sur la nouvelle classe ecologique*, Paris: Editions La Decouverte 2022.
30. Christopher Hitchens, "The Old Man," *The Atlantic* (July–August 2004). https://www.theatlantic.com/magazine/archive/2004/07/the-old-man/302984/
31. Ibid.
32. Karl-Heinz Dellwo, "Subjektlose Herrschaft und revolutionaeres Subjekt," a talk in Leipzig on January 12, 2021. (Quoted from the manuscript.)

33. This absence of a predestined subject of change will also lead to a new form of narratives. Kim Stanley Robinson's *The Ministry for the Future* (2020, usually characterized as "hard science fiction") opens up a new path. It mixes narrative fiction (which follows an international organization named the Ministry for the Future in its mission to act as an advocate for the world's future generations of citizens as if their rights were as valid as the present generation's) with emphasis on scientific accuracy and non-fiction descriptions of history and social science. What is also so refreshing about this book is that, after the deluge of apocalyptic visions, it imagines what is basically an optimist vision: if we pull our strength together, we have a chance of achieving something.
34. See Mladen Dolar, *Od kod prihaja oblast?* (in Slovene), Ljubljana: Analecta 2021, p. 167.
35. See Alexander Mitcherlich, *Auf dem Weg zur vaterlosen Gesellschaft* (1963), new edition Weinheim: Beltz Verlag 2003.
36. In premodern societies, the Master is also a servant, but he serves an authority external to the body politic of its subjects: a leader serves a transcendent authority like a God.
37. See Dolar, op. cit., p. 174.
38. Ibid., p. 123.
39. Jacques-Alain Miller, "La psychanalyse, la cité, communautés," *La cause freudienne* 68 (February 2008), p. 109.
40. Ibid., p. 112.
41. See Alexandre Dumas, *The Man in the Iron Mask*, Ware: Wordsworth 2001.
42. Catherine Malabou, in *Afterlives*, ed. by Peter Osborne, London: CRMEP Books 2022, p. 179.
43. Ibid., p. 179.
44. Etienne Balibar, in *Afterlives*, op. cit., p. 182.
45. Malabou, op. cit., p. 178.
46. Ibid., p. 179.
47. Balibar, op. cit., p. 184.
48. See Isolde Charim, *Die Qualen des Narzissmus. Ueber freiwillige Unterwerfung*, Wien: Zsolnay 2022.
49. Alain Badiou / Elisabeth Roudinesco, "Appel aux psychanalystes. Entretien avec Eric Aeschimann," *Le Nouvel Observateur*, April 19, 2012.

50. Personal communication (April 2013).
51. Hannah Arendt, "The Crisis of Education," in *Between Past and Future*, New York: Viking Press 1961, p. 191.
52. Aaron Schuster, "Beyond Satire," in William Mozzarella, Eric Santner, Aaron Schuster, *Sovereignty Inc. Three Inquiries in Politics and Enjoyment*, Chicago: The University of Chicago Press 2020, p. 219.
53. "Das Rheingold," Wikipedia, The Free Encyclopedia, https://en.wikipedia.org/w/index.php?title=Das_Rheingold&oldid=1153891126
54. Roger Scruton, *The Ring of Truth*, New York: Abrams 2017, p. 53.

Index